G
28

I0984387

Inside the Vatican

Inside the Vatican

GEORGE BULL

HUTCHINSON
London Melbourne Sydney Auckland Johannesburg

To Caroline

Hutchinson & Co. (Publishers) Ltd

An imprint of the Hutchinson Publishing Group

17-21 Conway Street, London W1P 5HL

Hutchinson Group (Australia) Pty Ltd
30-32 Cremorne Street, Richmond South, Victoria 3121
PO Box 151, Broadway, New South Wales 2007

Hutchinson Group (NZ) Ltd
PO Box 337, Bergvlei 2012, South Africa

First published 1982
© George Bull 1982

Set in Baskerville by Bookens, Saffron Walden

Printed in Great Britain by The Anchor Press Ltd
and bound by Wm Brendon & Son Ltd,
both of Tiptree, Essex

British Library Cataloguing in Publication Data

Bull, George
 Inside the Vatican.
 1. Vatican City – Social life and customs
 I. Title
 945'.6340928   DG800

ISBN 0 09 140070 8

Contents

Illustrations

The Modern Popes

Pius IX (Giovanni M. Mastai Ferretti) 1846–78

Leo XIII (Gioacchino Pecci) 1878–1903

(St) Pius X (Giuseppe Sarto) 1903–14

Benedict XV (Giacomo della Chiesa) 1914–22

Pius XI (Achille Ratti) 1922–39

Pius XII (Eugenio Pacelli) 1939–58

John XXIII (Angelo Giuseppe Roncalli) 1958–63

Paul VI (Giovanni Battista Montini) 1963–78

John Paul I (Albino Luciani) 1978

John Paul II (Karol Wojtyla) 1978–

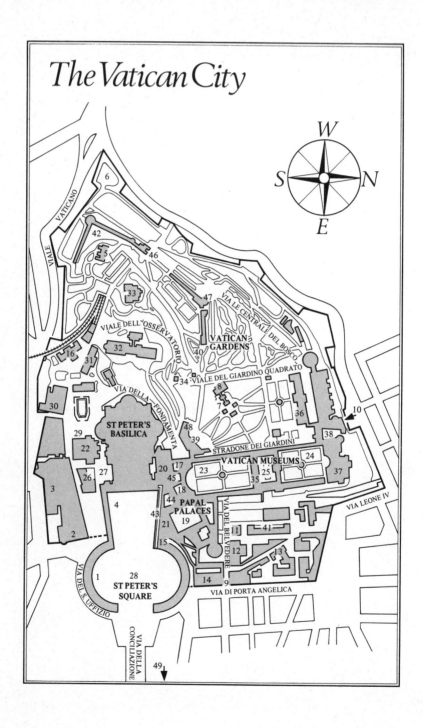

The Vatican City

THE VATICAN CITY

KEY

1 Bernini's Colonnades
2 Palace of the Holy Office
3 Audience Hall
4 Arch of the Bells
5 First Vatican Radio Building
6 Heliport
7 Casina of Pius IV
8 Pontifical Academy of Sciences
9 Gate of S. Anna
10 Public entrance to the Museums
11 Post and Telegraph Office
12 Polyglot Printers
13 Offices of *Osservatore Romano*
14 Swiss Guards' Barracks
15 Bronze Doors: entrance to the Apostolic Palace
16 Railway Station
17 Cortile della Sentinella
18 Cortile dei Pappagalli
19 Cortile di San Damaso
20 Sistine Chapel

21 Papal Apartments
22 Sacristy of St Peter's
23 Cortile del Belvedere
24 Cortile della Pigna
25 Cortile della Biblioteca
26 Teutonic College
27 Piazza dei Protomartiri Romani
28 Obelisk of Caligula
29 Piazza di Santa Marta
30 Palazzo San Carlo
31 Mosaic Factory
32 Government Palace
33 Ethiopian College
34 Statue of St Peter
35 Vatican Library and Secret Archives
36 Pinacoteca
37 Cortile Ottagono
38 Cortile delle Corazze
39 Fountain of the Sacrament
40 Fountain of the Eagle

41 Belvedere Palace
42 Wall of Leo IV
43 Bernini Corridor
44 Cortile del Maresciallo
45 Cortile Borgia
46 Grotto of Lourdes
47 Vatican Radio
48 Palace of the Mint
49 To Castel Sant' Angelo

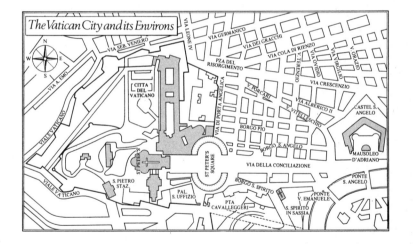

The Vatican City and its Environs

Prologue

Hilaire Belloc, in *The Path to Rome*, tells how Almighty God asked St Peter about the world and what people were doing there, and, on learning that those on their knees were praising and praying to him, decided to let it all continue. For me, the Vatican has primarily a religious significance, as it must have for all Catholics. Important as the Vatican is to the world's spiritual progress or survival, it is also a powerful political institution rooted in a tiny sovereign state in Rome, administered by several hundred dedicated officials at the centre of a worldwide ecclesiastical network. I instinctively think of it in layers of images far more complicated than those of a simple power-house of prayer.

The Vatican is immensely rich, not in terms of its financial accounts, but in the historical and cultural value of its territory, its palaces, churches, monuments and museums. From the outside, it presents a rather daunting circumference of medieval towers and bastions, Renaissance statues, domes and fountains, baroque columns and façades. The Piazza and Basilica of St Peter's, the Papal Palaces flanking the oval piazza, and the ancient walls teem with curious, precious things, like the decorated margins of a profusely illuminated manuscript. Inside the living Vatican are fresh, unexpected perspectives of St Peter's and the city of Rome; woods and gardens and villas with surprising splashes of architectural and sculptural fantasy; miles of busy corridors and halls; and edifices performing every sort of formal and domestic function. The artistic wealth of the Vatican is not just in the museums and in the grand, breathtaking works of the great artists who planned its buildings and filled them with sculptures and paintings. In the Pope's quarters of the Palace, in the apartments of cardinals and bishops, in the offices, reception areas and ceremonial rooms is a vast centuries-old inheritance, only partially catalogued, reflecting discriminating patronage and assiduous collecting of every kind of art and craft.

From the pinnacle of Michelangelo's dome, your eye can in an instant take in the main features of the Vatican complex rising towards the north and the west. But it takes years to begin to grasp the extent and richness of the physical possessions packed into this modest territory. Their significance is not comprehensible in material terms: they are symbols of stability and permanence. They reinforce the atmosphere of suspended time. Many of the treasures are hidden from public view, but the openness of Bernini's colonnade, inviting strangers to approach the Vatican and climb the great steps to enter St Peter's, reflects the generous attitude of most of the custodians of the Vatican's culture. Numerous scholars have not only been assisted assiduously in their research at the Vatican Library and Secret Archives, but also have been allowed to seek for particular historical items among the priceless stores of the treasury of St Peter's or the sacristy of the Sistine Chapel, and have been delightedly watched.

The face of the Vatican is benign, whether it is the Pope giving his blessing to the world, a cardinal president and archbishop secretary of one of the 'ministries' receiving a bishop, or an official welcoming a special delegation from abroad. The courtesy and charm which characterize the attitudes of most of the Vatican's personnel, from high-ranking prelates to door-keepers, chauffeurs and petrol-pump attendants, are stiffened by a certain nervous tension on everyone's part in the face of undue inquisitiveness. The formalities for going to and fro through Vatican territory are no trouble. Security measures and the guards responsible for them are rarely heavy-handed. But the more familiar the Vatican and the people who work there for the Papacy and the Church become, the more apparent are the little streams of suspicion and sometimes even fearfulness, for the Vatican is a tightly structured and disciplined organization dealing with the most sensitive areas of religious conscience and moral behaviour, and providing careers for life.

The Vatican is also a very Italian institution, despite the

advent of a Polish Pope who is Slavonic in temperament but very Roman in faith. There is in the atmosphere of the Vatican a certain volatility and excitability, balancing the *gravitas*. There are eye-catching contrivances or human dramas on display most of the time, sometimes arresting and beautiful, sometimes tawdry. The Vatican, beginning with St Peter's Basilica, encourages you to accept a certain human coarseness along with the awe that must be felt under Michelangelo's dome and over St Peter's tomb. Because the Vatican is so Italian, and because the Papacy is very old, it fosters a thin strain of world-weary cynicism, even among its faithful servants. I have never met a prelate with the sad, sceptical kind of faith expressed by Browning's Bishop Blougram, 'We called the chess-board white, We call it black. . . ,' but I have talked quietly with not a few inside critics, who worry over the Vatican's methods and prejudices, and hold their tongues.

The image of an Italianate Vatican changes in the light of the growing number of non-Italians brought into the administration. The kindliness and intellectual breadth – quite often the holiness – of many within the Roman Curia itself also softens the impression of stiff, reactionary prejudice. Inside the Vatican walls, I feel especially conscious of the lines thrown out from this small centre to all parts of the world, and of its genuine catholicism of race and class.

Around the Pontiff, in broadening circles of influence and responsibility, the Vatican's administrators create an environment of loving, responsive loyalty and devotion to the Holy See. The object of their faithful service is personalized in the Pope, but it is also directed to the other institutional pole of the Papacy, the Roman Curia, which has its own profound sense of guardianship of the Catholic faith. John Paul II has shown that he is no prisoner of the Vatican in any sense. In his determination to sharpen the edges of Catholic belief – to clarify a fuzzy image of the Church – he has attracted the needle of Vatican conservatism strongly towards him. It is a fascinating and rather paradoxical situation, promising dramatic and unpredictable developments.

This book is about the Holy See and the Vatican City State. It is written for people who may or may not be Catholics, or Christians, but who are curious about the mysterious-sounding institutions of the Vatican and the day-to-day lives of those who control and operate them. It seeks to explain the main structures of the complicated ecclesiastical government inherited by Pope John Paul II, and the attitudes and aims of the Pope's collaborators in the administration of the Catholic Church. It looks inquiringly at the Vatican's physical and organizational framework – the buildings, the monuments, the ministries – with a journalist's inquisitive and sometimes, no doubt, innocent eye. It is, above all, an explanation of the life of the Pope.

The material has been gathered from many years' extensive reading and involvement in the Catholic Church, from many discussions and interviews carried out inside the Vatican, and from correspondence with Vatican officials, papal envoys and interested observers in different parts of the world. Wherever I can, I let Vatican officials speak in their own words. I have tried to give accurate impressions of the way they look and react, of their personal tastes and environment, and of the nuances of their official positions. Frank but sympathetic writing about the personalities as well as the policies of the Vatican is still quite rare, because of the closed nature of the organization, and the traditional insistence that the Holy See should be exempt from any kind of sociological scrutiny. I have found the reserve melt away through patient wooing.

I first visited Rome and the Vatican in 1950, the Holy Year, where in St Peter's Basilica I saw my first Pope in the frail, white-robed figure of the ascetic, almost weightless-looking, Pius XII. Squeezed among several thousand tourists, including many ruthless, sharp-elbowed nuns, I heard the Creed sung in Latin in a glorious, emotional atmosphere of triumphal awe. I returned to a changing Vatican when John XXIII was Pope in the early 1960s, to gather material for a book on the Second Vatican Council. It was a time of rare religious controversy and crisis for many millions of Catholics, as the theological ripples started to spread out from Rome. Then, for this book, I paid successive visits to Rome, starting in the autumn of 1977 for talks with officials of the Roman Curia and with many people associated in one way or another with the Holy See. And, of course, all Rome has yielded innumerable comments on Vatican affairs.

Because of the deaths of Paul VI and John Paul I, there were three Popes on the throne of St Peter in the same year – 1978.

The election of Karol Wojtyla, the first non-Italian Pope for nearly five centuries, in the autumn of 1978, sent shockwaves through the Vatican, and these are still being experienced as they fan through the whole of the Catholic Church – a Church once again on the move. The importance of this for the world as a whole, not just the 732 million baptized Catholics more directly affected by the teaching of the Holy See, needs no stressing.

These pages were going to press when Pope John Paul II was shot and grievously wounded as he blessed the crowd in St Peter's Square, on 13 May 1981. Ten days later, his doctors said his life was no longer in danger: a remarkable confirmation of the Pope's robust physical and mental constitution, without which he would hardly have survived.

After the murder attempt and extensive surgery, it seemed that the Pope might have to change the style of his pontificate. His global travels, with their importance for the moral influence of the Vatican and the future of the Papal primacy, might have to be curtailed. But the international reaction to the events of May 1981 put beyond doubt the hold of the Pope on the world's affections, the important position of the modern Papacy, and the fascination of the Vatican for both its followers and critics.

The debt of gratitude I owe to many of those who work for the Holy See and the Vatican City will be obvious from the pages that follow. They have all been generous with their time and responded to oral or written questions always courteously and fully, if sometimes rather guardedly. In one or two cases, there was a plea for anonymity. I hope that the tone of voice comes through even so, as well as the significant content of what was said.

A list of acknowledgements is not appropriate on top of this general note of thanks. But I must record my gratitude to Adrian Turner, whose clarity of mind saved me from errors all of my own about the Papacy and whose generously shared knowledge of the Vatican can be as entertaining as it is encyclopedic.

The encouragement to write *Inside the Vatican*, and the original idea for the book, came from Jim Cochrane, of Hutchinson, who has been a most constructively demanding editor.

17

1

Inside the Walls

I have walked scores of times on my way to the Vatican over the sluggish, muddy Tiber by the Sant'Angelo bridge, past the ten chunky angels made to designs by Giovanni Bernini. These marble statues were put in place in 1688, the year of England's Glorious Revolution and the exile of King James II (who as Duke of York had sold New Jersey to two settlers in America, four years previously).

The ancient Roman bridge at this spot was named after the Emperor Hadrian, who also built Hadrian's Wall in Britain, for the defence of that distant province against the northern barbarian tribes. Lucrezia Borgia crossed the medieval bridge in procession in the Jubilee Year of 1500, watched jealously from the nearby castle by her father, Pope Alexander VI. Downstream, today's noisy traffic hurtles across the Ponte Vittorio Emanuele, built early this century to continue one of the great arteries of modern Rome, the Corso, and named after the first King of a united Italy, Victor Emmanuel II.

With such diverse evocations spanning two thousand years, history, secular and religious, seizes the imagination of the visitor to the Vatican, as it must do continuously the mind of the man who inherits the chair of St Peter and the papal patrimony.

The Pope is likely, when priest or cardinal, often to have made the same way as the student or visitor towards St Peter's Square, from one of Rome's many Pontifical Colleges or religious houses. Once over the bridge, the direction is past the fortress of Castel Sant'Angelo – originally the Emperor Hadrian's mausoleum, it is now an historical, monumental and military museum, chockful within its cylindrical walls of peperino and travertine with vivid reminders of the Papacy's past: the criminal court and dungeons as well as the frescoes, loggias and living quarters.

Most notorious among the ghosts of the past is that of the goldsmith and sculptor, Benvenuto Cellini, who fled to the castle in 1527 on the same day as the Medici Pope, Clement VII (1523–34), as they both sought safety from the fury of German and Spanish imperial troops. During the sack of Rome, Cellini helped melt down the Pope's gold and hide his jewels; and later he suffered imprisonment in the cells and broke his leg escaping from the battlements.

The *passetto* or gallery in the wall stretching from the Vatican Palace to the castle, along which Pope Clement fled with his cardinals (his white vestments hurriedly covered to make him less conspicuous) still stands today, long fallen into disuse. The area between the castle and the frontier of the Vatican State has changed out of recognition within the past fifty years.

The normal route to the Vatican, after crossing the river by the bridge of Sant'Angelo, used to be by the Borgo Nuovo. It was known as Via Alessandrina in Cellini's time, when Luther passed that way from his Augustinian convent. It was one of four streets running from the west of Castel Sant'Angelo. Opening halfway into the Piazza Scossa Cavalli, it led past the ancient church of Santa Maria Traspontina, the still older Palazzo Giraud (now Palazzo Toreonia), Palazzo dei Penitenzieri and Palazzo dei Convertendi (on the site of a house once owned by Raphael) to a small piazza abutting on St Peter's Square. At that point, for hundreds of years, the stupendous dome of St Peter's suddenly loomed to fill the vision of the pilgrim or tourist with the awesomeness of an artfully staged miracle.

To commemorate the Lateran Treaty (the Conciliation), Mussolini demolished the old curving streets of the Spina dei Borghi. In place of their broken-down buildings, a very wide, grandiose thoroughfare was driven, straight as a military road, towards St Peter's.

The avenue was completed in Holy Year, 1950, and flanked (as an afterthought) with stone benches and imitation obelisks. These narrow the road for the still dauntingly broad stream of one-way traffic which hoots its way towards St Peter's. The historical resonance can still be sensed through the noises of the street and the cafés which share shop space with the garish clutter of coloured pictures of the Pope, fig-leafed Davids, and painted and carved Madonnas. You may encounter the Belgian Cardinal Suenens, strolling ruminatively towards St Peter's Square, or glimpse the Holy See's representative in London, Archbishop Bruno Heim, being driven fast in the same direction in a tiny car by a plump English priest.

The Carmelite church and the three *palazzi* of the Borgo Nuovo have been carefully preserved, though the Palazzo dei Convertendi was actually transplanted to its present site. It now houses various Vatican offices, and a fine collection of icons. On the left, the south side, of the Via della Conciliazione, round quiet courtyards, are the religious houses of the Salvatorians and the Sons of Mary Immaculate; and the Hotel Columbus, owned by the Knights of the Holy Sepulchre, is the former Palazzo dei Penitenzieri. On the north side, the Via della Conciliazione ends with a bulge of dull modern office buildings and shops. At the corner, large glass doors lead to a press-conference centre and the press office of the Vatican, in the Piazza Pio XII which has usurped the old, charmingly named, Piazza Rusticucci.

Mussolini was not the first to think of driving a new road through the old Borghi, where Saxons once settled and Henry VIII had his embassy, to the threshold of the Vatican. When Stendhal crossed the Sant'Angelo bridge in a barouche in 1827, to glimpse St Peter's at the end of a narrow street, he wrote:

> Napoleon had announced the project of marking his entry into Rome by the purchase and the demolition of all the houses that stand on the left side of this street. He said once that this decree would be signed by his son; but the world has resumed its petty pace, and the constitutional régime is too prudent ever to indulge in such a mad expenditure.

The ancient, brick bastions of the Vatican, towering rather threateningly round most of the state, constitute the main stretch of its frontier. The border on the east, however, facing the Via della Conciliazione, is formed by the open edge of St Peter's Square and the huge Bernini colonnade. No passports are needed to cross, and there are no formalities, although the soldiers can lay hands on modern weapons.

The thousands of people who enter the Vatican every day, on foot, in cars of in lorries – the cardinals and bishops, friars and nuns, the day workers, official visitors, tourists and resident guests – pour in through the Arch of the Bells, to the left of St Peter's, leading past the great sacristy to the Government Palace and the gardens; through the doors to St Peter's itself; through the ancient bronze doors leading to the main entrance to the Apostolic Palace; through St Anne's Gate, leading to the Vatican's complex of offices, workshops, stores and barracks; and through the entrance to the museums, about a quarter of the way up the slope of the Viale Vaticano.

The Arch of the Bells is the main entrance for cars (though there is very brisk commercial traffic through the Porta Sant'Anna). The road leads round the back of St Peter's through the Cortile della Sentinella, where it is joined by the road from Porta Sant'Anna coming from the direction of the museums. After the Cortile del Pappagallo, the road takes you to the Cortile San Damaso, where those visiting the papal apartments or the offices of the Vatican's Secretariat of State alight and use the lift.

It takes nearly three quarters of an hour to walk, following the uphill route of the Viale Vaticano a good part of the way, along the circumference of the city. I do not know that any Pope has been round, though Wojtyla, the most sporting of Popes since the Alpinist, Pius XI, might well have done so.

The entire state measures just over 108 acres (44 hectares), in an uneven quadrilateral, a trapezoid, of which a third is paved with courtyards and squares, a third, on the slope's edges and running uphill, is laid out in varied gardens, and a third has been annexed by all styles of building for worship, administration, living and pleasure.

The marshy area by the Tiber was in classical times called *Ager Vaticanus*, which may derive from the name of an Etruscan village. On this ground, between today's buildings of the old Holy Office and the sacristy of St Peter's, the Emperor Gaius Germanicus, or Caligula, built a circus and a hippodrome, and erected an obelisk imported from Egypt, and now – thanks to Pope Sixtus V (1585–90) – standing in St Peter's Square. Here in the first century AD, after the burning of Rome, the Emperor Nero tortured and burned the Christian martyrs. St Peter was crucified and St Paul beheaded. And here, near a spot straight down from where the main altar of the Basilica has been built, the first Pope's bones were lodged and venerated.

The basic *raison d'être* of the Vatican is the tradition that St Peter was buried on the site of the church of Constantine, which was scrapped during the Renaissance for the building of the Basilica of St Peter's. The Vatican is first of all a tomb. Here was the final burial place of Peter and of other early Christians, then a place for worship and administration. Only in the fifteenth century, after the return of the Popes from their exile in Avignon and the end of the Great Schism, did it become the usual papal residence.

By then, the lines of its future architectural development had been clearly drawn. A turreted wall, part of which still remains, had been built by Pope Leo IV (847–55) around the old church and its outbuildings. In 852, it was consecrated by seven cardinals leading a procession of priests, sprinkling holy water. The wall established the Leonine City, and fortified it against the Saracens. A second, inner wall and additions to the palace and offices of the Curia were added in the early thirteenth century by Pope Innocent III (1198–1216), arguably the greatest of the medieval Popes, initiator of the Fourth Crusade, hammer of the Albigenses of Provence.

The Orsini Pope Nicholas III (1277–80) started work on a new two-storey palace whose plan and dimensions provided form and inspiration for the successive outbursts of building and embellishment from the time of the early Renaissance to the twentieth century. The Sistine Chapel stands on the old Palatine Chapel of the Middle Ages. The courtyard of San Damaso was the private garden, *hortus secretus*, of the medieval and Renaissance Popes. The first walls of Nicholas III still stand below the loggias added by Bramante and Raphael.

The visitor to the Vatican looks first to the huge dome, the *cupolone*, of St Peter's; then his eyes are drawn to the windows of the Palace, in the wing overlooking the right-hand colonnade of St Peter's Square.

The Pope, standing between the open metal shutters of his own window, saying noonday prayers from his balcony on Sundays and Holy Days, sees the crowd held tightly between the two huge semicircular stone colonnades, each with its four rows of Doric columns creating broad covered passages round the square and bearing on their high balustrades 162 baroque statutes of saints. Bernini's scheme, when the colonnade was begun in 1657, envisaged a third arm of columns on the east of the square. They were never built. The arms remain open.

Surprise and charm are added to the almost embarrassing grandeur of the colonnade by the obelisk in the middle of the square, resting and held by its own 320 ton weight on four lions and a tall plinth, by the two plain splashing fountains, and by the two round porphyry slabs from where each series of columns looks to the eye like one.

On historic occasions, such as the announcement of the choice of a new Pope or the funeral of an old, St Peter's Square is packed with 300,000 people or more. Most of the time there are just the pigeons, and tourists moving in eddies towards the Basilica, or slumped in ones and twos at the feet of the columns and pilasters. When the square is empty, glistening with rain or smouldering in the summer heat, it can seem lifeless and drab, despite the loveliness of patches of dove-grey and silver in certain lights, and its setting of intense, light-blue skies and dark-green cypresses on the hills. It needs to be filled with people, the Roman crowds jostling the strangers, to create its atmosphere of warmth as the familiarly sacred gathering-place for those who want to see the Pope, to touch him, the Holy Father.

From his apartments in the Palace, his home and his office, the Pope is ultimately responsible for, and personally regulates, the activities of the Holy See and the Vatican State. Physically, the domain can be divided into several distinct groupings, viewed as they might be by the Pope in a helicopter rising from the top of the hill, from the Vatican's own modest heliport in fact, on the site of the old tennis court used by the staff of the British Legation to the Holy See who were incarcerated in the Vatican during the Second World War.

Since it is outside his bedroom, and since his personal part of the Palace was built carefully so as not to spoil the view, the Pope looks at St Peter's every day.

Pope Paul VI loved and knew a lot about Michelangelo. He used to enjoy the exterior of the Basilica's drum, as he stared at it from his apartments, noting the perfect effect of the twin columns, despite their missing statues.

23

A namesake among Pope Paul's predecessors, Pope Paul V
Borghese (1605–21), who had a passion for adding to Rome's
buildings, especially fountains, also lengthened the nave of St
Peter's and added to it a facade designed by Carlo Maderno.
On the frieze of Maderno's portico, which was finished in
1612, is the only inscription on the exterior of the church. This
blatantly commemorates the initiative of Paul V, to the shame
of the Borghese family, who are still reproached for it.

On the balustrade are the statues, nearly 19 feet high (6
metres), of Jesus Christ carrying the cross, St John the Baptist
and all the Apostles save St Peter, whose statue is in the church.
These statues and two large clocks (only one of which works)
meet the visitor's eye as he crosses the piazza and looks for the
dome and drum of St Peter's. The collaboration of Paul V and
Maderno changed the design of St Peter's from a Greek to a
Latin cross, and the façade prevents Michelangelo's dome and
drum from having the effect he planned.

But St Peter's was still and has remained the most imposing
and flamboyantly Catholic church in the world, in size the
most impressive, in appearance the most beautiful amalgam of
Renaissance and baroque structures. It is not the Pope's
episcopal seat as Bishop of Rome (which is the Basilica of St
John Lateran), nor his parish church (which for the Vatican
City State is the little church of Sant'Anna by the gate of that
name). A memorial chapel in honour of the first Pope was
transformed by Constantine into the first glorious church of St
Peter's, a patriarchical basilica for the Pope in his role of
Patriarch of the West, and a centre for the whole Catholic
Church for ceremonies and celebrations.

The Pope, governing St Peter's through one of the bodies of
the Palatine (or Palace) Administrations, represents the point
at which the ceremonial function of the Basilica reaches its
apogee. For him, St Peter's is a constantly vivid symbol of the
power and responsibility of his office, and a reminder of his
personal mortality.

After the announcement of his election, the new Pope comes
to the central balcony of St Peter's to give his apostolic blessing
to the city of Rome and the world: *urbi et orbi*. He used to be
crowned within the Basilica at the high altar near the bronze
statue of St Peter, but recent Popes have been installed outside
the Basilica. He addresses the crowds in St Peter's Square

frequently from the loggia above the main entrance, and celebrates Mass at the principal altar on feast days. At Easter especially, he officiates in the Basilica at the high ceremonies of the Church. The tombs of most of his predecessors are in the crypt or the vaults of the Basilica; and his own body will lie in state in the church after his death.

The history of St Peter's, like the history of the Palace where the Pope lives, is present to his eyes in architecture and sculpture which record the extraordinary interaction over many centuries of spiritual and aesthetic aims and of papal patronage and artistic energy. Behind the massive structure of the St Peter's of Michelangelo and Bernini is the memory, like the sinopia of a fresco, of the church built by Constantine, with its huge nave, five doors – the main one of silver – flights of marble steps and mosaic interior and façade.

In the crypt or grottoes under the present floor, you can stand in what still exists of Constantine's Basilica. Below are the tombs and monuments, recently excavated, of Romans and Christians, some deliberately clustered round the tomb of the Apostle Peter; all around in the crypt are monuments to the Popes, including England's Adrian IV; above, through the skylights, you can catch fascinating glimpses of the new Basilica, and a still more enhanced sense of space upwards to the distant dome.

The first serious thought of replacing the decaying Basilica of Constantine was entertained by Pope Nicholas V (1447–55), who was excited by the grandly ambitious plans of Leon Battista Alberti for the whole of Rome. Julius II (1503–13), persuaded that a new St Peter's would be appropriate for his tomb, procured plans from Bramante, whose design made the Basilica in the form of a Greek cross, with a large hemispherical cupola at the centre, surrounded by four smaller cupolas. After Bramante's death, Sangallo, Raphael and Fra Giacondo da Verona produced a new plan and, when Raphael and Giacondo died, Sangallo and Baldassare Peruzzi produced yet another.

Sangallo raised the floor level for the new Basilica, leaving the space which would become the Vatican crypt. When Sangallo died, full of foreboding, Michelangelo in 1547 gloomily accepted the position of chief architect from Paul III. He remained responsible for the tremendous enterprise till his death seventeen years later, serving in turn Julius III, Paul IV, Pius IV and Pius V.

Michelangelo, harassed by rival factions and stuck miserably in the morass of intrigue and corruption fostered by the great building project, gave more emphasis to the massive central space of the Basilica. He left a model for the dome, and took the work as far as the completion of the drum in 1564. Enough had been done when he died that same year to ensure that St Peter's, especially in the flowing exterior lines of the pilasters and columns and windows, would bear his imprint.

Pope Sixtus V, who thought the Basilica without its dome resembled a headless body, found the money to enable Giacomo della Porta and Domenico Fontana, starting in 1588, the year of the Spanish Armada, to complete Michelangelo's work. Within two years, they built and clad the cupola (a modified version of Michelangelo's original plan which dangerously heightened the curves of the two shells), erected the columns of the lantern, and added the ball and cross to its summit.

Under Pope Paul V, what remained of the old Basilica of Constantine was finally destroyed and the nave of the new St Peter's extended. Maderno's portico was finished in 1612. Some splendid reminders of the old church remained, including Filarete's bronze doors which were used for the new central doorway, and Giotto's mosaic of the *Navicella*.

When the new Basilica was consecrated by Pope Urban VIII (1623–44), the main altar was raised in height at the same time, in preparation for the building of Gianlorenzo Bernini's luxuriant *baldacchino* or canopy, for which the bronze mostly came from the portico of the Pantheon. By the time Bernini died in 1680, the Basilica of St Peter's was fully built and formed. The internal decoration was nearly completed, after decades of frenzied and sometimes lifelong activity by architects, sculptors, painters, goldsmiths, carpenters and artisans of every craft and trade, working in wood, metal, stone, gold, stucco, mosaic and glass, in teams rising in peak years to seven or eight hundred.

One of the stucco workers, a Rocco Solaro, scrawled his name on the drum of St Peter's. Bernini had no need to sign his theatrical masterpieces of the *baldacchino* and the *Cathedra*, the enormous throne in the tribune enclosing the wooden chair –

once thought to have been St Peter's – inlaid with ivory and held up by huge statues of the four doctors of the church. With these massive ornaments, he achieved the metamorphosis of St Peter's from a Renaissance to a baroque temple.

Bernini's work on St Peter's turned Michelangelo's spiritual abstractions into a timeless setting for unabashed and beautiful 'propaganda' on the primacy of the Popes. On the frieze under the drum of the Basilica letters six feet high proclaim in Latin one of the three key Petrine texts: 'Thou art Peter and upon this rock I will build my Church and to you I will give the Keys of the Kingdom of Heaven.'

There are only a few pictures in St Peter's. The affirmations of Catholicism, planted among the twenty-nine altars and 148 columns, are mostly in stucco and marble and bronze. The smooth right foot of Arnolfo di Cambio's bronze statue of St Peter is still being kissed by the faithful. Charmingly, the Barberini bees, symbol of the family's munificence, swarm in the gold and black monument to Urban VIII. The flamboyance of one towering monument after another is relieved by gentle reminders of the human foibles of the Popes and the artists who served them. The humble Pope John XXIII had his coat-of-arms represented in inlaid marbles by Giacomo Manzù, who made the bronze doors for one of the Basilica's five entrances. The gleaming Virgin and dead Christ, the *Pietà* which was boldly put on show in the United States in 1965 and damaged by a madman with a hammer in 1972, is the only statue Michelangelo ever signed, because he overheard some country visitors saying it was done by someone else.

Before the Second Vatican Council, the spirit of the ceremonies held in St Peter's matched the exalted claims for the Papacy implicit in the decoration and the architecture of the building. Theological and ceremonial emphases have changed, but the Basilica of St Peter's remains the most eloquent and powerful symbol of papal power and prerogatives. Its very size is a religious statement.

The measurements of St Peter's are given differently in various sources. The scale is breathtaking. The length of the Basilica is usually given as 186.36 metres, or nearly 612 feet. The interior transept is 449 feet long. The great dome, divided into sixteen compartments corresponding to the windows in the drum, measures 138 feet in diameter and reaches a height

27

of 394 feet above the floor of the Basilica. The barley-sugar columns of Bernini's *baldacchino* are 95 feet high.

After eating grapes in the shadow of the great obelisk in the square, Goethe remarked that St Peter's had made him realize that art, like nature, could abolish all standards of measurement.

But, at the busy time for religious services in St Peter's, I find my sense of awe softened by the queues of humans waiting patiently outside the confessional boxes signposted for different nationalities, and the murmur of dozens of Masses being said in a matter-of-fact way at the altars. Even the Pope coming in might scarcely distract people.

The piazza in front of St Peter's was given its unique appearance by Bernini, who defined its elliptical shape with the encircling arms of the colonnade. Maderno planned the northern and Fontana the southern fountain.

The enormous sacristy, along a corridor from the Basilica, was constructed on the orders of Pius VI, who died a prisoner of the French during the revolutionary wars. The work of Carlo Marchionni, who finished it in 1784, it houses three chapels and the often looted but still richly endowed treasury of St Peter's, stored with sacred relics, vestments, chalices, candelabra and ornaments in precious metals, including the *Crux Vaticana*, a gift from the Emperor Justinian II. In the same building are the archives of St Peter's.

Below the sacristy and the Basilica are the Vatican grottoes. Originally formed by Renaissance builders below the level of the Basilica of Bramante and Michelangelo and above the church of Constantine, these hold the tombs of nineteen Popes.

The grottoes inspire awe and the Basilica's atmosphere is usually very solemn. It is a relief to come across the *sampietrini*, as workers for the governing body of the Basilica (the Reverenda Fabbrica di S. Pietro) are affectionately called in Rome and in the official documents. As the skilled maintenance men of the world's biggest Christian church, they are responsible for the continuous repairs and alterations needed to the fabric and its contents, and for erecting the scaffolding, platforms and barriers required for St Peter's endless ceremonial functions.

You could almost hear the sigh behind the remark in the

Vatican's yearbook (*L'Attività della Santa Sede*) that, in the year of the three Popes (1978), the *sampietrini* and all the personnel of St Peter's rendered extraordinary services night and day erecting sarcophagi, building altars, preparing the Basilica and the piazza for exceptional crowds, as well as scurrying around on their normal jobs.

It was a group of *sampietrini* who, during the pontificate of Pius XII, started the work of excavating under the crypt of St Peter's. They first of all unearthed a disconcerting little statue of Bacchus. Then the excavators broke through the foundations of the Constantinian Basilica to reveal a double row of mausoleums and a graveyard under the high altar containing what is believed to be the grave of the first of the Popes, St Peter himself.

The Vatican Palace, in the north-east of the Vatican State, is a heterogeneous group of buildings of all ages and purposes, stretching in a perplexing jumble from St Peter's Square to the walls on the northern edge of the city and the public entrance to the museums. Its historical heart is the enormous, gaunt courtyard of San Damaso, overlooked by the papal apartments. Eight other courtyards are ranged at varying distances and angles round about.

When I think about the interior of the Palace, the first place that usually comes to mind is a small and beautiful bathroom: the entrancing and mildly scandalous closet of Cardinal Bibbiena, designed and painted by Raphael, which is near the offices of the Secretariat of State, and which was shown to me by a young *monsignore* before we went to meet his cardinal.

Images also return of the domestic appearances of recent Popes: Pius XII, frail and almost translucent; the burly John XXIII, grumbled at for not getting down to his paperwork; John Paul I, who shyly gave me a book in Venice and showed me the rooms of two previous Patriarchs and Popes a few months before he took the throne; and John Paul II, a delighted histrionic figure reluctant to leave the window after saying the rosary for the crowds. Behind these, back to St Peter (a thought that can strike you like a physical blow as you look at the living Pope), stretch a line of Pontiffs who came to create the palaces in surges of building mania using the energies and talents of a long procession of painters, sculptors, architects and craftsmen. The edifices of the Apostolic Palace reflect an astonishing continuity of religious patronage, which transformed the original fortress-like nucleus of papal residence and curial offices into the richest concentration of art in the world and a unique centre of international diplomacy and administration.

The entire complex includes about 1400 chapels, halls, galleries, and private and office apartments. The Museums and the Monuments, the Vatican Library and the Secret Archives, the papal apartments and offices cover about fourteen acres of ground excluding the gardens.

The area linking the Papal Palace and the square of St Peter's assumed its present intricate form in the seventeenth century, chiefly through the genius of Bernini and the patronage of successive Popes with resonant Roman associations: Paul Borghese, Urban VIII Barberini, Innocent X Pamphilj and Alexander VII Chigi. As well as creating the ornate interior of the Basilica, and the great colonnade for the piazza, Bernini devised the breathtaking *Scala Regia* in the Palace.

Bernini's stairway is a miracle of structural ingenuity and spatial beauty. It is the ideal way to enter the residence of the Popes with a heightened awareness of their worldly as well as their spiritual magnificence. Approached either from the atrium of St Peter's, or the bronze doors and the portico of Constantine, it thrusts upward in two long flights of marble steps between pilasters, panels and columns supporting architraves and barrel-vaulting, all placed at gradually diminishing intervals to yield a marvellously elongated and graceful effect.

My visits to the offices of the Vatican near the Pope's rooms are usually through the bronze doors and then to the right and up flights of steps towards the courtyard of San Damaso. I have walked down the *Scala Regia*, after sauntering through the Vatican Gardens on the other side of the Palace. It is a descent from a timeless world.

At the top of the great stairway is the *Sala Regia*, the ceremonial centre of the Apostolic Palace. It is a vast, barrel-vaulted hall with painted walls which makes you feel rather exposed as you walk across its marble floor, and which was recently the scene of what an amused John Paul II called a 'surrealist' event, when over a thousand Catholic students sang to the Pope in Polish and Italian. Its doors open on to the *Scala Regia*, the sacristy, the Pauline Chapel and the Sistine Chapel. The Swiss Guards are always on duty.

In the *Sala Regia*, you are near to the quarter of the Vatican where the Popes had their first home in the original Palace, overlooking on three sides the present Cortile dei Pappagalli, and where in the fifteenth century Pope Nicholas V employed Fra Angelico. The Sistine Chapel, linking the springtime of the Renaissance with Michelangelo's classicism and despair, is one of the most evocative religious monuments in the world. It is the Vatican Court chapel, where in modern times the Conclaves are held for the papal elections. It is also a corridor from one part of the Palace to another, and now and then the neck-craning crowd of tourists opens like the Red Sea as a stream of *monsignori* come in from one door and out by another. It has precious frescoes by Botticelli, Luca Signorelli, Rosselli and Perugino and, of course, sustains the historic majesty of Michelangelo's stupendous paintings of the *Creation* on the vault and the *Last Judgement* over the high altar. It was built to the measurements of Solomon's Temple by the blatantly nepotic Della Rovere Pope, Sixtus IV (1471–84), chiefly to improve the defences of the Palace.

To the north of the Palace, Sixtus's successor Innocent VIII (1484–92) planned a loggia and garden which grew into a fine summer villa, called, for its splendid views of the countryside, the Belvedere. Julius II, who willed his structures not to be built but to grow 'as if by magic', employed Bramante to make a new façade for the Apostolic Palace, looking towards Rome, and to begin the construction of two elaborately planned, three-storeyed corridors from the Palace to the Belvedere pavilion. These powerful works of art and engineering – the long loggias stretching from the Palace to various terminal points uphill, rising with spiral staircases, ramps and piazze like a series of locks – formed the spectacular Belvedere courtyard, which was completed after Bramante's death and was used for tournaments, plays and bull-fights.

Save for the hubbub at the entrances, and the occasional noise of parties and receptions, the Vatican Palace is a serene haven of hushed corridors and lowered voices. In the private rooms, only the ringing telephones and animated conversations convey the busy transactions of the mornings and late afternoons. Wherever you go, you feel conscious of the proximity of the Pope and his hold on the affections of all those working there. It is ironic that one of the most violent of Pontiffs, by commissioning a new Palace, determined the context in which peaceable modern Popes would live their day-to-day lives. The Pope was Sixtus V (1585–90), a Franciscan inquisitor who cracked down on clerical discipline, and had the severed heads of local bandits exhibited on the Sant'Angelo bridge. The architect was Domenico Fontana, who, as well as moving the great obelisk of Caligula to its present site in front of St Peter's, built the Palace of Monte Cavallo (the Quirinal), a new Lateran Palace, and the new Library, the Hall of Sixtus V, which unhappily divided in two the vast Belvedere courtyard.

Fontana's Palace develops to the east the extensions of the old Apostolic Palace which had enclosed the San Damaso courtyard with two wings, and left open the view of St Peter's. A shorter wing was built on the east of San Damaso, and a new four-sided Palace arose round the new courtyard. Under Pope Clement VIII, this Palace was completed with the building of the lofty Clementine Hall decorated by Giovanni and Cherubino Alberti and Paul Bril, which acts today as the vaulted vestibule to the Pope's private rooms.

Fortress, residence, pleasure-dome, the group of buildings erected over five centuries round the original offices of the Curia of the Pope, after a century's pause following the death of Pope Alexander VII, provided for modern times the architectural shell for the earliest scientifically organized and richest museums in the world. The long, straight arms of the Belvedere corridors stretching towards the north were modified in the nineteenth century by scores of extensions and renovations which turned the Vatican into an incomparable showplace for the art of all times and cultures.

The way to the Pontifical Museums, after a climb along the outside of the Vatican walls to the Viale del Vaticano, is through a massive doorway cut in 1932 through the northern part of the huge, sloping walls. The surroundings outside, despite the ornate doorway, are drab and neglected, as if the breach were meant to be unobtrusive. Inside is one of the most curious ascents in the world, a double ramp winding like a corkscrew for going up and coming down, rather uncomfortably, in the same space.

The works of art inside the museums are a powerful, controversial demonstration of the instinctive humanism of the Popes, even the Pontiffs who now and then censored the nudity of some paintings. For the visitor, the museum authorities have made exploration easier in recent years by adopting a system of pre-selected itineraries. Follow the right colours of letters marked on the floor, and you can either see all there is on display, or complete about two-thirds of the entire tour, or contemplate just the Sistine Chapel.

The medieval and Renaissance Popes laid the foundations and built most of the structures. Pope Julius II arranged in a garden of the Belvedere a group of statues that formed the nucleus of the great future collections. From the eighteenth century onwards, nearly every Pope added something to the architecture of the museums, re-arranged them, or enlarged the collections. Pope Clement XIV (1769–74) laid the foundation stone of a new museum (the Pio-Clementine) and built the octagonal courtyard on Julius II's Garden of the Statues. Pius VI (1775–99) demolished the chapel of Mantegna but also built an inter-connecting series of spacious halls looped like lace from the extended Gallery of the Statues through the Hall of Animals, the octagonal Hall of the Muses, the *Sala Rotonda* (domed like the Pantheon) to the Hall of the Greek Cross and the *Scala Simonetti* on the axis of the Belvedere loggia. Pius VII (1800–23) took the sculptor Canova's advice to build a new wing for the Vatican's collections of ancient statues. This changed the Vatican landscape once more. The New Wing, the long corridor parallel to the Sistine Library, opening on to the Cortile della Pigna of the Belvedere, sharply modified Bramante's conception for the grandiose Belvedere, already divided into two and now into three courtyards, the Cortile della Pigna, the Cortile della Biblioteca, and the diminished Cortile del Belvedere.

However, the New Wing is classically beautiful and functionally apposite: a triumph and an innovatory achievement in museum history. Sky light from the barrel-vaulting of the long corridor falls on twenty-eight niches for the statues and on rows of columns and brackets for Greek and Roman busts. Halfway along is a domed ceiling supported by four arches.

The effect of the interior and the austere façade is cold, calm and luminous.

The urge to build, like the American drive to seek new frontiers, moves the spirits of modern Popes as urgently as it has ever done throughout the centuries. Pope John XXIII – who threw open from within the Vatican new metaphorical windows on the outside world – commissioned a modern new building to house the collections of the Gregorian Pagan Museum, the Pian Christian Museum and the Missionary and Ethnological Museum. Built to the west of the Cortile della Pigna, parallel to the Viale Vaticano, and opened during the pontificate of Pope Paul VI, it is a functional, adaptable building with bold, flowing lines, generously open to natural light from the gardens and the sky.

Talking to me in his offices at the Museums, shortly before the death of Pope Paul VI, Dr Redig de Campos mentioned that the four Popes he had served had all been keenly interested in the arts. An American, he added, had once argued with him that the Church should sell many of the treasures of the Apostolic Palace and give the money to the poor. 'Here,' said de Campos, giving the critic a few lire, 'would be your share. . . .'

Parts of his domain remind the Pope of his predecessors' stormy courtship of science as well as art. Pope Gregory XIII (1572–85) built the Tower of the Winds (where he had his observatory), which from the north of Ligorio's Belvedere corridor provides a pulse-quickening view of the ancient city of Rome and the flank of St Peter's. The walls of the room at the top of the tower still bear the markings to record the moving of the sun on which the reform of the calendar in 1582 depended.

The casina (or pavilion) of Pius IV, is a gem-like palace fringed by palm trees in the Vatican Gardens. John Paul II used to walk past the white, fresh-looking building, hesitating, in the early months of his pontificate, whether to go in or not. In the end, he decided to wait for a plenary session of the academy, when he toured the premises and spoke about his passion for science to its members, who had been commemorating the centenary of Albert Einstein.

Until fairly recently, the gardens of the Vatican were barred to the public. Pope Pius XII did not even like to see the

34

gardeners when he walked there. Nowadays, informal tours are arranged for small groups of visitors. But the gardens and the buildings within them retain an atmosphere of arcane privacy. You feel like an intruder, stepping on the dreams of Popes who walked up the slope of the hill and prayed by the grottoes and fountains.

As you walk through courtyards and woods, you are likely to stumble across the unexpected and the forgotten. When I was there in 1978, I saw the stooped figure of Cardinal Josyf Slipyi, long exiled in distance from the Ukraine and in time from his eighteen years in a Soviet labour camp, walking across the grass, under a wide-brimmed black hat, and saying his breviary. I learned, from my escort, about the near-miss on St Peter's by a German bomber pilot during the Second World War.

On your way to the gardens, you pass, in the south-east corner of the Vatican's territory, a string of buildings, all very familiar to the Pope, including the Palace of the Holy Office which is, in fact, just outside the Vatican State but ranks as part of it.

The Holy Office, or the Inquisition, was established in the sixteenth century by Pope Paul III to combat heresy. The Pope is no longer its prefect, and the Holy Office has been renamed the Sacred Congregation for the Doctrine of the Faith. The relationship between the Pope and the Congregation is still exceptionally intimate.

Beyond the old Palace of the Holy Office (one side of which faces the Pope's window across the front of the Basilica) is the newest of Vatican buildings, the Nervi Audience Hall. It was renamed Pope Paul VI Hall, after the death of Paul. It is half in and half outside Vatican territory, and one of the most important and impressive architectural projects in at least two centuries of Vatican history.

The audience hall was where I last saw Paul VI at one of his regular general audiences, when he was weak but vibrant, and appealing for the release of his friend the kidnapped Italian Premier, Aldo Moro. At the end, a frail figure in white hobbled away, soon to learn that Moro had been found dead in a street across the Tiber.

There are security men dotted around the audience when the Pope appears in the hall. He makes a clear target, dressed

35

in white and presented carefully for everyone possible to see. In the piazza, when the Pope walks or is driven through a surging sea of humanity, security is more of a nightmare still.

Pope Paul built the hall as a place for him to meet people – traditionally the vast crowds came into St Peter's Basilica – and expound his ideas. It seats normally just over 6000 but can be adapted to take 12,000 people standing. Paul commissioned the design from the architect Pier Luigi Nervi, who at first shrank from putting up a huge modern building on functional lines cheek by jowl with St Peter's. Sunken lightly into the ground, the audience hall turned out unobtrusive and perhaps inoffensive. It seems to have floated to its site.

It is vaulted in a double parabola and arranged so that the man on the rostrum can be seen from every point. The lighting adds to the effect of spaciousness and airy calm. The two huge oval windows, by the Hungarian artist Giovanni Hajnal, are ribbed and coloured to continue the lineal flow of the ceiling. The first audience in the hall was on the eighth anniversary of Pope Paul's coronation, when it was blessed and inaugurated. At the back the vast flowing figure of the Risen Christ in a forest of jagged and thrusting bronze, by Pericle Fazzini, was cast ready for Pope Paul's eightieth birthday in 1977. Nervi disliked the windows made for his building and would not come to the ceremony. When Nervi died in January 1979, Pope John Paul II praised his bland reinforced concrete structure for its elegance and daring, harmony and functionality, and he used the building for his first big party in the Vatican, an evening birthday celebration to which he asked 6000 of his compatriots, in May 1979.

As well as a suite of rooms for private audiences of the Pope (at least one of them has a set of three papal thrones), for larger meetings, including those of the Synod of Bishops, the audience hall enfolds a smaller hall efficiently equipped for simultaneous translation into six languages including Latin, for television and press coverage of events.

The Teutonic College, between the audience hall and the sacristy of St Peter's, served for many centuries as a hospice and a burial ground, the Campo Santo Teutonico, whose history goes back to Charlemagne. Today it has strong Irish connections and contains a house for student priests, the *camposantini*, a museum of antiquities and the restored Renaissance church.

The college stands to one side of the Piazza Protomartyri Romani, the Square of the First Roman Martyrs, where a marble disc marks the original position, in Nero's circus, of the obelisk (then one of a pair) which now stands in St Peter's Square.

On the upper floors of the sacristy are residences for the canons of St Peter's. Beyond it lies the Piazza di Santa Marta, the second largest square in the Vatican, across which the Pope's car will speed when he is coming from the Palace, round the back of the Basilica, to the audience hall of the main piazza. The British Legation lived in the hospice of Santa Marta during the Second World War. Nearby, again on the edge of Vatican territory, is the Palazzo San Carlo, housing the offices of the Pontifical Commission for Social Communications, where I first met Pope John Paul's fellow-Pole and close friend, Archbishop Andrzej Deskur. In front of the Palace and the surrounding buildings, used for residences and offices, stand the city's three casually attended petrol pumps.

Beyond the formal garden in the Square of St Martha is the small, ancient church of St Stephen of the Abyssinians. Next, a little further on the road which climbs to the summit of the Vatican Hill, is the Vatican's mosaic factory.

From here, the full stretch of the Vatican Hill, crossed by broad empty roads and winding paths, comes into full view. From every point of the gardens the dome of St Peter's is visible, and it is from the edge of the gardens that the full magnificence of Michelangelo's powerful conception of the Basilica can be grasped.

The gardens were wilder and more extensive before the burst of new building prompted by the settlement between Pius XI and the Italian government in 1929. A writer on the Vatican, George Seldes, observed at the time that a spring had been found in the hill, for mixing mortar, and that all the hurly-burly was 'making the sacred hill as tremulous as a Sheffield steel plant'. One of the largest buildings (the work of the architect Giuseppe Momo, a friend of Pius XI, who also built the Vatican Railway, the Ethiopian College and the Pinacoteca) was the Government Palace, completed in 1931.

This large, white, rather pretentious edifice in brick and stone was intended as a seminary but converted to the headquarters of the Pontifical Commission which governs the Vatican City State under the Pope, and the civil administration, the *Governatorato*, with its numerous offices. The *Governorate*, or government building, is the residence of Cardinal Sergio Guerri, the affable Pro-President of the Pontifical Commission, and has served as a guest-house for important state visitors. It rises over a large basement store for goods of all kinds, the exports and imports of the Vatican City, including the cars and cigarettes that can be bought in the *maggazino*. The offices transact a bemusing variety of supervisory activities ranging from salaries to security. Outside, the *Governorate* looks as sleepy and anonymous as a government building in Whitehall.

Near by, the Vatican's railway station presents, save on rare occasions, a still more comically slumberous aspect. Popes have used it sporadically, since it was built at the end of a branch line from Viterbo in the early 1930s, as when Pope John went in 1962 to the holy places of Loreto and Assisi; and a choir from the Sistine Chapel is charged on such occasions to sing psalms. But the station's activities nowadays are confined to taking out the products of the Vatican's mosaic factory, or bringing in the commercial goods.

On the façade of this ornate construction of marble and stucco, embellished with high Ionic columns, are two bas-reliefs showing Elijah in his chariot and St Peter with his miraculous catch of fish. Near Elijah are black marks on the wall left from the explosion of the bomb that might have hit St Peter's and was jettisoned but not apparently aimed deliberately by a German pilot.

The government building has its own piazza, and facing it a shrubbery and a flowerbed with the arms of the reigning Pontiff picked out in blooms as cheerily as in a municipal garden. Other Vatican buildings, functional, fanciful and decorative, are dotted around the hill, which culminates at the summit in a point like the tip of a spear, enclosing the heliport field. The Ethiopian College, one of Rome's score or so of ecclesiastical colleges under pontifical control, surmounted by loggias, stands in a secluded angle of garden formed by the long Avenue of the Observatory. The office of Vatican Radio's director general, and its 'No 1' studio, are in a pseudo-palace built by Pope Leo XIII and the keep of the old walls of Nicholas V, of which there are solid, well-preserved stretches sloping parallel to the present western walls of the city. The Palazzina Leone XIII was originally built as a summer residence for the Pope on the highest part of the Vatican Hill. Later, it was part of the Vatican Observatory.

Another tower of the walls of Nicholas V was restored by Pope John XXIII for his own peace and quiet and has been used as a guest house for visitors such as Athenagoras I, the Patriarch of Constantinople. Cardinal Mindszenty, the late Primate of Hungary, stayed there after ending in 1971 his fifteen years exile in the American Embassy in Budapest. Pope John Paul II moved to the tower for a while when his apartments were being reorganized and the ceiling repaired in 1979.

Every structure in the Vatican Gardens is liable to serve as a toothing-stone for another building and a fresh purpose. Halfway down the hill to the west of St Peter's, the remains of a tower, possibly once part of the wall built by Pope Innocent III, form part of the House of the Gardener, headquarters of the Board for Archaeological Studies and Research. Further down, the headquarters of the Pontifical Academy of Sciences has been located, since 1922, in the building abutting the original casina of Pius IV. The casina's two main buildings, facing each other across a courtyard, are the richly stuccoed villa and the loggia with fountain and lily-pond.

An orderly mind recoils from the view of the gardens as it unfolds on the ascent to the tower of Pope John, and the descent to the Palace of the Mint and the building (commissioned by Pope Paul V) linking the gardens with the Apostolic Palace. They reach after French and English effects of orderliness and naturalness but remain obstinately Italian gardens, frustrated by the play of heat and the lack of overall design.

The pleasures come in patches of charming vegetation and contrivance. Scrunchy gravel paths and green walks lead past box hedges and tall palms, willows and banana trees. There are rockeries of succulents and coral.

Above all, the fountains, grottoes and statues of the gardens reveal and display the naive pieties that form an essential element in the appeal of the Papacy to people hungering for

39

visual symbols of faith in the miraculous and the eternal. Papal pride is implicit in two great fountains, built by the Dutchman van Santen in the period of the Counter-Reformation: the huge Fountain of the Rock, with its massive stone eagle, and the Fountain of the Sacrament, surmounted by a great stone dragon from the Borghese family's coat-of-arms. Between the fountains, fed by water from Lake Bracciano, in one of the quietest spots of the gardens, full of shade and marble seats, is a statue of St Peter (apparently caught up in a moment of stunned revelation after his deliverance from prison) by a French artist – a woman – Amalia Dupré, which originally formed part of a monument commemorating the First Vatican Council and the declaration of papal infallibility. The jumble of religious and artistic works include items sent by the faithful as gifts to the Pope: a representation of the grotto of Lourdes, where St Bernadette saw her vision of the Virgin; a copy of the statue of Our Lady of Guadalupe, who appeared in Mexico to the Indian Juan Diego, and imprinted her image on the apron he wore, when he shook the roses from it.

Pope Paul VI built himself a roof garden for his recreation (it is hidden by a false roof). Pope John XXIII loved parts of the gardens, especially near the tower. Pope John Paul I had little time to explore them, though he is said to have gone there to weep over the mountains of paperwork loaded on him by his officials. Pope John Paul II immediately saw their potential for the construction of a swimming pool, though the one he has had built is at Castel Gandolfo. The gardens are the most ordinary part of the Vatican, showing its most human face.

The most prosaic entrance to the Vatican, the only one with traffic lights, yields the most lively human interest, if you stand and wait by the gate of St Anne, the Porta Sant'Anna, in the Via di Porta Angelica, to the right of Bernini's colonnade, before the Viale Vaticano.

In the middle of the little street, the Via del Belvedere, a Swiss Guard occasionally directs the traffic, questions strangers, greets and salutes (when it is appropriate) those whom he knows. Lorries, vans and private cars pass constantly through the gate, and crowds of visitors of all sorts stream along the pavement. This is the noisy spot where you can still best see the various traditional garments of monks, friars and nuns – the brown robes and sandals of the Franciscans, the black habits of the Benedictines, the white of the Dominicans – the flashes of purple and red signifying the rank of bishop or cardinal, the shaven heads and long beards, the varying gaits, gestures and, now and then exotic, clothes of clerics from all over the world as they go in and out of the Vatican.

If the visitor to the Vatican is of the clergy, the salute depends on his badge of clerical rank. Cars are identified by number plates and a diplomatic car earns a salute. Laymen on foot are identified by their style of dress: a rosette denoting a papal knighthood, especially with a silver backing (Knight Commander) or gold backing (Knight Grand Cross), gets a salute; so does a morning coat. Blue jeans do not, at any time. I have always been saluted, at least when *leaving* the Vatican by the bronze doors or the Arch of the Bells. At Porta Sant'Anna you never know, but it is, as a Vatican diplomat put it to me, rather the tradesmen's entrance. At the Arch of the Bells or the main entrances to the Vatican Palace, the Swiss Guards wear their best dress. At the Porta Sant'Anna they wear only their alternative, non-gala dress of blue and black.

The northern corner of the Vatican City, between the Basilica and the Palace and the museums, is rarely visited either by the Pope or by the tourists who come to see him. None the less, the Pope is always concerned about what goes on there, in the commissariat, and especially in the offices of the Vatican Press. Those hurrying along the Via del Belvedere are going to work in the offices and shops of the district, or heading for the Vatican Library and the Secret Archives, or choosing this route, as I have done, to make their way under the subway into the courtyard of the Belvedere and up to the offices of the Secretariat of State in the Palace.

The Pope's parish church, on the right after the gate, is called Santa Anna dei Palafrenieri. It was built in 1573 for the papal grooms (*palafrenieri*) by the influential baroque artist Giacomo da Vignola, Michelangelo's successor as architect of St Peter's. Opposite the oval church are the comfortable barracks of the Swiss Guards.

Along the Via del Belvedere, past the Swiss Guard and the security guard, on the corner of the road leading to the right, the Via Pellegrino, is the Vatican's printing concern, the

Tipografia Poliglotta Vaticana, which occupies the old stables of the disbanded Noble Guard. Next door is a chemist's shop, run by the *Fate Bene Fratelli*, the Hospitallers of St John of God, an old nursing order of brothers under vows to work for the sick; the pharmacy is modern, sweet-smelling and usually crowded.

On the opposite side of the curving street is the self-service food store and the offices and printing works of the *Osservatore Romano* and its associated papers and publications. The daily newspaper was founded in 1861, and bought for the Vatican by Leo XIII in 1890. You can hear the clattering letterpress from the street. Near by, close to the walls, are a huddle of workshops and the city generating station.

Nearer the courtyard of the Belvedere is another cluster of buildings containing the post office, the health centre, the telephone exchange, and the public offices of the Vatican Bank. The car park, between these buildings and the old walls of Bramante, was built over a second Roman necropolis which was scrupulously excavated and preserved.

The people who buy stamps in the post office, cash their cheques in the bank, make use of the car park, can, by favour, include the occasional visitor such as myself. Normally, however, this part of the state is like a private village, full of bustle and local drama, but inward-looking and closed to the scrutiny of outsiders who do not work or live in the Vatican.

Scattered throughout Rome are buildings used by the Holy See to exercise its government of the Church. They stand outside the sovereign state of the Vatican on Italian territory but are exempt from Italian taxation and possess diplomatic immunity. They are intimately associated with the Popes and their history.

About 170 acres of territory are outside Italian jurisdiction. The buildings are all within a few miles of the Vatican, except for Castel Gandolfo, in the Alban Hills nearly twenty miles to the south-east of Rome. As well as the Pope's summer residence at Castel Gandolfo, and the building of the old Holy Office, they include the offices attached to the Basilica of St John Lateran, St Mary Major, St Paul-outside-the-walls and St Laurence-outside-the-walls; the Palace housing the headquarters of the Jesuits, in Borgo Santo Spirito; the Palace of the Apostolic Chancery; the Palace of San Calisto in Trastevere; the Palace of the Propaganda Fide (the Congregation for the Evangelization of Peoples), Piazza di Spagna; and the Hospital of the Infant Jesus on the Janiculum Hill. Several other institutions, such as the Gregorian University and the Biblical Institute, are free from Italian taxes or the possibility of expropriation.

Castel Gandolfo is one of the *castelli Romani* – the old towns and castles, overlooking the *campagna*, and famous for their wine.

Most intimately associated with the institution of the Papacy, and the claims and emotions of the Popes themselves, is the complex of buildings of the Lateran, notably the Basilica and the Palace. For about a thousand years, before exile in Avignon, the Popes lived in the healthier atmosphere of the Lateran Palace, rather than across the Tiber in the Vatican. Until 1870, the Popes were crowned in the Lateran Basilica. In February 1929, the Lateran Agreements were signed in the Council Hall of the Popes at the Lateran Palace. Every year, the reigning Pontiff used to conduct an Ascension Day ceremony of blessing from the arched loggia of the Basilica.

Conscious of the highly charged historical significance of the Lateran to the Romans, Pope John XXIII and Pope Paul VI ordered its complete restoration to serve as the headquarters of the vicariate of Rome, the pastoral and administrative centre of the Pope's own bishopric, which was moved from the Palace of San Calisto. The Pope's vicar general (since 1558 always a cardinal) lives next to the Palace. He has his own Curia and auxiliary bishops.

Over the façade of the Basilica of St John Lateran, linking its history to the Donation of Constantine, are the words: *Sacrosancta Lateranensis ecclesia omnium urbis et orbis ecclesiarum mater et caput* – this is the cathedral both of Rome and of the world.

The Lateran Basilica's architectural and religious history is enmeshed with that of the growth of the medieval Papacy to the height of its power. Five ecumenical Councils were held there, including the Fourth Lateran Council, opened by Pope Innocent III in 1215, which was attended by the representatives of two emperors and five kings, made preparations for the

43

forthcoming crusade, defined the absolute unity of God, Catholic doctrine on the sacraments, and the supremacy of Rome.

Destroyed twice by fire in the Middle Ages, the Cathedral has been reconstructed and extended in every century since. The magnificent Basilica, 426 feet long, is a stupendous treasure-house of Christian art from the Gothic to the baroque and of Early Christian and classical echoes and artefacts: works by Giotto, Giacomo da Vignola, Filarete, the *cosmati* marble and mosaic workers; the bronze doors of the ancient Senate House of Rome; the heads of St Peter and St Paul; the tombs of the great Popes Innocent III and Leo XIII; the last chapel to be built for a noble Roman family, the Torlonia. The papal altar, in the transept, contains a table on which, according to legend, St Peter said Mass and where now only the Pope may do so.

The Lateran Palace, on the actual site of the old residence of the Popes, was reconstructed for Pope Sixtus V by Domenico Fontana in the sixteenth century. Its imposing art collections – the Christian, Profane and Ethnological Missionary Museums – were transferred to the Vatican when it became the headquarters of the vicariate of Rome.

The destruction by Sixtus of what was left of the old building in his frenzy for re-building and town planning can be regarded as an act of vandalism, judging by the remains of the former Palace. These include the *Triclinium* or tribune and the *Sancta Sanctorum*, the ancient private chapel of the Popes. This chapel of St Laurence is crammed with relics, including the oldest of all images of Christ, a sixth- or seventh-century painting on wood covered with silver. Leading to it is the *Scala Santa*, the twenty-eight marble steps, protected by boards, which are by tradition the staircase trodden by Christ in the house of Pilate, and which the Catholic faithful climb on their knees. The spectacle is conducive to faith for some; to others, as it did to Charles Dickens, it crystallizes all the old fears of Popish superstition. Remarking that the staircase was steep, and that one man cheated by helping himself up with an umbrella (on a fine day) he expostulated, after his visit to Rome in the 1840s, 'I never, in my life, saw anything at once so ridiculous and so unpleasant, as this sight – ridiculous in the absurd incidents inseparable from it; and unpleasant in its senseless and unmeaning degradation.'

The Lateran complex, like the Vatican, fuses the spiritual elements of the Papacy with their expression of worldly pomp and beauty. Outside Rome, another extra-territorial possession brings past and present together in a less portentous way.

A Pope may die in the villa at Castel Gandolfo, as did Pius XII tragically, in 1958. Pope John XXIII offended the inhabitants of the village when he threatened to spend more time in his refurbished tower in the Vatican Gardens rather than always make the routine journey there for summer and winter retreats. The tourist traffic is considerable, and the villa possesses a large hall which can be used for audiences of up to 8000.

The audience hall, built for Pius XII, was inaugurated by Pope John XXIII in 1958. On Sundays, from the balcony of the Palace, the Pope says the Angelus above the courtyard crowded with visitors. In his latter years, Pope Paul VI used to return to Rome from Castel Gandolfo by helicopter for the general audience on Wednesdays.

Before 1870 Pope Pius IX used to be seen riding a white mule along the terraces of the villa, followed by cardinals in their scarlet robes. Castel Gandolfo was not visited by Popes from 1870 till after the Lateran Treaty, when Pius XI restored most of the property, including the Villa Barberini. In his first full year as Pope, John Paul II had a swimming pool (50 feet by 82 feet) built. He said, when the expense was remarked upon, that it would be less than the cost of a new Pope.

The Palaces of Castel Gandolfo, and the town with its 3000 inhabitants, have been associated with the Papacy for nearly 400 years. Near the site in the Alban Hills was once a villa of the Emperor Diocletian, persecutor of the Christians. The ruins can still be seen today. The Roman Savelli family sold an old castle and its land at Castel Gandolfo to Pope Urban VIII in 1596. The present villa was built for Pope Urban to the design of Carlo Maderno and on the advice of his doctors. The old battlements are still visible. It was extended by Pope Alexander VII and completed by Pope Clement XIII.

Castel Gandolfo covers about a hundred acres of land, and includes the Pope's Palace, the Cybo Villa and Palace, and the Villa Barberini. The Pope's own villa, with roomy and richly furnished interiors, looks like a fortified bastion against the world, and is architecturally dull compared with the Villa

Barberini. But his apartment has a magnificent view of the lake and hills. Near by are the two domes of the Vatican Observatory (manned by Jesuits), which was transferred to Castel Gandolfo by Pius XI in 1935.

In the grounds are French and Italian gardens and a famous sheltered walkway, decorated with frescoes. This is the magnificent cryptoporticus of Domitian's Palace, over a hundred yards long, which housed hundreds of homeless people in the Second World War. A farm yields produce and livestock for local convents or sale in the Vatican. The view over the Roman countryside, especially from the terrace of the Italian gardens, is breathtaking. Most visitors to Castel Gandolfo use the lift and so miss the main 'staircase', a strange corkscrew ramp designed for the convenience of donkeys.

The healthy air of the Alban Hills turns the Palace at Castel Gandolfo into an essential holiday refuge for the Pope from the stifling Roman heat of summer. With him go a small group from the Papal Court, and a few Swiss Guards whose job it also is to close the main doors of the villas on the death of a Pontiff.

2
Around and About the City State

A sullen storm raged over the Vatican on Monday 18 July 1870, as a few hundred crimson- and white-robed cardinals, bishops and abbots voted in St Peter's Basilica on the decree declaring the Pope infallible: the historical constitution, *'Pastor aeternus.'*

Thomas Mozley, a correspondent of the London *Times*, in an excited letter home described vividly how:

'Placet', shouted His Eminence or His Grace, and a loud clap of thunder followed in response, and then the lightning darted about the baldaccino and every part of the church and the conciliar hall, as if announcing the response. . . .

The result of the voting – 533 to 2 – was greeted with cheers and clapping by the bishops who had remained for this momentous public session of the First Vatican Council. A new ultramontane course was set for the Catholic Church.

War between Prussia and France was declared the very next day, 19 July. At the beginning of August, the French Emperor Napoleon III recalled the garrison he had stationed in Rome to safeguard the territory of the Papacy. Victor Emmanuel, whose drive to unite all Italy in one kingdom had been blocked by the Austrians in the north and by the Pope in the shrunken Papal States, sent his army against Rome early in September, after news had reached Turin of the French defeat at Sedan. On 20 September, after a few hours of bombardment, the Italian troops marched into Rome through two breaches in the Aurelian Wall, each side of the Porta Pia, not far from where the British Embassy is now. Pope Pius IX ordered the papal forces, including the Swiss Guards and volunteer Zouaves from all over Europe, not to fight. A plebiscite brought the Papal States into the kingdom of Italy.

The old Rome of the Popes evinced considerable nostalgia. Augustus Hare wrote that in three years the ancient characteristics of the city had perished, and he accused the new government of barbarism and injustice. The Rome depicted by Piranesi or described by Byron vanished, along with the markets and white bullocks of the Campo Vaccino, the altars of the martyrs in the Colosseum, the processions of cardinals and monks through the streets, and even the *pifferari*, the pipe-playing shepherds from the hills. A rich, still half-medieval culture was erased (and a kind of literary counter-culture, from Joachim du Bellay to G. G. Belli, soon went with it).

Five successive Popes after 1870 willed to stay as the prisoners of the Vatican, refused to accept the Law of Guarantees offered as a settlement by the Italian government, and maintained their own diplomatic relations with other states, including Britain (whose legation to the Holy See was set up in 1914). Their policy proved vital to the preservation of the unique status of the Holy See in the world today. The last of the five 'prisoner' Popes, Pius XI, after several years' negotiation resolved the 'Roman question' and regularized the relationship between the Catholic Church and the Italian State.

Today, the Vatican City State provides a small territorial base for the Holy See, whose claims to sovereignty and independence have been recognized since the earliest days of Christian history. The claims are separate from the territorial position of the Vatican, and the distinction is vital to an understanding of the Papacy.

The Vatican City State came into being on 11 February 1929 when the Lateran Pacts were signed by an elated Benito Mussolini for Italy and Cardinal Pietro Gasparri for the Holy See. The documents included a treaty of conciliation, a concordat for relations between Church and State in Italy, and a financial agreement. On a chill, rainy day, with bells ringing, in the Council Hall of the Lateran Palace the Duce and the cardinal signed the documents with a gold pen that had just been blessed by Achille Ratti, Pope Pius XI.

The pacts gave the Holy See complete sovereignty over a new nation, established in order to support and symbolize its freedom and independence. They were ratified in June 1929, and the new state was implicitly recognized by the thirty powers which had diplomatic representatives accredited to the Holy See.

The size of the new state, which at one stage was intended to include part of the area between St Peter's and the Tiber, was cut down at the very last minute by Pius XI, who wanted the Vatican to be seen to be as small as possible. (The excluded area is associated with the early Kings of Wessex who were in the habit of resigning and going to live in Rome.) Geographically, the new nation comprised the Vatican Palaces, the gardens, the Piazza and Basilica of St Peter's and several nearby edifices. Various buildings and the splendid papal summer residence at Castel Gandolfo obtained extra-territorial 'Holy See' status. For the adornment of this parcel of territories, the adventurous Pius XI at once embarked on fairly grand programmes of building and decoration. He commissioned the Vatican Picture Gallery; he thought at one stage of moving the Vatican Observatory and its astronomers to the brilliantly clear air of the Ethiopian plateau.

The new state was defined as an elective monarchy under the Supreme Pontiff, who possessed complete legislative, administrative and judicial powers. Its constituent laws were promulgated when the Lateran Agreements were ratified: they include the Fundamental Law of the State, which defines its character and its public institutions.

Under the Lateran Treaty, the Italian state is forbidden to tunnel in the ground under the Vatican, and aircraft are forbidden to fly over the city state. (There are no such restrictions regarding space satellites.) The Hague Convention of 14 May 1954, organized by UNESCO, protects the whole of the Vatican territory as a world cultural heritage.

The flag of the Vatican, the papal banner – fluttering as never before throughout the world during the travels of Paul VI and John Paul II – consists of two vertical fields: one yellow, hanging nearer the flagstaff, the other white with the papal tiara and keys. Within the state, no inhabitant may possess landed property, as the Vatican City is the private domain of the Holy See, under the supreme administration of the Pope. The laws and customs of the state are a hodge-podge of medieval and modern elements. For the Holy See, the important element is that the Vatican City should be visibly recognized as an independent sovereign entity in international law.

The Vatican City State is not vital to the sovereignty of the Holy See (which remained intact after 1871, when the Italian government's Law of Guarantees deprived the Pope of his old sovereign rights over 5000 square miles of territory). It performs a series of practical functions, from providing the physical base for the activities of the Holy See to preserving the unique artistic heritage of the Papacy. It lessens the possible threat of domination of the Papacy by a secular power. But it is essentially a symbol of the independence of the Holy See, a useful fiction of fading significance in recent times. Important as the Vatican is to the world's spiritual progress or survival, the Holy See, whose residence it is, is also a powerful political institution which has found lack of territory and people no impediment to dealing with the most important of sovereign states on equal terms, and which itself supports, rather than is supported by, a small sovereign state in Rome, administered by dedicated officials at the centre of a worldwide ecclesiastical network.

Citizenship of the Vatican is as paradoxical as many other aspects of the state. Under the constitutional law of the Vatican, there is no law of nationality, but there is a principle of citizenship. Citizenship is conferred on the basis of a legal bond between an individual and the city state. Vatican citizens must be permanently employed or live permanently in the Vatican (and the close relations of a citizen living in the Vatican can enjoy citizenship while they stay there). Those now in possession of Vatican citizenship number about 400, of whom 160 or so are representatives of the Holy See abroad.

There are some, not many, holders of Vatican City State passports; most passports issued by the Vatican are for diplomatic purposes, on behalf of the Holy See. (Holding a Holy See diplomatic passport does not make you a permanent citizen of the city state, or give you the right to enter or reside there.) The passports are carried by curial cardinals and the Vatican's representatives, and can also be obtained by non-curial cardinals. The Swiss Guards carry Holy See service (or non-diplomatic) passports.

The Pope becomes the sovereign ruler of the Vatican City State at the same moment as he is canonically elected the

Supreme Pontiff of the Catholic Church. There are no separate ceremonies associated with his becoming head of the state, though almost at once he goes to meet the staff formally and he is close to them all the time. The state has diplomatic relations with several international organizations, governmental and non-governmental. These were fostered especially after the Second World War, when the Holy See tended to place more stress on the role of the city state than it does today. The organizations to whose activities the Vatican endeavours to contribute a spiritual dimension even when its practical involvement is clearly limited include the Universal Postal Union, the International Union of Telecommunications and the International Wheat Council.

The settlement of the 'Roman question' was the reward for some agile diplomacy by Mussolini and Cardinal Gasparri. For the Catholic Church it provided a neat contrivance for the maintenance of the dignity as well as the independence of the Holy See: the artificial but legally valid state of the Vatican City, with territory, population and sovereignty. It has a government, and its affairs have to be conducted like those of other little states, distinct though it is with its neutrality, its absolutism and its religious purpose.

The governor of the Vatican City from 1929 till his death in 1952 was a layman, Camillo Serafini, former head of the numismatic cabinet of the Vatican Museums and brother of a famous cardinal. He used to answer directly to the Pope, but an administrative body of three cardinals and a clerical secretary was set over him in 1939. The government of the Vatican City State is today regulated by a law which came into force in July 1969. Under this, the Pope exercises legislative and executive powers through a commission nominated for five years. It comprises seven cardinals, with Cardinal Casaroli, in his role of Secretary of State, as president. The lay delegate working with the commission and responsible for the day-to-day running of the government is nominated by the Pope. At present he is Marchese Don Giulio Sacchetti.

Marchese Sacchetti is the chief executive of the Vatican City State, with wide responsibilities for staff, public works and general order. His formal job is to communicate the wishes of the Pontifical Commission to his officials. The pro-president of the commission – Cardinal Guerri – lives in the government building, over the shop, and is in close contact with the administration. The full Commission normally meets at least twice a year, to inspect and approve the budget, and to agree to any important building schemes, or other projects.

Marchese Sacchetti is also assisted by a Council of State (*Consulta*), of which he is president. Along with three honorary councillors, it has twenty-four members, many of whose names are rich in historical association with the Papacy. Prince Colonna heads the list, followed by Prince Torlonia, Prince Massimo, Prince Del Drago and Marchese Patrizi.

Sacchetti is a distinguished representative of those upper-class Italian families which have a centuries-old tradition of personal service to the Popes. They are still socially distinct, he tells me, in Roman life, though their *usi e costumi* – ways and customs – have changed. He is a tall, deliberate man, with a rare but warm smile, speaking the best Italian, *lingua Toscana in bocca romana* – Tuscan words on Roman lips – and a slow but sure English. He has handsome, rugged looks, and wears an air of reserve and well-tailored suits. Looking every inch the superior functionary, he reinforces the impression of Englishness with his degree in agriculture and his real love of the land. He farms extensively around Tarquinia. The marchese enjoys holidaying in England and Scotland, going around the castles, but spends most of his life in Rome near the Vatican, where the Sacchettis have a huge, beautiful *palazzo* in the old Tuscan quarter on the Via Giulia. The family migrated to Rome in the sixteenth century; among their ancestors was the wry fourteenth-century storyteller, Franco Sacchetti. The Sacchettis must have regarded many of the papal families they served as *parvenus*.

Don Giulio Sacchetti continues the family tradition very happily, and finds the service of the Holy See a pleasure and privilege. For normal Vatican working hours he sits at a large, antique desk in a spacious office on the second floor of the drab government building that houses the Vatican State's General Secretariat, the offices of the Pontifical Commission and the bureaux of its technical and economic services. At the top is Cardinal Guerri's flat. The tall windows of Sacchetti's room look on to the back of St Peter's, framing an absorbing view of the cupola and drum.

As Special Delegate for the State, Sacchetti is responsible to the cardinals' commission for a payroll of about 1400 people. He will tell you that, in the words of Pope Pius XI, the Vatican City State is simply a small parcel of land necessary for the sake of the independence of the Church. Running the state causes him no great headaches. The budget usually balances. There may sometimes be murmurs over wages and conditions, but labour relations are usually tranquil.

Religiously, the Vatican City State is part of the diocese of Rome, but it has its own religious administration under Bishop van Lierde, who has been vicar general to five successive Popes.

Judicially, the state's system is run by a judge, acting in the name of the Pope; a Court of First Instance; a Court of Appeal; a Court of Cassation, concerned with defects of judicial form or procedure. There are about forty lawyers involved altogether, and they are not kept very busy with Vatican work. For the judge, a few civil cases crop up every year, involving, for example, the issue of a summons or two, or procedure for establishing a death. Many scores of criminal cases (involving Italian law) come before him each year, chiefly from the Vatican Security Department, and concerned mostly with road traffic offences.

Sharply divergent from normal states in its aims, the Vatican City State shares many convenient features with them. As well as its own passport, its use of the pontifical flag and its own railway, it mints its own coinage and medals, and prints its own stamps, partly as an earnest of sovereignty, partly because they are lucrative, partly to spread a religious message.

An agreement made with the Italian government in 1930 puts the Italian Mint (the mint of the Papal States, before 1871) at the disposal of the Vatican for producing its own coins, and the Vatican may use no other mint for coinage. The Vatican coins must be of the same size, metal content, and nominal and intrinsic value as corresponding Italian coins. Under a revised agreement in 1962, the total value of Vatican coins issued in any one year is not to exceed 100 million lire (about £50,000), rising to 200 million at a time of *Sede Vacante* – between pontificates – and 300 million when a Council is inaugurated.

Vatican coinage is legal tender in Italy and San Marino, but I have rarely found it in my change. Recent mintings have included a medal to celebrate the journey of Pope John Paul II to Poland (on sale inside the Vatican and kept in some quantity for the Pope's own use). An attractive series, issued in 1979, commemorated the anniversary of the election of Pope Paul VI. Seven coins, dated 1978 and ranging from 500 down to 5 lire, bear the coat-of-arms of the late Pope on the obverse and scenes from the Gospels on the reverse. These issues are sold to the public in St Peter's Square; Vatican officials and outside dealers can order them in advance.

Vatican stamps are used rather than simply collected. They always provide lively splashes of colour on envelopes that may be cheerfully franked *'Gloria in Excelsis Deo'*. Among philatelists they have tended to arouse generally lukewarm interest, though the fashion may change. The stamps are not valid in Italy, nor are Italian state stamps valid for postage from the Vatican. Since 1929, the Vatican Post Office has supplemented regular issues of stamps for each pontificate with a plethora of special commemorative items – for Holy Years, for the elections and deaths of Pontiffs, for religious anniversaries, for specific charitable purposes. The first airmail stamps were issued in 1937. Ingeniously, their designs represented the Holy House of Loreto, which flew to Italy from Nazareth; the dove flying with an olive branch back to the ark; Elias's chariot *en route* for heaven; and St Peter.

There were six issues of stamps in 1978, the year of the three Popes. Various philatelic events in 1979 commemorate the fiftieth anniversary of the foundation of the Vatican City State; for instance, the issue of 100,000 sets of six illustrated postcards and the use of a special cancellation. In 1980, two of the special series commemorated St Benedict, Patron of Europe, and Bernini. The philatelic and numismatic office is one of eight offices administered by the General Secretariat of the Vatican City State government. The others are for legal affairs; personnel; accounts; posts and telegraph; imports and exports; security; pilgrim and tourist information.

About eighty marriages are registered in the Vatican each year. The reason for some of them is shown on the marriage certificate, which has a large space for 'full details of all the children to be legitimated by this marriage'. Most Christians get married in their own parish, where they are already known; but it is difficult for a couple who have been together for many years, and have had children, to reveal in a public ceremony that they are only now marrying.

All the activities of the Vatican City State are performed, under the supervision of Marchese Sacchetti and the general secretary, Vittorio Trocchi, by a staff of which about 90 per cent are laymen and women. Including a salaried lay staff of 180, they work for the Secretariat, the Vatican Monuments, Museums and Galleries, the Technical Services Department, the Health Department, the Vatican Observatory, the Archaeology Department and the Pontifical Villas. Covering a wide range of social background, though most of them are Italian, the employees of the city state maintain the physical structure and services, and sustain part of the variegated culture, of the Vatican State and Holy See.

When he replied, 'About half' to the question: 'How many people work in the Vatican?' Pope John XXIII may have been prevaricating as well as making a good joke. There is no simple answer to questions about how many people are employed in the Vatican City.

The departments of the Roman Curia employ about 3000 people compared with the 1400 mostly laymen employed by the government of the city state of the Vatican. About 350 people (retaining their own nationality) are authorized to live in the city state and nearly 3000 reside in extra-territorial or tax-exempt properties of the Holy See.

The Swiss Guards, a few Jesuits of Vatican Radio, the handful of cardinals and archbishops, the city-state workers, the Holy See domestics, the students at the German College, the nuns – all the different groups brought into being by the phenomenon of the Holy See – create a mosaic of colourful life, with an intensely bright centre of pageantry and power.

The pontifical march for the Vatican, which was composed by Gounod and became the official wordless hymn of the Holy See in 1949, begins '*Allegretto maestoso* . . . .' The surroundings of those who work for the Holy See in the Vatican and its extensions throughout Rome are also still often charming, but the majesty of ecclesiastical life has been attenuated by inflation and the prudence of the modern Popes. The old papal nobility, the 'black' aristocracy, which used to impart a semi-feudal aura and a glow of past glory, has largely faded away. Its social significance has dwindled along with its claims to innumerable ceremonial and executive functions within the Vatican. There is still scope in the secular administration of the city state for important laymen; but it was noticeable that Pope Paul VI left many places in the bureaucracy vacant.

When non-Italians at the Vatican were rare, an intimate social life flourished among the families of the ecclesiastics of the papal government, brought along, like the brothers and nephews of Eugenio Pacelli, Pope Pius XII, to help out with the Church's earthly business. Among the 'Gentlemen of his Holiness' of the Pontifical Family, there are still four Pacellis. Today, the many foreign priests and sisters often find existence in Rome difficult and lonely. They tend to huddle close to their national colleagues or the headquarters of the religious orders.

The papal government of the Curia still ticks to an Italian tempo, and its atmosphere is generally more akin to that of a family than of a secular civil service. There is a sense of really belonging or not. There are fervent emotions and loyalties to individuals; sudden rises to favour and abrupt falls from grace; secure touchstones of faithfulness, notably the encyclical *Humanae Vitae*.

Prelates who present a genial face to the world can reveal sometimes more severe aspects of their personalities when dealing with domestic matters on their home territory. It is sometimes the other way round. Correspondence in the files of the Vatican's Secretariat of State shows Mgr Giovanni Benelli, when he was the most important member of the Pope's team, granting permission to one of the lay officials to keep a cat at his family apartment, and so bending the rules which forbid pets. The cats behind St Peter's have, incidentally, set going some controversy over whether they would be Holy See or Vatican City cats, and who should control them.

Curial cardinals live in a large number of special – but not necessarily very grand – penthouses and apartments, including a few inside city-state territory, and scores along the Trastevere and the Via della Conciliazione or the Piazza della Città Leonina.

Lay people working for the Holy See may have apartments in a grandiose Roman palace such as the Vatican-owned Palazzo San Calisto in a charming, murky part of Trastevere, but most find their own accommodation. The lay officials do not really count in the hierarchy, though they can wield influence especially when they are Italian and well connected. Some are sarcastic about the amateurism of the clerical officials placed over their heads; some confess to feeling shocked at the ambitious careerism evident among some clergy. All those I know have succumbed to the attractions of the climate, the rich disorder of Roman life and the magnetism of the papal office.

Social life is an important part of Roman, and therefore of Vatican, culture. It moves on various distinct lines, which occasionally intersect. In Rome, social circles revolve round the Quirinal, the Italian government; the film set; the curial officials; the religious orders; some of the old aristocracy.

Employees of the Vatican pay no income tax and no customs duty on the petrol or goods they buy at the Vatican shop, and if they are non-Italian they enjoy allowances up to 15 per cent on their monthly salaries. These ranged from 850,000 lire (say, £425) at the top of the Curia down to 300,000 (about £150) in 1979. Health and pension facilities are good, but paid for by deductions from wages. During the 1970s Italian wages raced ahead, while inside the Vatican only cost-of-living increases were granted. But reasonable increases were forthcoming in 1979–81, bringing a cardinal's salary to about 1.5 million lire.

Cardinals are not above pointing out how little they are paid, but most ripples of economic and social discontent occur lower down the slopes of the vineyard. In 1975 there was an uproar, to no effect, when the Vatican bakery was closed down. Pope Paul VI did set up an Office for Labour Relations for the City State, but in 1980 some of the lay employees at the Vatican, feeling that traditional benefits were no longer enough to offset rising living costs, formed a union.

Life can be Spartan for those on the lower rungs of the Vatican ladder, but for all employees of the Holy See, from cardinals to doorkeepers, the thirty-three-hour week and numerous religious holidays allow generous time away from the office. It is spent on pastoral work (practised conscientiously by all the cardinals I have met and urged on all curial priests by Pope John Paul II); on leisure pursuits; or on another job.

Outside a block of Vatican offices in Via dell'Erba, not far from St Peter's Square, a tall, grey-suited *commesso* informed me that he had been in the Vatican service – first as a doorkeeper or *usciere* – for twenty-nine years, and so had seen five Popes, and many more cardinals, come and go. Very dignified at the base of the pyramid, he reminds you of the Vatican's role in providing jobs for hundreds of Romans and their families.

I was on my way to lunch inside the Vatican, in the Palazzo dell'Archiprete, with one of the several cardinals who live within the walls. Beyond the huge, forbidding wooden door of a building behind St Peter's Basilica, to the south, a lift whirs you to an apartment full of the personal treasures of art and friendship accumulated during a lifetime spent mostly in the Vatican's diplomatic service. There is an atmosphere of fragrance and light. From the white marble-floored hall, where your eye is drawn by the vivid colour of a red biretta, past the cardinal's private chapel, you pass to a sitting room with red damask sofa and chairs and pictures into a princely dining room, where five successive courses are served by two white-clothed sisters. The food is excellent. The tablecloth is immaculately white, and sets off beautifully a display of yellow flowers. The first preprandial drinks from a solid decanter, the crisp white wine accompanying the meal, the brandy (and a *bonbon* from a little silver dish) loosen tongues. The host, who is abstemious himself, says grace and lets the conversation among his five guests (two of them budding Anglican priests with cautious umbrellas) meander through the subjects of Vatican finance or religious toleration. But he breaks into it often with his own robustly tolerant opinions.

This cardinal's table is well known for the stimulating variety of the guests who are regularly invited to it. You meet all kinds there – sportsmen, musicians, even journalists – and mostly people from outside the Vatican. He and his way of life represent some of the gentle features of a unique kind of civilized society which the Vatican City State helps to sustain. I am glad it still exists.

The physical defence of the Vatican City State is the responsibility of the young Swiss from Catholic families who serve as the Pope's soldiers and are seen by most visitors to the Vatican in twos and threes on duty at the entrances: one standing to attention with a pike; another wearing a sword, ready to interrogate the stranger; and, beyond the bronze doors, a sergeant seated at a table.

The corps of the Swiss Guard, *Cohors Helvetica*, is the only surviving unit of the old armed forces of the Papacy. The Swiss Guards come under the direct authority of the Pope (though they can be called on if needed by the government of the city state) and are exclusively charged with the safeguarding of the Apostolic See. When the Pope goes to celebrate Mass in St Peter's, or off to St John Lateran, or down to Castel Gandolfo, they go too.

The magnificent Noble Guard and the Palatine Guard have vanished from the scene. The former were officers chosen, in recent times, from among all the Italian aristocracy; their commander (the last being Prince Don Mario del Drago) was appointed personally by the Pope from the noble families of Rome. Before being disbanded by Pope Paul VI, they numbered nine colonels under their commander and standard-bearer, and a booted and helmeted detachment was permanently on duty to escort the Pope. The unpaid Palatine Guard, also disbanded by Pope Paul, came from all kinds of social background but were always of Roman birth. Their duties were to act as a guard of honour for the Pope on special occasions. The last public appearance, so to speak, of both the Noble Guard and the Palatine Guard, was at Castel Gandolfo in August 1970 when the British Minister to the Holy See, Desmond Crawley, presented his credentials.

Today, under the Central Security Office of the Vatican, the drably dressed Civil Guard, successor to the old *Gendarmeria Pontificia*, is responsible for policing the city and some of the Vatican's Roman properties.

Legatees of the martial traditions of the Papacy, the Swiss Guards rank as one of the offices of the Curia within the Papal Household and are entrusted with the protection of the person of the Pope and the defence of his territories. Under their commander (Colonel Pfyffer von Altishofen), the guards can muster a hundred at full strength, including four officers, a chaplain, twenty-three non-commissioned officers (*sottufficiali*), sixty halbardiers and two drummers. The most familiar of their uniforms is the billowy Renaissance costume of dark-blue, orange and yellow stripes.

The guards must obey only their colonel, one other officer and their sergeant, who all wear identically coloured plumes. Other officers are supernumerary, and their orders can be ignored.

New recruits are sworn in at an impressive annual ceremony, attended by the Swiss Ambassador to the Quirinal. Each recruit holds the standard in one gloved hand, raising the other gloved hand aloft, with two fingers and thumb outstretched (representing the Trinity), while he swears in his own language – French, German or Italian.

A special agreement between Switzerland and the Holy See controls recruitment. The Holy See accepts only Swiss more than twenty years old who have already done their national service, and whose military record is unblemished; in compensation, serving Swiss Guardsmen are exempt from reserve service at home.

The guards are real, not Ruritanian, soldiers, disciplined and dedicated. They are always Catholic and usually of middle-class origins. Most of them serve for two years, and then return to Switzerland, where there are several associations of former guardsmen in different cities. (This helps with the recruiting, which has to be discreet.) There is also a pensionable long-service term of eleven years plus nine.

The barracks of the Swiss Guards are just inside the Vatican, near the Porta Sant'Anna. The building is old but the quarters have been modernized and made reasonably comfortable, with the mostly bachelor troops living two to a room. The salary of an ordinary guardsman is about 500,000 lire (say £250) a month, which is a sharp improvement over the position a decade ago, when uncertainties about the future made recruiting difficult. There is a month's annual leave; free board and keep; and an entitlement to cheap petrol.

For those who serve many years in the guards, the motivation is one of a 'personal calling'. The phrase was used by Sergeant Hans Roggan, when I talked to him about the unusual profession of papal soldier. He was on duty the first time we met, wearing uniform and patrolling at the foot of the stairs leading to the San Damaso courtyard in the Apostolic Palace, where he kept a wary eye on people going to and fro. He has been in the Swiss Guards over twenty-five years. In uniform, he wears a row of papal medals: Cavaliere di San Silvesto, Pro Ecclesia e Pontifice Cross, the Benemerenti medal. . . .

Hans Roggan, who is married to an American, and so has his own family apartment in the Vatican, emphasizes the vocational element in his job. 'I joined to serve the Pope and the Church.' He enjoys the wide range of contacts and friendships that the work secures, and he likes Rome, for its art above all, despite the city's violence, which troubles him.

Roggan is a cheerful, stocky figure, very relaxed in manner. He remarks that the Swiss Guards seek most of their friendships with non-Italians and find that the Italians working in the Vatican naturally tend to band together, to keep to their own groups and families. The guards on duty and at home within the Vatican are jealous of their traditions. A few years ago, they showed some resentment when an 'outsider' was made their commander. Now they have one of their own again.

The guards are mostly German-speaking and their official language is German. Their professional life is one of drills, parades and guard duty. They seek their social life in Rome, where they are warned to be 'discreet' and keep a sensible low profile. They must be back in their barracks by midnight when the city state locks up; if not, they have to ring the bell and have their names taken.

They add a skein of colour to the day-to-day activities of the Holy See, an alien element in the Italian culture around them, serving under arms for the Pope's sake. Like that of most others who work at the Vatican, theirs is a very personal loyalty.

3
Life and Times of the Pope

Thousands of people who never enter Vatican buildings, even the Basilica, simply stand in St Peter's Square, staring at the high window of the Palace, slanted a few hundred yards behind the colonnade, where the Pope appears. A solitary figure in white, he looks down always interestedly as the crowd stirs and responds to whatever he says or does. At general audiences, he moves among the swarming crowds in the piazza.

The Vatican is given animation as a tiny sovereign state, and the administrative and spiritual centre of Roman Catholicism, only through the presence of the priest who wakes up in his bedroom on the top floor of the Palace.

Even a gregarious Pope such as John Paul II opens his eyes each day an inescapably isolated man, although destined to spend it in almost unceasing human contact. Election as Pope brings a life sentence of physical estrangement from one's own people, which sharpens the solitude that must be the lot of someone designated Christ's representative on earth. The natural instinct of the cardinals from whom a Pope is chosen is to push the cup away.

This has not always been the case. There is a story of a Pope who, when cardinal, always kept a large fishing-net on view at his home in order, he said, never to forget the humble origins of St Peter. After his enthronement, it was soon noticed that the net had disappeared, 'What need of the net,' he said when questioned, 'now that the fish is caught?'

Paul II (1464–71) the Venetian Pietro Barbo, disconcerted the cardinals on his election by first wanting to take the name 'Formosus' – a reflection, they thought, of the pleasure he took in his own handsome looks. Julius II, the warrior Pope, was overjoyed by his election in 1503 and could hardly wait to put on his new vestments. Ten years later, the Medici Pope Leo X, is said to have confided to his brother Giuliano that, since God had given him the Papacy, he meant to enjoy it: *'Godiamoci il papato, poichè Dio ci l'ha dato.'*

After the Council of Trent in 1563, the personal lives of Popes came mostly to be free of scandal. But the ostentation and pomp associated with the claims of princely dominion persisted until the upheaval of the Second Vatican Council of 1962–5. Then, one after the other, many of the ambiguous trappings of papal magnificence began to be shed. In recent years, there has been a metaphorical bonfire of the tinsel and symbols of secular empire and spiritual triumphalism, fuelled by inflation and stretched resources as well as changed religious attitudes. The old armed forces of the Papacy, with their panoply and weapons – the guard of honour, the gendarmes, the Palatine Guard – have been disbanded; the fans of ostrich plumes, the *fabelli*, waved before the Pontiff as he was carried aloft on his portable throne, the *sedia gestatoria*, are gathering dust.

The simplification of papal life and ceremonial under Pope John XXIII and Pope Paul VI was partly a natural adaptation to the growing informality of modern times; partly a reflection of the seismic theological changes in the Roman Catholic Church which were revealed and codified at the Second Vatican Council. Pope John Paul I, when he came from Venice to begin his brief reign in 1978, chose not to wear the papal tiara; he was modestly installed as pastor rather than crowned as Pontiff.

There are nine tiaras among the papal treasures. One of these triple crowns – used in the coronation of Pope Pius X (1903–14) – shaped like a hooped beehive and ornately embroidered, is decorated with 32 rubies, 19 emeralds, 11 sapphires, 529 diamonds and 252 pearls. Pope Paul VI had a tiara given to him for his coronation by the city of Milan. He wore it for the last time on 13 November 1964, and let it be known he was giving it to the poor. It was subsequently bought by Cardinal Spellman, Archbishop of New York.

On the day of his installation, 22 October 1978, Pope John Paul II recalled the decision of Paul VI; now was not the time 'to return to a ceremony and an object considered – wrongly – to be a symbol of the temporal power of the Popes. Our time calls us, urges us, obliges us to gaze on the Lord and immerse ourselves in humble and devout meditation on the mystery of the supreme power of Christ himself.'

Symbol of temporal power or not, the tiaras with their Byzantine and worldly associations will remain in store. No future Pope will be crowned in the loggia of St Peter's and hear the traditional words: 'Receive the tiara adorned with three crowns, and know that thou art father of princes and kings, ruler of the world, vicar of our saviour Jesus Christ.'

Once the new Pope has accepted his election by the cardinals and announced his choice of name, he is led to a small room near the Sistine Chapel and robed as Pope, choosing one of the three sizes of silk soutane that have been laid out, and putting on a white silk sash, red slippers and scarlet cape. The room is known as the Chapel of Tears.

Angelo Roncalli, the fatherly John XXIII, thought that his life as the servant of the servants of God was a 'real martyrdom'. Giovanni Battista Montini, the sensitive, self-aware Paul VI, regarded his inheritance from John as a terrible burden. Albino Luciani, the self-effacing John Paul I, responded cheerfully in public to his unexpected election in September 1978 but prayed for God to forgive the cardinals what they had done to him. These three Popes had known the heartache of realizing that, though they might have some of their own *famiglia* with them, they would never return from the Vatican to live in their homes among their own people in the north.

Cardinal Karol Wojtyla was elected Pope and took the name John Paul II on Monday, 16 October 1978. As he prepared the homily for the first Sunday Mass as Pope during the days following, he thought about the works of the great Polish writer and patriot, Henryk Sienkiewicz, and especially of the novel *Quo Vadis?*

Written in 1896 and partly inspired by Sienkiewicz's sight of the Basilica of St Peter's, *Quo Vadis?* contains several layers of meaning. It is set in ancient Rome in the time of the Emperor Nero. Its celebration of the triumph of the spirit (the persecuted Christians) over brute force (the rulers of imperial Rome) also points with hope to the triumph of the persecuted

Poles of the nineteenth century over the occupying armies of
Russia, Prussia and Austria. To cite Sienkiewicz is to plead
implicitly for national and religious freedom.

Explicitly, however, Pope John Paul II quoted his compatriot
to convey the emotions he had felt on his election. He recalled
that no doubt the first Pope and Bishop of Rome would rather
have stayed by the lake of Genesareth with his boat and nets
than have journeyed to the heart of the Roman Empire. Then
he told the story handed down in an ancient tradition – and
given 'magnificent literary expression' by Sienkiewicz – of
how, when fleeing from Rome, Peter had a vision of Christ,
and on asking '*Quo Vadis, Domine?*' – 'Lord, where are you
going?' – had been told that He was going to Rome to be
crucified again. 'Peter went back to Rome, and stayed here till
his crucifixion.'

Cardinal Wojtyla arranged the night before the meeting of
the Conclave which elected him for an early return flight to
Cracow. Instead, he became Pope, at the age of fifty-eight. He
would never return to Poland for good. Even one return visit
might (though it did not) prove impossible. He wrote in his
first 'message to the world' of the 'fearful yoke' borne by his
predecessors and now imposed on him. Karol Wojtyla is the
first-ever Pope from Poland, the first non-Italian Pope for 450
years, and, though grey-haired, the youngest for 150 years.

It was exceptional when Pope John XXIII left the Vatican by
train to pray at Assisi, on the eve of the Second Vatican
Council, but Pope Paul VI travelled on a series of remarkable
pilgrimages, to America, the Holy Land and India. The present
Pope showed from the first his determination to travel, but
even he will remain inside the walls of the Vatican for most of
his reign, perhaps over several decades.

In time, the Pope comes to feel at home in the vast spaces of
the Palace and its surroundings, to which he adds his own
distinctive artistic and architectural contribution, and where
he will be buried. He modifies protocol to suit his own
sensibilities and stamps his own strong personality on the lives
of all those who work and live in the Vatican. Over the smallest
state in the world, which is both his house and his place of
exile, he is absolute ruler.

The cardinals, in October 1978, were looking for a healthy
Pope, a traditionalist in theology, a man with the qualities of a

leader, but with pastoral experience and the human warmth to sustain the benign impression created by Pope John Paul I. A Pope from Communist territory might be provocative, but why not, when everything else fell into place? Yet there was clearly a lot of manoeuvring, and the white smoke swirled from the chimney of the Sistine Chapel only after several, perhaps eight, ballots.

The cryptic politics of the Catholic Church come into play at every Conclave. There are factions of sorts, alliances and allegiances along the lines of racial, national or continental origin, of temperament, of theological and socio-political persuasion, even of self-interest. None the less, the cardinals and the Catholics whose leader is being chosen believe that the electors are guided by the Holy Spirit.

An Italian cardinal who has taken part in two papal elections and been considered a candidate himself, said to me emphatically, resting his hand over his heart, 'In a Conclave you can feel the assistance of the Holy Spirit. You know you are taking part in something beyond ordinary understanding and that certain human beings are being used by divine providence to choose Peter's successor. The Roman proverb often comes true: the man who goes into the Conclave a Pope comes out a cardinal . . . .'

Many people close to Cardinal Roncalli, the future John XXIII, including his friends and assistants, did not think of him even as a candidate. When in 1978 I discussed who could be the next Pope with the patriarch's secretary in Venice, he said to me vehemently that it must be a pastoral and holy priest, but he had not the slightest inkling that it would be the man we had just been talking to, Albino Luciani.

The man elected Pope is psychologically transformed. He may have to accept the powerful momentum of the Curia in a fashion that prompted the rueful remark of Pope John's: 'I am only the Pope here . . .' but he starts his reign as head of the Catholic Church fortified as well as awed by the belief which the present Pope constantly reiterates: 'I am Peter.' When Cardinal Wojtyla became Pope, he seemed to adopt instinctively a new gesture – a rapid, outward and upwards movement of the arms, powerful and authoritative – that he had never used before.

Despite his new *persona*, a Pope brings to his daily life in the

Vatican the quirks, habits and ideas formed by the influence of his own birth and upbringing. These affect the style of his pontificate, in small domestic details as well as large issues of policy. The home life of a Pope is a compromise between the settled ways and preferences of a mature, sometimes old, man and the ancient protocol and prejudices followed by those who are dedicated to his service and closest to him.

Of the three men who were Popes in 1978, Giovanni Battista Montini came to the papal throne from an upper-middle class, northern Italian background. His devoutly Catholic father was a wealthy landowner who once edited a Catholic newspaper and represented Brescia in the Italian Chamber of Deputies. His mother, to whom his devotion was intense, was a strong-willed Catholic activist, from the lesser nobility. She had three sons. Montini, who became Pope at the age of sixty-six, was Jesuit-educated, ordained a priest when twenty-three, and spent most of the middle years of his life working in the Secretariat of State. Long years of office routine in the Curia reinforced the systematic and diplomatic aspect of his mind, though his stint as Archbishop of Milan gave him insight into human, pastoral needs.

Towards the end of his pontificate he tended to procrastinate and to sound more and more querulous, but he still 'gave' himself immensely in public and displayed privately the wit and spontaneity which had always been natural to him. He loved beautiful things, such as fine book bindings and paintings. He was frail but resilient, intelligent but intellectually unadventurous, scrupulous and sensitive. These qualities affected the important policies of his reign, notably the cautious, sincere implementation of the Second Vatican Council; his determined personal endorsement of the encyclical *Humanae Vitae*; the condemnation of the rebel 'traditionalist' Archbishop Lefèvbre; and the pursuit of international influence in the cause of peace.

Pope Paul VI's daily life reflected the gentleness and orderliness of his nature. An instance of his kindness is that, in order not to upset the aged Cardinal Ottaviani, who was living in the old, beautiful Holy Office building, which could have been demolished to be replaced by a new audience hall, he had the audience hall built on its present site instead. He had a quiet wit. When Bishop van Lierde (a stickler for formal detail) failed to turn up in time to join the Pope's suite for an audience, Pope Paul turned to another bishop and said, 'Do you think it will be *valid* without him?'

Montini was in constant pain from arthritis during the last years of his fifteen-year pontificate. In public, the obvious physical suffering compounded the impression of anguish conveyed by the fears he expressed for the Church and the world. In private, he could still be warm, and at times light-hearted. He was a spontaneous joker. When Cardinal Suenens, one of the most dignified of cardinals, took a close personal interest in the 'charismatic movement', Pope Paul greeted him with raised arms and a boisterous 'Hallelujah!'

Albino Luciani, John Paul I, came from a working-class family in the Dolomites. His father was a bricklayer, who used to migrate for work to Switzerland before finding a job with the glassblowers of Murano. Luciani entered a minor seminary at the age of eight, was ordained at the age of twenty-three, and studied theology at the Gregorian University in Rome. He became a bishop at forty-six but did not go to Venice as Patriarch till he was fifty-seven. He was elected Pope (like his predecessor) at the age of sixty-six. Luciani was sensitive and spontaneous. He hated bombast. In Venice, his reticence, disapprobation of wealth and showiness, and lack of oratorical flair robbed him of real popularity. After the austerities of Pope Paul VI, his smiling, vulnerable-looking charm won a delighted response when he was presented as Pope. If Luciani had not become a priest, he would, he said, have been a journalist. His book *Illustrissimi* – letters to saints, writers and fictional characters including G. K. Chesterton, Dickens, Mark Twain and Walter Scott – is a sweet confection with nuggets of shrewdness and common sense. He was too delicate for the Papacy and died of heart failure after a reign of thirty-four days.

A curial cardinal once said to me as we reminisced about Luciani, 'He died of humility. . . . When his assistants asked Pope John Paul I to use the *Sedia Gestatoria* they used a novel kind of argument: if he accepted the wish of the faithful to have a better view of him at the audiences, he would be making an act of humility, since he felt confused and somewhat ashamed at being carried on people's shoulders.' Luciani's changes in the life-style of the Vatican would have been towards simplicity and decorum.

Karol Wojtyla was born in the small town of Wadowice near Cracow in 1920, only a year after the creation of the first free Polish state for nearly 150 years. His father was a retired army captain; his mother, whose looks he inherited, died when he was nine. His brother died a few years later and Karol, nick-named Lolek, lived only with his father during his teens. He went to grammar school, then to the Jagellonian University in Cracow, to study Polish philosophy. After the German invasion, he worked in a quarry (both to support his father and avoid deportation), joined in a kind of 'underground' theatre, and, after the wrench of his father's death, enrolled in a clandestine seminary in Cracow.

Wojtyla was ordained a priest in 1946 and then studied in Rome at the strictly disciplined Angelicum University (run by the Dominicans), improving his French by living at the Belgium College. He returned to Communist-ruled Poland in 1948, and during the years of Stalinist pressures pursued a brilliant university career till he was made a bishop in 1958. In 1964 he became Archbishop of Cracow. Pope Paul VI created him cardinal in 1967 at the unusually early age of forty-six.

To the Papacy, Wojtyla brings intensity, physical robustness and restlessness, intellectual curiosity trammelled by scholastic disciplines, and theatrical versatility. He is seen to combine the comfortably avuncular presence of Pope John XXIII with impressive physical fitness and good looks. He is short and thick-set, like a rugger forward. The expressions on his face are as changeable as English weather, but it is a strong face. The Pope's Renaissance versatility (poet, philosopher, singer, sportsman) distract attention from the more important strands of character and experience that he brings into the Vatican – his self-awareness, his Slavonic emotionalism, his Polish nationalism, his unswerving sense of Roman Catholic orthodoxy, and above all his conviction that a firmly led, united Church is essential to defeat forces hostile to Catholicism, especially atheistic Communism. He is certain that diversity and experimentation can prove dangerous. As John Paul II settled into office, his words and actions increasingly confirmed his determination to discipline the Church in its beliefs and practices, and to maintain his own freedom of initiative in international negotiation and personal travel.

Most of the Pope's time is spent in the private papal apartment of the Apostolic Palace, with constant excursions to the Basilica of St Peter's, the audience hall and the Vatican Gardens. The Pope's own suite of rooms is on the top floor, and most of the windows overlook the right-hand colonnade of St Peter's Square, from the north.

The Pope's own way to the papal apartment is usually by lift from the courtyard of San Damaso. The lift starts in the basement which, since the Vatican is built on a hill, is level with the Belvedere, to which there is an exit. The ground floor is San Damaso. The first floor is the level for the *Sala Ducale*, the Borgia Apartments and the Sistine Chapel. The second floor is the level for the papal state apartments – the library and the entire suite for audiences, including the *Sala Clementina* and the Consistorial Hall – and also the Raphael Rooms. The third floor is that for the Secretariat of State and the Council for the Public Affairs of the Church. It is also the level of the papal *private* apartments, but in the way is the top half of the two-storeyed *Sala Clementina*. On the third floor a broad, bright gallery stretches in one direction to the offices of the Secretariat of State, and in the other to a hallway and the rooms on two floors which have been the preserve of the Pope and his personal attendants since the time of Pius X.

On the top floor, there is a small library, an office for the private secretary, the Pope's own study and bedroom, chapel and dining room. Near by are rooms for the Pope's valet–chauffeur and a cloistered room for the bevy of Polish sisters of the Maria Bambina Order, who cook for the Pope, clean the apartment and do his laundry. On the floor below are the chief secretarial offices. The Pope's main library is in between the two floors. On the roof, discreetly concealed from observation by a false roof, is the Pope's trellised garden of walks, fountains and shrubs.

The austere effect of the Pope's own chapel is heightened by the white marble walls, where the *Stations of the Cross* are by Lello Scorzelli, and by slabs of light and colour falling from the interior stained-glass windows. Pope Paul VI would start his own day by saying Mass here each morning, among works donated by contemporary Italian artists. He had the library-study, or audience library, refurnished and brightened up early in his pontificate. He had good, restrained northern Italian taste, and the clutter of old papal collections, furniture and busts was replaced by a few, comfortable antique chairs and tables and seventeenth-century oil paintings. The walls were painted cream, and the white and black marble floor was brightened up with a few rich carpets. A tapestry after Raphael shows Christ commissioning St Peter.

Popes dress in red or white. The wardrobe of Pope Paul VI contained several white cassocks, a red and white cloak, two red hats and several white *zucchetti* or skullcaps, as well as many white shirts, clerical collars and pairs of shoes, in red or white, size eight and a half. Typically, Pope John Paul II will wear a white caped cassock, a *zucchetto* and a pectoral cross, together with a fascia or sash, for his day-to-day appearances.

Every new Pope rings the changes, sometimes thunderously. Pope Pius XI, following the easy-going years of Benedict XV, gave the Curia a spring-cleaning in the 1920s. He forced the women coming to his audiences back into high-necked dresses, with skirts down to the ground; and he ate very dull meals. Pope Paul VI, with his stressful inheritance of commitment to the reforms of the Second Vatican Council, rewrote the rules and regulations of the Curia with the scrupulous care he gave to all his duties, sometimes inserting comments, underlinings and marginalia in his thin, spidery handwriting in the papers sorted for him by the Secretariat of State. Above all, he began to travel internationally, outside the Vatican and Rome.

Pope John Paul II has not greatly altered the furniture or furnishings of the papal apartments, but the style and pace of his daily life and contacts are sharply different from Montini's. In the first few weeks of his reign, the Romans began to call him the festive Pope. The changes proved more serious than this implied. In 1979 Vatican staff began to murmur in rather a dazed fashion about the unflagging energies of the Pope and the demands his quick metabolism and foreign travels were making.

There are many subtleties and paradoxes in the character of Pope John Paul II. He can listen patiently, his heavy head to one side or sunk in his hands, but he knows his own mind and is not very susceptible to argument. His artistic responses are

71

verbal rather than visual. He is not so interested in his immediate surroundings as in what lies beyond for him to explore. He is a natural actor who instinctively responds to the invitation of a stage. He shows his liking and respect for people all the time. He looks at all those he meets, never through them. When he plays to the gallery he is both amusing and amused, intrigued by the response and by his own reaction to it. Whether seen by a Catholic as the Supreme Pontiff or by a non-Catholic simply as a holy religious leader, he always seems genuinely accessible. On his visit to Poland in 1979 he left among the people, especially the young, the feeling that he had been speaking to them from the heart in a way they had not experienced from any other public figure. He is ready to invite free and open discussion on all kinds of subjects, from the way nuns should dress to the treatment of priests who lose their calling. But, at the end, he insists on discipline and conformity, on clarifying and codifying the rules of religious behaviour and belief, like a leader preparing for battle.

John Paul II's skill with people, both with individuals and crowds, is spontaneous, like his readiness to touch, shake hands, hug or kiss. It is not calculated, but he is aware of its effect.

The Pope's love of music is a very physical, social emotion. He joins in singing when a choir performs in St Peter's Square below his window. His poetry illustrates the deeply reflective aspects of his nature, and a great depth of religious feeling fused with humanism and patriotism. The verses are packed with idiosyncratic images and metaphors, using strong physical detail, and they surge with impressions of movement.

The Pope's emphasis on human rights is directly related to the Catholic Church's struggle for survival in Communist countries. It is the theme he stresses in all diplomatic dealings with the Soviet Union and Eastern Europe. During his own visit to the monastery of Jasna Gora in Czestochowa, he linked people's right to religious freedom to the Church's right to freedom of communication and organization.

Diplomats who have met John Paul II recall, even after brief encounters, the warmth of his greeting and his very relaxed treatment of protocol and ceremony. His unforced friendliness seems to them more on the human plane than the reserved holiness of Paul VI or even John XXIII. A typical experience was that of the South African minister who was taken by the arm after the formal proceedings of his meeting with John Paul II to a table on which a large atlas was open at the map of South Africa. The Pope pointed at it and asked the minister to tell him about his country.

John Paul II has created startlingly fresh images of the figure of the Pope, pursuing the active sportsmanship important to his bodily and mental health, jumping in and out of jeeps and helicopters, travelling with journalists and officials to deliver impassioned addresses in spectacular settings throughout the world. Thanks to the modern technology which he relishes, he can direct affairs in the Vatican when he is travelling. (The Camerlengo of the Holy Roman Church is in charge when the Pope is absent, and also during the so-called *Sede Vacante*, after the death of a Pope. The present Camerlengo, Cardinal Paolo Bertoli, tells you modestly that his duties are mostly social and when the Pope is away 'there is not a lot to do. The offices run themselves and the Pope can easily be kept in touch.') None the less, many decisions tend to be deferred when the Pope is out of Rome, and you can sense the tension mount with the flurry of activity that follows his return.

John Paul II's energy and determination profoundly affect the physical and emotional life of the Apostolic Palace and the relationships between the Pope and his immediate circle. It is, for example, difficult for those near him to feel as affectionately protective as they did towards Pope Paul VI in his troubled old age. John Paul's living style gives full rein to his dedication to physical exercise. He goes to Castel Gandolfo as often as he can and the living quarters there are open most of the year, not just at set holiday periods. His daily round at the Apostolic Palace follows more or less the traditional pattern, though he is an earlier riser than was Paul VI, and he often breaks away from routine.

For an hour and a half after getting up, usually at five o'clock following five hours' sleep, the Pope prays by himself. Whatever he prays, he is always seen with a rosary in his hands. A small group of attendants, including his two secretaries and his group of Polish nuns, join him at Mass in the private chapel at seven. He normally has a good breakfast, Polish style, and enjoys talking with someone over the meal. Sometimes the breakfasts are more English than Continental and the sizzle of frying has been heard in the Apostolic Palace, even though John Paul was noticed to have lost weight after he became Pope. After breakfast, he starts the day's reading, very attentively, before the audiences, which he conducts in a relaxed and affable manner, begin at eleven o'clock. One of the visitors he sees in the morning may find himself invited to the midday meal, which is always a social occasion, and will include Polish as well as Italian food.

Pope John Paul II uses the Vatican Gardens for brisk exercise most evenings. He likes to wear tennis shoes, and pace one of his secretaries. He talks to anyone he meets. The Pope converses easily in several languages, though his French is better than his English and his German than his French – which is why, for example, Cardinal Hume usually talks to him in French and the diplomat, Archbishop Heim, in German. He is passionately fond of singing (in an agreeable baritone) when the occasion presents itself.

There is a faint echo of Prince Florizel in Wojtyla's slipping away from the Apostolic Palace not infrequently, with a secretary, to dine at one of the universities or colleges, preferably among Polish friends. When they catch sight of him, the Swiss Guards sink to one knee as they salute.

No matter how relaxed and friendly he may be, the Pope is always on duty. He is jealously guarded by the celibates around him. Now and then, information about his attitudes and activities seems to flow freely from the Apostolic Palace. Then, suddenly, the old shutters of secrecy are noiselessly brought down. But Roman gossip never stops.

I savour the story, from a past reign, of how Pope John XXIII (who liked talking to his own cronies and sometimes did so very indiscreetly) signalled the man standing at the door with some palms to leave them there, while he himself went on with his monologue. This would hardly do for the visitor. He was carrying out the solemn annual commemoration of the time in 1586 when the 320 ton obelisk of St Peter's Square was saved from crashing because a sailor from Bordighera, despite the threat of death for anyone breaking the silence, shouted out 'Water the ropes', just in time. The village thereafter has had the privilege of bringing palms to St Peter's for Palm Sunday. The more Pope John irritably waved to the villager to leave the palms, the more obstinately he waited for a properly elaborate reception. For how long can one forget one is Pope?

The Vatican's atmosphere of prayerful matter-of-factness has seemed absolutely native to Pope John Paul II since he first spoke to the Italian crowd in St Peter's Square after his election. To an incredible extent, the life of the Pope is a life of continuous public and private prayer, and in quiet parts of the Vatican one feels not so much a sense of religious revelation as the utter naturalness of acceptance of the supernatural, as in Galilee.

Traditionally, the Pope has a very special relationship with the Romans, which is extremely emotional as well as theological. He is their own bishop, the Bishop of Rome. Between him and his people in the diocese is a layer of ecclesiastical officialdom: a cardinal vicar, an archbishop viceregent and a number of auxiliary bishops; but he tries to get close to them physically, in the parishes. John Paul II has been very assiduous about this. He visited about eighteen parishes during the first year of his pontificate, to talk to as many of the thousand and more priests and their parishioners as possible. He always reminds them that Christ wanted the Church to be where St Peter founded it.

During the course of the year, the Pope makes appointments to an extraordinarily high number of offices. The word about whom he has chosen, for what position, goes round the Vatican remarkably swiftly, and then spreads through the ecclesiastical world of Rome, inviting incredulity, despair or delighted relief. In 1979 and 1980, the well-publicized appointments of Pope John Paul II always seemed surprising. Whether thought of as terribly conservative (Cardinal Oddi to the Sacred Congregation for the Clergy) or imaginatively promising (Fr., now Bishop, Agnellus Andrew to the Commission for Social Communications) and, although taken on advice, they became more and more clearly his own decisions. Among the appointments with very large religious and political implications was that of the Jesuit biblical scholar, Fr. Carlo Maria Martini, as Archbishop of Milan, an enormously important diocese of the Catholic Church.

The Pope's most worked-over communications to the world are the encyclicals, apostolic letters and apostolic constitutions, perhaps a dozen or more of these each year. As well, he signs a

75

hundred or more letters and telegrams on subjects such as the death of a cardinal or a flood disaster, makes over a hundred discourses and homilies, delivers sixty or so scheduled and sometimes unscheduled 'Angelus' messages at his window, and speaks at several hundred special and general audiences. The ceaseless outpouring of comment, exhortation and prayer is intensified during the Pope's travels.

The Pope's formal duties at home are broadly liturgical, ceremonial, pastoral, administrative and political. In each of these areas, he must choose friends and advisers whose own attitudes and ideas can be influential, sometimes decisive, in the development of his pontificate.

Close to the Pope is a slim, quietly spoken priest from Northern Ireland who has an exceptional closely guarded knowledge of the Pope's way of life and the place where they live. This is Fr. John Magee, English-speaking secretary first to Pope Paul VI and now to Pope John Paul II. The Pope's other and principal secretary is a Polish priest in his early forties, Fr. Stanislaw Dziwisz, a railwayman's son who had worked with Cardinal Wojtyla for a dozen years in Cracow.

It was Fr. Magee, then sharing secretarial duties with the Italian Mgr Pasquale Macchi, who looked for Pope John Paul I in his chapel in the early hours of 29 September 1978, and then entered the bedroom to find the Pope lifeless in his bed, with the light still on. (Following protocol, he had to move abruptly from his rooms in the papal apartment, until he returned once again to serve the new Pope.)

The private secretaries of the Pope, who see more of him than anyone else, are on the staff of the Secretary of State, listed among the Grade II *officiali minori*. Their importance depends not on their formal position in the hierarchy of the Curia, but on their access to the Pope and their personal relations with him. In the Vatican, the position a man holds goes only some way to indicate his influence. The private secretaries, living close at hand to the Pope, gain an intimate insight into his character and are the most bound to secrecy of all Vatican officials. Pasquale Macchi, who worked with Pope Paul VI for over fifteen years, broadcast after Paul's death about the Pope's actions and feelings when he appealed to the Red Brigades terrorists to spare Aldo Moro's life; but such revelations are few and far between.

With some members of the papal government, the Curia, the Pope has very close relations based either on personal predeliction, the nature of their office, or both (as in the case of the Secretary of State, Cardinal Casaroli).

In general, he is likely to form close ties with certain members of the *Famiglia Pontificia*, the Pontifical Family which, with the *Cappella Pontificia*, or Pontifical Chapel, makes up the Papal Court largely for purposes of ceremony and protocol.

Mingling elements related to the Pope's position as both head of the Vatican State and head of the Holy See, these two offices of the Roman Curia are less grandiose but still colourful derivatives of the old Papal Court which still flourished with some magnificence up to the time of Pope John XXIII. The *Annuario Pontificio* for 1965, the last year of the Second Vatican Council, devoted eighteen pages to the member bodies or individual members of the Pontifical Chapel, all those who formed the Pope's cortège at public functions. They included the Sacred College of Cardinals; the College of Patriarchs, Archbishops and Bishops ranked as 'Assistants to the Throne'; Princes, Assistant to the Throne; His Holiness's Majordomo; the assessors and secretaries of the Holy Congregations; the Apostolic Pronotaries; the Master of the Sacred Palace; the College of Advocates of the Sacred Consistory; the Apostolic Preacher; the Confessor of the Pontifical Family; the College of Procurators of the Sacred Apostolic Palaces; the clergy of the Pontifical Chapel; the Macebearers; and the papal messengers.

The Pontifical Family, all the functionaries of the Papal Court with duties recognized by protocol, covered ten pages of the yearbook, and included the Palatine Cardinals; the members of the Noble Secret Antechamber; the Secret Chamberlains of Cloak and Sword; the Noble Pontifical Guards; the Swiss Guards; the Papal Gendarmes; the Private Chaplains; the Apostolic Preacher; the doctor of His Holiness; and the *bussolanti* or papal servants and attendants.

In movement, the Pontifical Family would create an unforgettable impression of worthy splendour and religious fervour. A British diplomat recalled from the days of Pope Pius XI an anniversary procession to High Mass in St Peter's:

> The great procession is now marshalled and ready for its slow march up the centre of the church to the High Altar. First

comes the Papal Master of Ceremonies, accompanied by the procurators of the ecclesiastical colleges and two Swiss Guards. Then comes the Capuchin Preacher to the Holy See, in his brown habit, the Father-Confessor, by tradition a member of the Servite Order, in black, then representatives of all the chief religious orders whose habits, plain black and brown and white, contrast with the monsignorial purple of those who follow, the chaplain bearing the Papal mitre, the judges of the Rota and Vatican legal officials carrying candles; then two of the deacons, one Latin, one Greek, who are to assist in the Mass to follow, and so on to higher and higher ranks of clergy. The Abbots, Bishops and Archbishops of the Latin rite are preceded by two clergy carrying staves decked with flowers; then come the Bishops, Archbishops, and Patriarchs of the various Eastern churches in communion with Rome, all in their traditional vestments. The procession begins to glow with more and more colour as the Cardinals come in their crimson robes, followed by a single figure, in black with silk hose and a white lace fichu, the Prince Assistant at the Pontifical Throne, always either Prince Colonna or Prince Orsini, the two great historic families, mortal enemies in the Middle Ages, but long reconciled and united in this traditional personal service to the Pope.

Then come the Papal Chamberlains, in their gala court-uniforms, surrounding the Pope aloft on his throne, over him a canopy held high by eight *monsignori*. The Pope is dressed in a robe of white silk, with a short cape of red velvet; his tiara seems heavy to bear for such a long time as the procession takes to reach its end. Accompanying the Pope, who gives his blessing to the kneeling crowds as he passes, are the Swiss Guards, some carrying staves representing the Swiss cantons, officers of the Noble and Palatine Guards, Knights of the Order of Malta in black with a white Maltese Cross, Knights of the Holy Sepulchre, in white with red crosses, two Privy Chamberlains carrying the *flabelli*, and the Dean of the Rota, who has the duty of holding the tiara when at length the Pontiff can take it off. Bringing up the end come the Papal Major Domo, various other Papal officials and the Generals of all the religious orders.

The Popes still have the Swiss Guards and the *Sedia Gestatoria*, the throne on poles. But for how long? Changes come slowly in Vatican ceremonial and protocol, but occasionally there is a leap forward. The functions and form of the Pontifical Chapel and the Pontifical Family were overhauled in 1967 as part of the general reform of the Curia by Pope Paul VI.

In recent editions of the *Annuario Pontificio*, the Pope's *cappella* and *famiglia* occupy far fewer pages. The chief casualties of reform were the papal armed forces. The work of the two offices was tidied up though traditional ceremonies and historical titles linger on: in the Pontifical Family, Prince Don Aspreno Colonna and Prince Don Alessandro Torlonia are lay Assistants to the Throne, for example. The functions performed by the Pontiffs' Ceremonial Congregation, the offices of the Majordomo, the Chamberlain, and the Heraldic Commission of the Pontifical Court were transferred to the *Casa Pontificia*, a new institution which revived an ancient name.

The Prefecture of the Pontifical Household (the *Casa Pontificia*) chiefly conducts the internal affairs of the Pope's own household in the Vatican and at Castel Gandolfo and arranges most of the Pope's meetings. Its officials are never far from the side of the Pontiff.

A beak-nosed prelate can usually be seen very near the Pope, with a few other seemingly permanent ecclesiastical dignatories, in pictures taken at papal audiences. When I first met him, Bishop Jacques Martin showed me one of these pictures in an album on his desk, stabbed at it and said with a flourish in his voice, *'Je suis là. . . .'* Bishop Martin and his office have to deal, under Pope John Paul II, with more unexpected eventualities than ever before: the Pope's decision to walk about among the crowds in the open air, for example; his lingering conversations when time is short; and his acceptance of invitations out of the blue to baptize babies or receive young visitors.

Bishop Martin sees the Pope, formally and informally, most days of the week. He is the only official with the right to enter the papal presence without being summoned, or without having to knock or ask permission. As Prefect of the Pontifical Household, he has a suite of rooms below the level of the Cortile San Damaso, to one side. They are handsomely furnished and have frescoed walls and ceiling, with sportive-looking cherubs and satyrs in one room, religious scenes including a fine triptych in oils in another.

Bishop Martin has a staff of eight who are mostly priests,

including a Christian Brother from Australia. 'The work is very simple,' he says, 'I have to organize the audiences of the Pope and the papal ceremonies.'

Papal audiences, however, are far from simple. The printed protocol for the reception of a head of state, for example, runs to about sixteen pages of instructions. Under the 'general arrangements' for the reception of Queen Elizabeth and the Duke of Edinburgh in October 1980, the Prefect of the Papal Household was instructed to summon the Pope's Almoner, the Vicar General for Vatican City, the Prelates of the Antechamber, the Assistant at the Throne, the Special Delegate of the Pontifical Commission for the Vatican City State, the State's Consultor, the Commandant of the Swiss Guard, the Gentlemen of the Pope, the Attachés of the Antechamber, the Dean of the Hall and the *Sediari*, the Guard of Honour of the Swiss Guard and the Pontifical Band.

For the arrival of the Queen and her suite of fifteen, a picket was drawn up at the Arch of the Bells, a guard of honour stationed in the San Damaso courtyard, and four guards placed on either side of the entrance to the lifts. Six guards and a sergeant were stationed in the second loggia and a platoon was posted in the Clementine Hall.

Greeted on their arrival in a Rolls-Royce by a fanfare and the Prefect of the Royal Household, the Queen and Prince Philip took the lift to the second loggia and walked in procession by strictly regulated stages to the Clementine Hall, shedding guards and diplomats at pre-arranged intervals en route to their meeting with the Pope on the threshold of his library.

Unusually, the Queen wore black for the occasion, in deference to papal traditions. As usual, the papal ecclesiastics wore red-trimmed cassocks with sashes, the civil dignitaries wore dress-coats with decorations, and the Swiss Guards their dress uniforms.

When the Pope receives a head of state there is always such elaborate protocol and ceremonial, though since 1967 the procedures have been less pompous. 'We try to avoid giving a *military* impression,' Bishop Martin says.

The regular visits to the Pope of the curial cardinals, and of the bishops on their '*ad limina*' journeys, are less elaborate in ritual but still demand punctilious decorum and protocol. Bishop Martin is usually on hand to greet the visitors, and has vivid recollections of particular encounters over the reigns of five Popes. He recalls the four visits paid to Pope Paul by Soviet Foreign Minister Gromyko, for example, 'presumably to discuss peace. . . .' He elaborates particularly on the attitudes of Pope Paul VI at such meetings. 'He loved to see people. He was an apostle, a teacher well versed in the psychology of modern man. He used to say to me before the general audiences: what can I give them? The only present I can give them is in words, *une parole.*'

Mention of the general audiences and pontifical ceremonies quickens the pace of the bishop's descriptions. Eager and animated, he speaks French very fast, gazing intently at you with light-blue eyes and courteously apologizing every time he bobs up to answer the telephone, which rings very often. He wears a plain black cassock and silver cross. He is thin, rather fussy and precise, and a little self-deprecating. He enthuses about the big papal gatherings as if they were balletic exercises, or opera or pageants on stage, as to some extent they are. Seeing Pope Paul VI on these occasions, he remembers, struck him as a strange and marvellous spectacle – *très curieux.* The frail Pope would call to one group after another, talking to the people in their different languages. '*Vraiment un spectacle universel.*'

Bishop Martin recalls how cold it was in the Holy Year, 1975, when they had to have Mass out in the open. 'There are always so many problems posed by the pontifical ceremonies, but I am not complaining. I love the work. I love seeing the vast audience . . . *c'est une comédie tout le temps*' [it is a piece of theatre, every time]. He refers to the 'illumination of joy' on the face of Pope Paul when he talked to a large audience or put his hand on the head of a child.

For the audiences and visits, the staff of the *Prefettura* have to do a great deal of liturgical preparation suited not only to different occasions (a beatification ceremony, or the election of a Pope) but to different nationalities, with meticulous translating, editing and publishing. The skills of Bishop Martin must also be those of diplomacy and tact; he has to keep an alert eye on the proceedings of the Pope's day, especially during forays abroad, and has considerable influence over who receives an audience (privately, or in a special group) out of the many thousands of people who request every week. Now and then his department inevitably upsets disappointed applicants and the queue for audiences can cause exasperatingly protracted delays.

Apart from official and general audiences, the Pope's receptions of various people are classified as scheduled audiences (for the curial officials), private, semi-private (*baciamano*), and group audiences. The private talks, usually held in the Pope's library, are nearly always restricted to ambassadors or heads of state, cardinals or bishops on urgent or important business.

The Pope will sit on a chair, his back to a painting by Perugino and two pairs of sixteenth-century bookcases, while his visitors sit on chairs at the edge of the carpet in front of him, one rising to make the formal introductory address.

Semi-private audiences are given to small groups of people with some special claim to privilege, who usually kiss the Pope's hand and have a brief exchange of conversation. The group audiences are for people visiting Rome for special reasons, perhaps a professional conference, canonization ceremony or an organized pilgrimage. The Pope usually makes an address relevant to their circumstances. These audiences are normally held in one of the halls on the second floor of the Apostolic Palace, under the Pope's personal rooms, including the Consistorial Hall, the Hall of the Throne, the Hall of the Popes and the Hall of the Small Throne. Rooms on the first floor near the *Sala Ducale* are also used. The Pope hands out medals, and photographs are taken. Regulations about dress stipulate some formality. Under Pope John Paul II, the occasions have become quite relaxed, as the Pope has brought some of the unpredictability of his behaviour in public to the smaller meetings. Always, however, he moves under the careful eyes of his close officials.

Bishop Martin illuminates Vatican life through his own career. Some forty years ago, he was the only Frenchman working in the Secretariat of State. Now there are five Frenchmen there. He studied at Santa Chiara and first joined the diplomatic service because the Secretariat of State needed a French-speaking editor. He knows intimately all the odd corners of the Vatican and the foibles of Popes. In the courtyard of San Damaso, he points out the infirmary built on the top floor for Pope Paul to have his prostate operation. The upheaval to palace routine was unbelievable. Recently, he stumbled across a little staircase near the Pope's apartments that had been forgotten for centuries. The bishop is part of the Vatican's atmosphere of timelessness, beautifully modulated routine and unquestioning piety. The way the great wall slopes under his window reminds you that the building was also a battlement. He lives comfortably inside the walls, and one of his extra tasks is to act as confessor to the Swiss Guards. So he has no problems, he jokes, when he comes home late after an evening out in Rome.

From his bedroom window, the Pope sees in an arc from left to right the Villa Medici, the Quirinal, the Victor Emmanuel monument (the 'Typewriter' as it is sometimes called) and, over and above, the building belonging to the great Vatican institution of Propaganda Fide. Pope Paul VI travelled often away from Rome, not because he did not like the sight from his window – he did enormously – but because he felt the call to plead for peace personally throughout the world. Pope John Paul II early in his reign showed that he was going to put journeys among the most important items of his personal programme along with mass audiences and pastoral work in Rome, and would not be deterred by any obstacles at the Vatican. The anxiety to be seen and heard internationally fits very well with his physical urge to keep on the move, and his theological view of the Papacy.

The Pope's journeys are politically and religiously significant. They are determined by the diplomatic aims of the Holy See, both tactical and strategic. But they can also spring from an attitude of true spontaneity that sometimes leaves his officials wishing he would reflect and rest a good deal more.

John Paul II's very first overseas visit as Pope – to Mexico – was in response to an invitation that had been extended to Pope Paul VI to attend the historically important conference of the Latin American bishops at Puebla; he used the occasion to balance the Vatican's commitment to human rights with its abhorrence of political violence.

The reasons for the Pope's return to Poland in 1979 were more personal, but also politically far-reaching. His patriotic determination to see old friends – his own Polish people – was complemented by the strong possibility of exerting profound pressure on the course of political life in Poland.

83

In contrast, the Pope's visit to Ireland, in the early autumn of 1979, was a response to the initiative of the Irish clergy themselves. To celebrate the centenary of the 'Apparition of Our Lady at Knock', Archbishop Joseph Cunnane had persuaded the Irish bishops to ask John Paul I to Ireland. On the Pope's death, it was decided to invite his successor. According to Cardinal O'Fiaich, Cardinal Archbishop of Armagh, the letter was delivered to John Paul II in December 1978 and 'when I visited the Pope just before Christmas, I referred to it, gave him books about Knock, and exhorted him to come. I wrote on Pentecost Sunday [2 June] reiterating the earlier invitation. I met His Holiness on two occasions during that month, in Poland and in Rome, on both occasions in the company of three different Irish bishops, and we spoke to His Holiness of the very warm welcome he would receive if he came to Ireland.'

The American bishops seem to have made the need of a rallying call for orthodoxy the basis for their invitation to the Pope to visit the United States in October 1979. His speech at the General Assembly of the United Nations on 2 October, on peace and human rights, continued the traditional involvement of recent Popes in that forum.

John Paul II went to Turkey in December 1979, visiting Istanbul and the ruins of Ephesus, and again following the path of Paul VI, to promote Christian unity between East and West and to pursue his campaign for human rights.

The bishops of England and Wales invited the Pope to visit England – in 1982 – when he gave an audience at his Castel Gandolfo summer villa to Cardinal Hume and Archbishop Worlock in 1980. The bishops of Scotland wrote to him a few days later; the Archbishop of Canterbury invited him to visit Canterbury, the first firm indication of a strong 'ecumenical' emphasis in the Pope's plans for Britain, where he agreed to travel extensively and, in Cardinal Hume's words, was assured of a 'warm welcome'.

Meanwhile, in May 1980 (the month of his sixtieth birthday), John Paul II toured six African countries in ten days, in a demonstration of his continuing fitness and his determination to assert the teaching authority of the Holy See: he stressed the importance of monogamous marriage and African tradition, and in a characteristic balancing act counterpointed his approval of Africanization of the Church with reminders of its vital unity in communion with Rome. In June 1980, the Pope returned to Latin America. He began 1981 with a marathon journey to the Far East, including strongly contrasted visits to the Philippines and Japan.

At times a photographer catches the Pope's face in contemplative repose, sometimes full of tiredness, deeply thoughtful if never utterly melancholy. As he travels, the impression he confirms is that of a man always in motion, whose sense of time and distance is peculiarly his own. He often passes among the crowds in an open vehicle after landing in a helicopter. For the long journeys, the jet aircraft which is provided by Alitalia or the relevant national airline is converted to provide his own personal cabin (where he can celebrate Mass) and space for his attendants, as well as room for the press. The Aer Lingus Boeing 747 flagship 'Saint Patrick', for example, which flew the Pope from Rome to Shannon and Shannon to Boston in 1979, had its upper deck compartment converted for papal use, with a four-seater table, a settee, and ceiling-to-floor curtaining to divide the dining and rest areas. A crucifix in wood was attached to the port side bulkhead. To his pleasure, the Pope's coat-of-arms was painted on the fuselage.

As well as making saints in Heaven – he must assent to the processes and conduct the final solemn ceremonies of beatification and canonization – the Pope also confers distinctions on earth. There are five orders of papal knighthood conferred directly through Apostolic Letter.

The Supreme Order of Christ, the chief of the pontifical orders, was approved by the fourteenth-century Pope John XXII as a continuation in Portugal of the suppressed Order of Templars. It has been an order of merit – not a religious order – since the fifteenth century, and was awarded only to Christian heads of state by Pope Paul VI.

The Order of the Golden Spur – among the most ancient knighthoods – was revived by Pope Pius X early this century and was also awarded only to Christian heads of state by Pope Paul, but subsequently among the Knights was the late Shah of Iran.

The Supreme Order of Christ and the Golden Spur are rarely, if ever, awarded these days. The Golden Spur (which

Mozart and Gluck held) was at one stage merged with St Sylvester (see below). It was also given in the sixteenth century to the Swiss Protestant ancestor (as Commander of the Swiss Guard) of the now Catholic Counts de Salis as a *hereditary* decoration. The Foreign Office chose a Count de Salis with his hereditary decoration as the second British Minister to the Holy See.

The Order of Pius (founded in 1847) is bestowed, for outstanding services to the Church or society, upon non-Catholics as well as Catholics. There are now four classes: the Grand Collar (restricted to heads of state), the Knights of the Grand Cross, Knights Commander with and without star, and Knights.

The Order of St Gregory the Great was founded by Pope Gregory XVI in 1831 for award to citizens of the Papal States. It has three classes of knights, with civil and military divisions, and is nowadays conferred on persons of distinguished or notable achievement.

Finally, the Order of St Sylvester (instituted in 1841 to absorb the since revived Order of the Golden Spur) has three degrees: Knights of the Grand Cross, Knights Commanders with and without star, and Knights. It is conferred, usually on the recommendation of a bishop, on those who have served the Church in some notable way.

All three normal orders (Pian, Gregory, Sylvester) are given to Catholics, non-Catholics and non-Christians in a carefully graded order of downwards progression: Pian Grand Cross, Gregory Grand Cross, Sylvester Grand Cross, Pian Knight Commander, Gregory Knight Commander, Sylvester Knight Commander, Pian Knight, Gregory Knight, Sylvester Knight. The Pian Grand Cross has been given to Dukes of Norfolk, and the system is rather like the British progression through the Bath, St Michael and St George and the British Empire. The Pian Grand Cross is also regularly bestowed on ambassadors to the Holy See after they have served for a number of years.

Knights of St Gregory have an eye-catching bottle-green uniform with silver embroidery (which they must buy themselves, at great expense, if they want to wear it). Knights of St Sylvester have a black uniform with gold embroidery.

There are two papal decorations. The Cross *Pro Ecclesia et Pontifice* was instituted by Pope Leo XIII in 1888; it hangs from the breast with a red, white and yellow ribbon. The first of a series of special medals called *Benemerenti* was awarded by Pope Pius VIII. Nowadays, this medal is issued by the reigning Pope to those who have served the Church with some distinction; it is worn from a ribbon of the papal colours, yellow and white.

One of the cardinals told me of lunching alone with Pope John Paul II in the Tower of Pope John, high up the hill in the Vatican Gardens; the Pope went very carefully through the discussion papers they had before them, in contrast to the accusations sometimes made that John Paul II does not listen. 'But he is more interested in some subjects than others. He is preoccupied with his pastoral work in Rome, and with the task of world evangelization. He is not so interested in all the topics that fascinate the liberal West.'

The best map to his own philosophical personality was provided by Pope John Paul II himself, a few days before Christmas, 1979. He was speaking in Rome at his alma mater, the Angelicum University, which he attended in 1946–8, as a student outside Poland for the first time in his life. In the presence of a group of old curial dignatories (Cardinals Parente, Ciappi, Philippe, Knox, Garrone) and of the Master of the Dominican Order, Fr. Vincent de Couesnongle, John Paul II affirmed his commitment to the 'perennial philosophy' of St Thomas Aquinas. The occasion was the hundredth anniversay of the publication of Pope Leo XIII's encyclical *Aeterni Patris*, which sought to reinvigorate philosophical study within the Catholic Church on the basis of Thomism. The address which John Paul II gave to professors and students at the Angelicum betrayed some signs of drafting by officials of the Curia (in the curiously desiccated language that can talk of Leo XIII as 'the immortal Pontiff'), but it is all the same a document vital to an understanding of the present Pope through its assertion of the pre-eminence of Aquinas as a Catholic philosopher. St Thomas, the Pope said, established the distinction between reason and faith 'and preserved their respective dignities in such a way that human reason soared to the loftiest heights . . . and can scarcely rise any higher, while faith can expect no further or more reliable assistance. . .'.

The first quality of St Thomas was 'his complete submission of mind and heart to divine revelation. . .'. 'How beneficial it would be,' the Pope added significantly, 'for the Church of

God if also today all Catholic philosophers and theologians followed the wonderful example of the *Doctor communis Ecclesiae*.'

The second quality of St Thomas was his 'great respect for the visible world because it is the work, and hence also the imprint and image, of God the Creator'. The third quality was his 'sincere, total and life-long acceptance of the teaching office of the Church, to whose judgement he submitted all his works both during his life and at the point of death.'

This speech of John Paul II provides a key to understanding the intellectual basis of his campaign for human rights. St Thomas, he remarked, said all that was essential with regard to the dignity of the human being 'even though much more still remains to be investigated in this field, one where the contribution of modern trends in philosophy can be helpful. . . .'

The qualification in this sentence seems an interesting reflection of the Pope's own open-mindedness with regard to the development of Catholic philosophy. None the less, the address confirms a keynote of the pontificate of Pope John Paul II: his utmost concern for the 'teaching office' of the Church, as embodied in the Papacy. It should probably have come as no surprise, then, that under John Paul II the Sacred Congregation for the Doctrine of the Faith acted to discipline several Catholic theologians such as Hans Küng; that the Dutch bishops were summoned to Rome in the spring of 1980 to a special kind of bishops' synod to discuss the re-establishment of pastoral and doctrinal discipline on Vatican lines; and that Pope John Paul II himself was soon being talked about as another Pius IX or Leo XIII (and so a disappointment to many 'liberal' Catholics), though very much his own man.

4
The Cardinals and the Curia

Early Christians recognized as Apostolic or Holy Sees the official 'seats' of the Apostles who founded the first churches. The word 'see' (derived from the Latin *sedes*, meaning chair) is still used for the residence of a bishop. The Holy See has come to mean specifically the See of the Bishop of Rome. In the law of the Catholic Church (Canon Law) and international diplomacy, the Holy See means the bishopric of the Pope in Rome along with the Curia, or Court, which helps him govern the Catholic Church.

The bishops of the Church, according to Catholic theology, rule their own dioceses by divine authority. However they may be chosen, the choice must be confirmed by the Pope. Together with the Pope, they exercise an authority over the whole Church, which is made visible when they assemble in ecumenical councils, of which there have been twenty-one, from the First General Council of Nicaea in 325 AD which defined the Godhead of Christ, to the Second Vatican Council in 1962, called by Pope John XXIII for the general renewal of the Church.

But the Pope, by virtue of his position as the successor of St Peter, also exercises by himself alone supreme power over the Church on divine authority. When he teaches on matters of revealed faith or morals, he can alone, as well as with the bishops, invoke the doctrine of infallibility, the divine guarantee that in certain carefully defined (and not easily ascertainable) circumstances he cannot err in his teaching.

The Holy See is the supreme organ of papal government, and is the body generally recognized as performing valid acts on behalf of the Catholic Church in international law. It is the one exception (apart from the Order of Malta) to the rule that only 'states' have legal responsibility in international law. Within the Church itself, the organization of the Holy See has grown over the centuries into a complicated hierarchical system embracing a Curia or civil service numbering more officials than ever before. With some important exceptions, the key advisers to the Pope are the curial cardinals, who live permanently in Rome, in or near the Vatican City.

Held in affectionate awe by most Roman Catholics, cardinals come in all shapes, sizes and ages, and are as diverse a group of men as any in the world. (The eldest I have ever met was Cardinal Carlo Confalonieri, still stunningly eloquent and good-looking at the age of eighty-seven, who was curious whether I would write 'bad or good things' about the Church.) Cardinals are appointed by the Pope to act as his chief assistants in the central administration. Collectively, they form the Sacred College of Cardinals.

Members of the Sacred College fall into three categories, cardinal bishops, cardinal priests and cardinal deacons. The classification goes back to early medieval times, when the Pope's advisers came from among the bishops of dioceses around Rome, and from the Roman parish priests, or were simply administrators. (The most famous example of the last is Gregory the Great, who was only a deacon when elected Pope, though he had had important diplomatic experience.)

Certain functions of the cardinal bishops and cardinal deacons make it convenient for them to reside in Rome; so members of the Curia are often appointed cardinal deacons, and some of them are subsequently made cardinal priests and later cardinal bishops. Residential bishops are appointed cardinal priests and remain such. Those who are neither members of the Curia nor residential bishops (Cardinal Newman, for instance, received special dispensation from living in Rome) are usually appointed cardinal deacons and also stay as such.

The cardinal bishops (for example, Cardinal Sebastiano Baggio, who is titular Bishop of Velletri) and the cardinal deacons (e.g. Cardinal Silvio Oddi who is titular Deacon of S. Agata in Urbe), usually the career men with records of administrative service at the Vatican, are normally promoted to the rank of cardinal straight from being nuncios or secretaries to one of the Sacred Congregations. They continue in full-time service at the Curia.

Before 1917, though it happened very rarely, laymen could be cardinals. (Cesare Borgia springs to mind as the most notorious.) Nowadays, the priests who become cardinals are usually already bishops, and if not they are consecrated bishops beforehand.

Present-day cardinals receive their 'title' from the old Roman basis of the Curia. Thus, Cardinal John Cody, Archbishop of Chicago, has the titular church of S. Cecilia; Cardinal Jaime Sin, Archbishop of Manila, the titular church of S. Maria ai Monti; Cardinal Gordon Gray, Archbishop of Saint Andrews and Edinburgh, the titular church of S. Chiara a Vigna Clara. Particular residential sees have long-standing associations with particular titular churches: successive Archbishops of Westminster have had St Sylvester in Capite.

The College of Cardinals used to be limited to seventy, but recent Popes have eagerly added to its numbers. It is now made up of six cardinal bishops, 103 cardinal priests, and seventeen cardinal deacons.

In the selection of particular candidates, past Popes have been swayed by the appeal of obvious sanctity, by nepotism, and by political considerations, sometimes coloured by the relationship of the Papacy to contemporary European governments. In modern times, the choice of cardinals is more predictable: certain usually primatial sees such as Vienna, New York, Westminster; the holders of certain offices in the Curia; and sometimes those it is expedient to waft upstairs. In the actual choice of the man for a particular see, the Pope's say is usually limited to picking from the *terna*, the possible candidates, and he is influenced by the wishes of the bishops, clergy and people. But the selection of cardinals is the prerogative of the Pope.

A cardinal is sometimes not publicly named but created *in petto* (secretly). This practice vanished under Pope Pius XII and Pope John XXIII, till Pope Paul VI acted to honour certain cardinals in Communist countries as a gesture of solidarity.

The composition of the modern Sacred College reflects above all the pressures on the Vatican for political and cultural internationalization. Italian domination of the entire Sacred College and of all the leading positions in the Curia has been eroded; the Italian cardinals lost their majority in the Sacred College in 1946. In 1965, at the end of the Second Vatican Council, about 70 per cent of the 103 cardinals came from European sees; twelve came from Latin America, nine from Asia, eight from North America, five from Africa, and one from Australasia. At the beginning of the reign of Pope John Paul II, about 50 per cent of the 119 cardinals came from European sees; twenty-three were from Latin America, nine from Asia, ten from Africa, fourteen from North America, and three from Australasia.

There are several kinds of consistory, or assembly, at which cardinals assist in the government of the Church and in the perpetuation of their own unique organization. They range from the 'secret consistory', at which they and the Pontiff are present with a host of officials and which may deal with the nomination of new members to their ranks or the formal petitioning for *pallia* (the woollen vestments signifying papal approval) for new archbishops, to rare public consistories, with bishops and diplomats present as well as ordinary Catholics, for ceremonial purposes. The steps in the creation of a new cardinal are fairly flexible but normally involve the notional assent of the college at various procedural stages to the choices made by the Pope.

Thus Pope John Paul II held his first secret consistory for the appointment of his fourteen cardinals, whose names had been announced in May, on 30 June 1979, in the Consistorial Hall of the Apostolic Palace. Fifty-two existing cardinals were present. Other secret consistorial business was transacted, including the nomination of bishops and archbishops and the nomination of the Camerlengo of the Sacred College. An hour or so later in the morning, in the Paul VI audience hall, the dean of the college handed the new cardinals their *biglietti*, certificates. The new cardinals then took their oath of faithfulness and obedience to the Pope and his successor. Then, the Pope went through the ceremony of imposing the biretta on the new cardinals kneeling before him, and assigning to each the title of a Roman see, in the presence of the other cardinals, many bishops, members of the diplomatic corps and 4000 of the faithful.

The next day, 1 July, the Pope concelebrated Mass with the new cardinals and gave them their rings in the Basilica of St

Peter's. And on 2 July, with friends and members of their families, they were received by the Pope in audience.

The ring given to a cardinal by the Pope on his election varies from one time to another. Pope Pius XII gave topazes in 1946. Cardinal Basil Hume showed me the ring he was given in 1976: a masculine gold ring of the Good Shepherd, heavy in the palm.

A prince of the Church normally wears a black cassock trimmed with scarlet but, in public ceremonies, he wears a cassock of scarlet or purple. His shoulder cape or *mozzetta*, worn for religious ceremonies, is scarlet or red, as is the square cape or biretta handed to him by the Pope.

Paul VI took the decision, which became effective in 1971, to exclude cardinals over eighty from being able to vote in future Conclaves for his successor as Pope or stay on in the Curia. This rather tied the officials in knots for the Conclave which followed. The over-eighties accepted that they were excluded from entering the Conclave and voting, but not that they should know nothing more than the outside world of what was going on. In particular, they wanted to know who the new Pope was before the public announcement, and so be able to pay him homage along with the younger cardinals. In the event, they were informed by their own 'hot line', a special telephone link.

The decision to exclude some of the cardinals from the Conclave was seen also as a reminder that the cardinals and their college, unlike the bishops, were a human and not a divine institution: that there could even be more changes and reforms to come in the method of electing a Pope.

Pope Paul VI certainly gave a great deal of thought to the possibility of including other than the cardinals in the election process. He had in mind particularly representatives of the Uniate Churches and the bishops on the Committee of the Synod of Bishops (most of them elected by the synod and therefore representative of the bishops as a whole).

He finally decided against, and the odds are against Pope John Paul II's making any significant changes in his turn. The present system provides for the absolute necessity of knowing which individuals are entitled to enter a Conclave and take part in an election. Any arrangement other than the College of Cardinals, such as the use of episcopal conferences, or voters elected by the Synod of Bishops, would risk bringing back the inconclusive results that often plagued the medieval church.

The Sacred College has a tiny secretariat of three and a dean of its own, the old and influential Cardinal Carlo Confalonieri. Its most important members, constitutionally and often politically, are the dean and the Chamberlain or Camerlengo of the Holy Roman Church (a post not to be confused with that of the Chamberlain to the Sacred College itself). In carrying on the routine administration of the Church through a commission of cardinals resident in Rome, during the inter-regnum after the death of a Pope, the Camerlengo makes arrangements in collaboration with the dean for the funeral of the dead Pope, and for the summoning and supervision of the Conclave to elect the new one.

In the elections of Popes, the cardinals as a corporate entity come into their own. They meet in general congregation to prepare the Conclave where up to the maximum number of 120 cardinal-electors will cast their votes. Pope Paul VI laid down the latest rules for the conduct of Conclaves in the document *Romano Pontifici Eligendo*, which elaborated a series of former regulations aimed at procedural certitude and absolute secrecy.

When a Pope dies, the cardinals who are already in Rome must wait fifteen days for the others to assemble and must enter the Conclave after at most another five days. They then must remain enclosed within the Vatican Palace, cut off from the outside world, until the election is made. (The cardinal penitentiary – dealing with matters of conscience – has the right to send and receive sealed letters while in Conclave.)

The Sistine Chapel is the election hall, with writing desks for the cardinal-electors crammed round the walls and a large table before the altar of the Last Judgement where votes are cast and the ballot papers counted. Accommodation is arranged in the apartments and corridors of the Palace, where the cardinals confer alone save for a handful of officials. They swear not to speak about the events that take place in the Conclave. The cardinals are trusted not to use cameras, tape recorders, radio transmitters or receivers, but the officials have to take an oath on this.

On the day the Conclave starts, the cardinals celebrate a Mass of the Holy Spirit in St Peter's and then walk in procession to the Sistine Chapel. An official inspection checks that all openings are sealed, the entrance to the Conclave area is closed, and the door is bolted on the inside and padlocked outside under the scrutiny of the Prefect of the Pontifical Household and the Commandant of the Swiss Guards. The following day, the election starts.

There are three ways in which it may proceed. 'Acclamation' is when the cardinal-electors all together and at once shout their choice of the same individual as Pope, an event that has not recently happened outside the novels of Frederick Rolfe. The normal method of election is by scrutiny, two votes being taken each morning and two each afternoon in the Sistine Chapel till one candidate receives a majority of two-thirds plus one vote. In difficult instances, the cardinals can agree unanimously to delegate a limited number (nine to fifteen) of themselves to make the choice; to change the majority rule from two-thirds plus one vote to an absolute majority plus one vote; or after protracted delay to limit the final choice to the two candidates who received the largest number of votes in the most recent ballot.

In the normal balloting and scrutiny system, the cardinals write the name of their candidate on a ballot form under the printed words *Eligo in Summum Pontificem* – I elect as Supreme Pontiff. . . . This is folded and borne aloft, between thumb and index finger of the right hand, to be dropped into a box before the altar by the cardinals in order of rank and seniority. Three cardinals chosen as tellers handle the counting of the votes. When they tally with the number of electors (if they do not, a fresh vote is taken), the results are announced for both the tellers and the cardinals to record.

Voting continues, afternoon and morning, till the new Pope is elected and the votes put into a stove to produce a curl of white smoke – the *sfumata* – for the onlookers in St Peter's Square. (In the past, the votes were burned either with or without straw. Nowadays, to ensure the right colour of smoke, there is always a chemical to hand labelled either *bianco* or *nero*. The confused signal on the election of Albino Luciani in 1978 was caused, apparently, by the amateur cardinals putting in so much *bianco* that at first the smoke came out very dense, and rather dark.)

The senior cardinal deacon announces the name of the new

Pontiff from the balcony of St Peter's, and the cardinals revert to their chief role as advisers of the Pope.

As heads of curial departments or – normally – leaders of their national Churches, individual cardinals wield considerable juridical and moral authority. Collectively, their power is at its greatest when they perform their age-old function of electing a Pope. In the extraordinary year of the three Popes – 1978 – they used this power to confound the predictions. The elections of Albino Luciani of Venice and subsequently of Karol Wojtyla of Cracow, although unforeseen by most pundits, followed logically from the common purposes and formations of the cardinals, while also reflecting the new geographical distribution of numerical power within the Conclave.

In the two papal elections of 1978, Italian cardinals were in a minority and European cardinals were outnumbered by those from other parts of the world, though still the largest block. A majority of the cardinals were seeking not for a curial but for a 'pastoral' Pope (as indeed most Popes have been this century).

Luciani emerged, during one day's voting, on the third or fourth ballot, with a strong majority. He had been a cardinal since 1973, and, though little known even in Italy, had impressed several cardinals from the Third World by his sympathy for their problems, as well as most of his fellow Italian cardinals by his orthodox piety. He had served for several years as a member of the Congregation for the Sacraments and Divine Worship, whose other members included Cardinals Knox, Seper, Arns, Felici, Pignedoli and Wojtyla. The cardinals' brief experience of Pope John Paul I confirmed their anxiety to see a pastoral Pope in the chair of Peter, and for obvious reasons one with an undoubtedly robust constitution and resolution.

Cardinal Wojtyla was elected on the second day of the Conclave and after perhaps as many as eight ballots. Once there was failure to agree on an Italian candidate – even, it seems, among the Italian cardinals themselves – the original supposition that an East European (like an American) would constitute too politically imprudent a choice was obviated by the already well-known spiritual and moral qualities of the Polish cardinal who had given a 'retreat' to the Pope and the

Curia in 1976, and whose book *Sign of Contradiction* had been suddenly in demand between the Conclaves. The cardinal-electors – nearly all of whom by upbringing and training tend to deeply conservative instincts and loyalties – showed imagination and courage as well as faith. Their successive choices of Luciani and Wojtyla may well have halted for a long time the underlying pressure for a widening of the electoral college.

The tremendous emotion of the climax to the cardinals' electoral deliberations, throwing into relief the uniquely heightened religious quality of the event, was expressed to me by Cardinal Hume. When the cardinals are 'nailed up', he said, they experience a tremendous sense of community, as they prepare for the very serious business that unites them in a common purpose. 'There is an almost tangible sense of being under the guidance of the Holy Spirit.' On the election: 'We realize the tremendous, the dreadful, thing we have done to one man.'

Cardinal Hume recalls his abiding memory from both Conclaves of the moment when the election is completed. 'The man chosen leaves the chapel dressed in the black and scarlet of a cardinal like the rest of us. Then after a while he comes back wearing the white cassock of Pope, the new supreme Pastor.' On the balcony, after first presenting an air (the cardinal searches for the words) 'of shy dignity, of tentative dignity', the new Pope suddenly seems transformed.

Most of the cardinals who have attended a Conclave cannot wait to return home, whatever their affection for Rome, where most of them have studied. (For Cardinal Hume, London – because of *The Times* and marmalade for breakfast – is preferable to Rome, 'where there is too much noise and too many priests . . .,' he says with mock seriousness.) The non-curial cardinals will be back from time to time. They are all members of the Roman congregations or commissions and travel to the Vatican regularly for the full meetings of these bodies.

Several American bishops, as well as all the American cardinals, have assignments as members or consultors of the Vatican congregations. Villa Stritch, the home of American priests working in the Curia, is easily visited by the American bishops. Archbishop Ernest Primeau, director of Villa Stritch since 1974, acts as unofficial liaison officer and sounding board for the American bishops with the Curia.

The influence of particular national Churches within the Catholic Church on the Holy See ebbs and flows, often in relation to personal factors, such as the relationship between Pope Pius XII and Cardinal Spellman or, on another level, the deep Slavonic loyalties of Pope John Paul II. Fundamentally, however, it depends on the numerical strength of Catholicism in the region concerned, and on the assessment by the Holy See of the degree of orthodoxy of the local church and its members. Despite attempts to 'internationalize' the Curia, it is still a very Italian institution, resistant to change and suspicious of outside influences. A non-Italian like Cardinal Wright, although at the head of a congregation, to the end was still regarded as really an outsider.

The Curia, none the less, is neither homogeneous nor static. It has evolved century by century from its beginnings in the synods of Roman priests on whom the early Popes relied for the government of the Church. Its first office was the Apostolic Chancery. In the Middle Ages authority was exercised under the Popes by consistories of cardinals. The structures of today's Curia were well established by 1588, when they were reformed and regulated by the disciplinarian Pope Sixtus V. A thorough-going structural reform of the modern Curia was initiated by Pope Paul VI in the Apostolic Constitution, *Regimini Ecclesiae Universae* (For the Government of the Universal Church).

Listed in order in the *Annuario Pontificio*, which indicates official precedence, the Roman Curia consists of the following bodies:

The Secretariat of State, and the Council for the Public Affairs of the Church.

The nine Sacred Congregations (numbering twelve before the reform of Pope Paul). These are: the Congregation for the Doctrine of the Faith (the old Holy Office); the Congregation for the Bishops; the Congregation for the Oriental Churches; the Congregation for the Sacraments and Divine Worship; the Congregation for the Clergy; the Congregation for Religious and Secular Institutes; the Congregation for the Evangelization of Peoples (Propaganda Fide); the Congregation for the Causes of Saints; the Congregation for Catholic Education.

The three Tribunals of the Curia are the Sacred Apostolic Penitentiary; the Supreme Tribunal of the Apostolic Segnatura; and the Sacred Roman Rota.

The three Secretariats are the Secretariat for Christian Unity; the Secretariat for Non-Christians; and the Secretariat for Non-Believers.

The Pontifical Commissions, Councils and Committees of the Curia include the Council for the Laity; the Justice and Peace Commission; the Commission for the Revision of the Code of Canon Law; the Commission for the Revision of the Code of Oriental Canon Law; the Commission for Social Communications; the Commission for Latin America; the Commission for the Pastoral Care of Migrants; the Council *Cor Unum*; the International Theological Commission; the Biblical Commission; the Commission for Sacred Archaeology; the Commission for Historical Sciences; the Commission for the Ecclesiastical Archives of Italy; and the Commission of Cardinals for the Pontifical Sanctuaries of Pompei and Loreto.

The offices of the Curia are the Apostolic Camera; the Prefecture for the Economic Affairs of the Holy See; the Administration of the Patrimony of the Apostolic See; the Prefecture of the Pontifical Household (dealing with the Pontifical Family, the Office for Pontifical Ceremonies, the Chapel of Pontifical Music and the Corps of the Swiss Guard); the Relief Service of the Holy Father; the Archive of the Second Vatican Council; the Office for Personnel Relations of the Holy See; and the Central Office of Statistics of the Church.

The Palatine Administration, under the authority of the Curia, includes the Reverend Fabric of St Peter's; the Apostolic Vatican Library; the Secret Vatican Archives; the Vatican Press; the Vatican Publishing House; and the *Osservatore Romano*.

These curious corridors of power carry titles loaded with portentous historical associations, or coined recently for new bodies called into existence by a new theological stance or a growth in the Vatican's international interests. The congregations and offices, the old sinews of the Church's government, are mostly situated outside the walls of Vatican City. The commissions and committees are a mixed bundle of the relatively new bodies, also with headquarters outside Vatican City, several in Piazza San Calisto. The psychological atmosphere and theological tendency and personalities of those employed can vary sharply from one body of the Curia to another; for example, between the Congregation for the Doctrine of the Faith and the Secretariat for Christian Unity. But they are all spokes of a wheel with the Pope and the Secretariat of State at the hub.

There are cardinal prefects at the top of each of the congregations, and cardinal presidents head each of the secretariats and nearly all the commissions and councils. The personnel of the departments of the Curia include members, officials and consultants (the Secretariat of State has only officials). The members of the congregations are all cardinals, plus (since a decree of 1967) seven diocesan bishops each on five-year terms (who have the right to take part in certain plenary sessions). Several of the other curial bodies have lay members, notably the Justice and Peace Commission and, as one would expect, the Council for the Laity. But all the curial departments are overwhelmingly clerical and dominated by cardinals and bishops.

Curial officials total about 500 priests and fifty laymen, with a scatter of religious and lay women. Especially important among the full-time official posts are those of *Sostituto* or Deputy at the Secretariat of State, the Secretary at the Public Affairs Council, and the secretaries of each of the congregations. These officials are normally archbishops, and the more able of them sometimes exercise more influence even than some of the cardinal prefects and presidents.

The departments of the Curia draw on the services of 700 or so consultors, who are engaged on renewable five-year terms. Many of the consultants to the congregations are members or officials of other curial departments. The secretariats, commissions and councils can call on about thirty lay consultors, from various walks of life, but most of their consultors are priests.

The historic document defining the present structure and powers of the Roman Curia, the Apostolic Constitution, *Regimini Ecclesiae Universae*, was promulgated by Pope Paul VI on 15 August 1967. The reconstruction, which sprang from the prompting of the Second Vatican Council, made the Curia more representative of the international nature of the Church by, for example, including diocesan bishops and lay people among the members of the departments.

The 'reform' of the Curia followed nearly four years' study and consultation by a commission of three cardinals. The Apostolic Constitution bore every trace of the subtle and anxious mind of Pope Paul, who closely supervised its final preparation; and the emphasis throughout its chapters was placed on the initiatives of the Pope.

The key, and to some extent conflicting, features of the reform were the strong coordinating, advisory and supervisory role given to the Secretariat of State, and the addition of diocesan bishops to the membership of the departments. Otherwise, the changes covered some re-drawing of the lines of departmental responsibility, several significant changes of name (for example, the Supreme Sacred Congregation of the Holy Office became the Sacred Congregation for the Doctrine of the Faith) and a limit of five years on the terms of office of the cardinals and bishops who are members of departments.

All the powers of the Curia are delegated to its members and officials by the Pope. His threefold authority as head of the Church – administrative, judicial and executive – is in broad terms deployed through the three different categories of curial department: respectively, the congregations and secretariats, the tribunals, the offices and commissions. Specific papal approval has to be given to exceptional decisions, but generally the departments act with considerable, albeit vicarious, day-to-day authority.

Under their cardinal prefects or presidents, assisted by their secretaries and under-secretaries, the permanent staff of the curial departments are divided into major officials, minor officials and lay personnel. Major officials and above are appointed by the Pope himself. The cardinal prefect, with the approval of the Pope, appoints the rest. Cardinal prefects, presidents and senior prelates must resign after five years in office but they can be re-appointed for a further term. Heads of department must resign when they reach seventy-five. On the death of a Pope, the terms of office of the cardinal prefects and presidents as well as of the secretaries come to an end. They are normally re-appointed by the new Pope.

Thus are all the threads gathered up in the hands of the Pontiff, whose portrait on paper or canvas graces virtually every office in the Vatican and all the Curia's assemblies.

The major and minor officials and the lay staff in the offices have their terms of employment – from hours of work to promotion – defined in detail by the *Regolamento Generale della Curia Romana*, the General Rules of the Roman Curia, applied in March 1968. The *Regolamento* with its forty-three pages, 130 articles and three appendices is a classic piece of Italian penmanship – grave, sonorous and bureaucratic, it announces that each article has been pondered by the Supreme Pontiff personally. The minor officials are divided into three grades – *minutanti, addetti* or *scrittori* – as are the lay subordinates – *commessi, ordinanze* or *uscieri*, and *ausiliari*. Physical, moral and educational criteria for appointments are scrupulously spelled out. Officials must make promises of secrecy and loyalty (in Latin for officials, in Italian for lay assistants). Responsibilities and duties are detailed: subordinate personnel, for example, have the duty of 'dispatching or delivering letters and packets, looking after the cleaning before officials arrive and after they leave, carrying out the tasks committed to them by their superiors, on behalf of the discastery to which they belong'. In their offices, priests must wear cassocks (a rule that has gone; the black clerical suit is more prevalent).

Hours of work are stipulated as thirty-three a week for the officials, thirty-nine for the lay helpers. Normal office hours in the dicasteries are from nine o'clock to one thirty, with arrangements for flexible timing to keep the offices open to four o'clock. 'Office hours must be faithfully observed so that, at the set hour, everyone is at his own place of work and at the disposition of the superiors.' Holidays, including the anniversary of the coronation of the Supreme Pontiff, his patron saint's day, and the anniversary of the death of his predecessor, are carefully listed.

The second part of the *Regolamento* describes the procedures for the various meetings of the dicasteries (e.g. cardinals speak first and then the other members) and defines spheres of competence.

The most important frequent meeting of a curial department is the weekly congress, attended by the cardinal prefect in the chair, the secretary and the under-secretary, along with appropriate officials. The congress discusses routine matters and decides what needs to be referred to the Pope or to another departmental meeting, the Ordinary Congregation or the Plenary Congregation. The former is attended by the cardinal, and by bishop members of the department if they are in Rome. The Plenary Congregation of a department is held annually, with all the members, cardinals and bishops, in attendance. Before this meets, to discuss departmental programmes or matters of important principle, the consultors to the department hold their own preparatory meeting in the Vatican. These departmental meetings, of varying degrees of solemnity, are held mostly in the Apostolic Palace or in the Palazzo delle Congregazioni.

All the heads of the departments hold regular meetings in the Apostolic Palace under the presidency of the Cardinal Secretary of State. This is an important practical aspect of the fascinating system of government applied through the Curia. Peter Drucker, in *The Concept of the Corporation*, a famous study of the management of General Motors, discerned a close parallel between that company's scheme of organization and those of the Catholic Church and of the modern army as developed by the Prussians, both renowned for administrative efficiency.

The Curia has elements both of a medieval court – with the monarchical principle indeed strengthened by the reforms of Pope Paul VI – and of a modern corporation, making exhaustive use of mixed committees. But the most remarkable organizational feature of the Curia is the system of, as it were, multiple directorships, through which a small number of prelates can dominate the Vatican departments, and especially the congregations. For example, when he was in the influential post of *Sostituto* or deputy at the Secretariat of State, Archbishop, now Cardinal, Giovanni Benelli was a consultor to the Congregation for the Doctrine of the Faith, the Congregation for the Bishops, the Commission for the Revision of the Code of Canon Law, and the Commission for Latin America, as well as a member of the Ecclesiastical Archives of Italy and the Commission for Migration. The Cardinal Prefect of the Congregation for the Bishops, Sebastiano Baggio, is *inter alia* a member of the Congregations for the Doctrine of the Faith, for Religious and Secular Institutes, for the Evangelization of Peoples, and for Catholic Education, a member of the Commissions for the Revision of the Code of Canon Law and the Interpretation of the Decrees of the Second Vatican Council, and President of the Commission for Latin America and the Commission for Migration.

This multiplicity of offices, which is especially typical of the heads of the Sacred Congregations, brings the benefit of rapid informal communications horizontally between the government departments of the Vatican and vertically between the members and the Pope.

Attempts to internationalize the Curia were increased during the pontificate of Pope Paul VI and are continuing today; but the effects have so far been rather blunted. The diocesan bishops, for example, are in Rome too infrequently to alter the character or greatly influence the proceedings of curial meetings. The same applies to cardinals appointed as members of commissions.

Cardinal Hume, Archbishop of Westminster, as a member of the Secretariat for Christian Unity and the Congregation for Religious and Secular Institutes (and also till 1980 the Secretariat for the Synod of Bishops, for which Wojtyla chose him as his successor when he became Pope) on average has been visiting Rome two or three times a year. I asked several other cardinals specifically to test their feelings about involvement in activities of the Curia. Among them, Cardinal John Dearden (Archbishop of Detroit for twenty years till 1980) notes that his participation in the work of the Congregation for the Sacraments came about in two ways: through general meetings held in Rome; and through correspondence in which matters were referred to the members of the congregation for a judgement and appraisal. 'Because of the intermittent nature of these activities, it is difficult to say how much time is involved in it. I have regularly gone to Rome for meetings that are called. The frequency of such meetings varies greatly. For the most part, the particular congregation with which I am associated holds general sessions no more often than once a year, and often at intervals that are even longer than that. In general,' Cardinal Dearden reflects, 'I am pleased with my association with the work of the congregation. I am confident that I enjoy a real participation in its work.'

In contrast, the reflections of Cardinal Suenens (who in 1979 submitted his resignation as Archbishop of Malines–Brussels and whose experience of the Curia is profound) are less sanguine. The list of members and consultors of the congregations is long, he says, but the number of those outside Rome attending the annual meeting of the congregation is limited. Many consultations are held by mail. 'The work of the congregations is still in the hands of the Roman offices. The consultors, who are called to Rome only once a year, do not have a real influence.'

A long distance from the episcopal centres of Europe and the United States in its preoccupations is Beirut in the Lebanon, the residence of His Beatitude Maximos V Hakim, the Melchite–Greek Catholic Patriarch of Antioch and all the East, of Alexandria and of Jerusalem. Maximos V (whom I first met in Haifa before his present appointment) is the head of the most widespread Eastern-rite Catholic churches which accept the primacy of the Pope and are in communion with Rome. He is elected by the Synod of the Melchite Church. In the vexed politics of the Middle East, he plays an active part as intermediary. He participated very forcefully in the Second Vatican Council, but his view of the Vatican is critically detached and puts the role of the Curia into yet another perspective.

Relations between the Melchite Church and the Vatican are governed by an 'Eastern' Canon Law, promulgated by Pope Pius XII, in which references to Rome are frequently stipulated. A commission at present working in Rome on the reform of canon law is expected to make it, in the words of the Patriarch, 'more in conformity with Eastern traditions'. It will probably be several years till the commission produces its final report but, in the meantime, the Patriarch comments that there has been a change in spirit since Vatican II. 'Our relations with the Vatican are now nearly all concentrated with the Congregation for Eastern Churches. Many things depend on persons.' The present prefect was certainly more open and understanding than his predecessor. 'But there is still a lot to be done to see Catholic patriarchs treated in the Vatican in the same way as the Orthodox. The Secretariat for Christian Unity is certainly more up to date than the Oriental Congregation!'

The Patriarch does not find it necessary to be in Rome often. An exchange of letters is more efficient. However, there is still, he thinks, too much centralization, and too many calls to go to Rome even for minor matters. Praising the work of the Holy

See for the cause of international peace, the Patriarch remarks that in fact it is very well organized, 'much better than many states'.

At the beginning of the pontificate of John Paul II the heads of curial departments, mostly cardinals, included seven from Italy, four from France and ten from other countries. Among the secretaries to the departments the balance in the key posts was still very much tilted towards Italians, although well over half of the secretaries were non-Italians.

The curial cardinals who live in Rome differ enormously in their life-styles. Some are almost recluses. A few enjoy splendid apartments and the social comforts that can go with them. More often, they live quite modestly, like the Camerlengo, Cardinal Bertoli, who has a cosy apartment overlooking the bus stop in the noisy, rather tatty, Piazza della Città Leonina, just outside the Vatican walls.

The religious attitudes of the curial cardinals can also range as widely as their living conditions and temperaments. One of them considers in a resigned, affectionate way that John Paul II is 'a pre-Vatican II Pope'.

There are many psychological and even economic reasons why the Curia has not changed into a truly international organization. It is, for example, less costly to employ personnel from the religious orders (who receive a special salary and can get board and accommodation from the House of their own order in Rome) than lay people or priests from abroad. Retirement is less of a problem too. A department such as the Congregation for the Doctrine of the Faith may and does ask the national colleges in Rome to suggest the names of student priests as possible officials. But, in the words of an English priest, working in the Curia as an under-secretary, 'that is not the sort of work that English priests usually want. They prefer pastoral work. . . .'

This raises troublesome issues about the role of the priest anywhere in the world, and it can seem tactless, to say the least, to press them in Rome where so many priests are officials. Most of them, including the curial cardinals, do certainly take up pastoral work of one kind or another, involving, in some cases, considerable effort and self-sacrifice. They might also argue that working for the Holy See is pastoral work in the final analysis, though that does nothing to relieve the sense of unease that a priestly bureaucracy creates. Meanwhile, the thirty-three-hour week for curial officials allows time for directly pastoral work in theory, but many of them have a second job, to supplement salaries that are rather low. Working in the Curia means working in Rome and living among Italians, possibly for the rest of one's life, a prospect which does not always attract non-Italian priests with life-styles very different from those of the Romans. The flow of fresh blood into the Curia also tends to be thinned by the commendable introduction of pension arrangements, to qualify for which the curial official has to be under thirty-five.

But, meanwhile, the Curia's conservative mentality is maintained, and there is no guarantee that, even if you started to hear less Italian and more American English or Spanish or French or Polish (least of all perhaps Polish) in the corridors of the Vatican, the old ways would be soon dispelled. Indeed, many who have been called from outside to serve the Pope within the Curia have become most traditionalist. An eminent example was the late Cardinal John Wright, a big, buoyant man of brilliant talents, whose career in the Curia rather disappointed Catholics who had seen him in earlier days as a powerful, intelligent liberal.

Disparagement or praise of the Curia, as I have reflected rather ruefully after quite bitter arguments, can arouse very heated feelings among loyal Catholics. On either side, one can cite numerous instances of organizational blunder and evasion, or of common sense and honest dealing. Overall, there is such a thing as the curial mentality, not so difficult to define but open to many, many exceptions. Let us say it expresses itself in profound and protective loyalty to the reigning Pontiff but tends almost to assume that its own voice is an extension of the papal authority itself. In theology, it tends to stress the Church's possession of the whole truth as expressed in set formulae, shrinks from encouraging the exploration of the development of doctrine, and cherishes the unity rather than the diversity of the Catholic religion. In organization, the curial mentality tends to favour centralization, hierarchy and the preservation of the status quo.

But, to be fair, the Curia is neither monolithic nor inert. Among the members and officials of the Sacred Congregations and Offices, traditionalism and conservatism are deeply entrenched, and this can produce anything from resistance to relaxation of the rules of confession to rejection of the slightest breath of criticism of *Humanae Vitae*. Error on the part of the Church is unthinkable for this cast of mind. But there are scores of curial officials who possess liberal instincts and philosophies, and, as an organization, the Curia can yet set its machinery whirring into movement to make tremendous changes, as it did to implement many of the decisions of the Second Vatican Council, especially as they affected Catholic worship.

Action by the departments of the Roman Curia can have profound effects on the religious and moral behaviour of millions of people. In the pattern of Catholic worship, for example, with decisive cultural as well as religious consequences, the Sacred Congregation for the Sacraments and Divine Worship, headed by Cardinal Tabera as prefect and the Reverend (later Archbishop) Annibale Bugnini as secretary, carried through massive liturgical changes which shook Catholic parishes throughout the world from Nairobi to Tokyo. Their liturgical revolution gave most Catholics their first intimations of the work of the Second Vatican Council.

In the moral sphere, few other religious bodies deal with such sensitive issues as the Sacred Roman Rota, which hands down decisions concerning individual petitions in connection with the establishment of nullity in marriage. (The Church holds fast to the indissolubility of marriage; nullity dissolves a marriage which is considered not to have been valid in the first place). The Rota has its own in-built appeal system, from a *turnus* of three judges to another *turnus*. Consanguinity gives rise to nullity and is dealt with by a local ecclesiastical court or the Rota. The dissolution – as against the nullity – of marriage is dealt with either under the heading of a dissolution in favour of the faith (the dissolution of what was a valid marriage between a baptized and an unbaptized person) by the Congregation of the Doctrine of the Faith; or under the heading of non-consummation, by the Congregation of the Sacraments.

The other Roman tribunals are the *Segnatura Apostolica* and the Sacred Penitentiary. The former is a Court of Cassation, dealing with the validity or invalidity of a decision given by the Rota: such appeals (on the grounds, say, of a procedural fault) are very rare. The latter deals with special questions of conscience, such as the granting of absolution to a priest who has been automatically excommunicated for 'attempting' a marriage.

The Sacred Roman Rota is the busiest and largest of the three courts. It is composed of twenty-one prelates, sitting under a dean, at present a Yugoslav priest, Mgr Heinrich Ewers, with a permanent Vatican staff of fifteen priests, and a training college for ecclesiastical lawyers. The court meets at offices in the Palazzo della Cancellaria to hear cases submitted by Catholics from all over the world. The Rota generally examines if there has been 'the lack of due discretion', one of the causes of which could be gross personal immaturity. Decisions are usually handed down only after protracted processes sometimes lasting years.

The Curia invites and defies comparisons with secular governments. Visiting its myriad offices and waiting rooms is like being with Alice behind the looking-glass. The profane is sacred, the sacred profane. The eternal is made matter of fact. Streams of proposals and instructions pour out to the world Church. Conversations are full of sweet reason but 'what we cannot speak about we must pass over in silence'; though one official speaks his mind, another will be suspicious of questioning, and another fearful of answering.

Sometimes it takes a little while for the ice to melt, as I found with Fr. Henri de Riedmatten OP, the secretary, before his death in 1979, of the Pontifical Council *Cor Unum*. He makes his appearance here chiefly as typical of Vatican officials scarcely heard of outside the Curia, and of modest rank and title, who yet possess pervasive and sometimes decisive influence. This Swiss-born and Oxford-educated priest, I was told, could 'make or break' the work of anyone writing about the Holy See.

As well as being secretary of *Cor Unum*, he was a consultor to the Congregation for the Evangelization of Peoples, the Pontifical Council for the Laity, the Pontifical Commission for Latin America and the Committee for the Family. I found him in the spring of 1977 near the San Damaso courtyard of the Apostolic Palace, up a winding staircase past the *Museo Lapidario*, in a little air conditioned office suite with a charming statue of the Madonna. (Just up the staircase was a way into the apartments of the Secretary of State.) Wearing the white robes of his order, with brown belt and black shoes, his eyes peering through glasses from a reddish, intelligent face, Fr. de Riedmatten warmed up after we had discovered friends in common from Oxford. He said in very good English, 'We don't lie at the Vatican, but we don't always tell.'

Fr. de Riedmatten's influence sprang from his eighteen years' service with the Curia, his nimble intelligence and his unmoving loyalty to the decisions of the Pope. He was one of the *periti*, or theological experts, appointed to the Second Vatican Council. He served in the Vatican diplomatic service, and in particular disseminated the policies of the Holy See regarding questions of population and birth control before and after his appointment to *Cor Unum* in 1971. This organization, under the presidency of the Cardinal Secretary of State, was founded in 1971 as a 'small affair' to provide a forum for the Holy See and Catholic societies in different countries for international aid and relief, for example, the British Catholic Fund for Overseas Development, the American Catholic Relief Services, and the German Misereor – the worldwide Caritas Internationalia. Its main task is to coordinate aid activities in emergencies. 'I travel', said Fr. Riedmatten, 'anywhere where there is destruction. . . .'

Another Dominican, Archbishop Jerome Hamer, born in Brussels in 1916, a long-serving official of the Holy See, has wielded more visible, if not more potent, influence through his position in a curial department whose history runs back over four hundred years to 1542. Its first definite name was the Congregation for the Holy Inquisition of Heretical Error. After absorbing the Congregation of the Index, it settled down as the Sacred Congregation of the Holy Office. Today it is called the Sacred Congregation for the Doctrine of the Faith. With responsibilities gently modified to suit the climate of the Church after Vatican II, its competence extends to all matters concerning the teaching of the Catholic faith and of morals, to questions connected with faith and doctrine, to studies, the examination and if necessary correction of new teachings, to the examination and condemnation of books, and to the judgement of crimes against the faith. It has the powers of a tribunal. Its procedures are secret.

The Holy Office's position in the Curia is central:

structurally overshadowed by the Secretariat of State but placed at the head of all the Sacred Congregations. In recent years it has summoned theologians such as the Dominicans Fr. Jacques Pohier and Fr. Edward Schillebeeckx to Rome to answer charges against their writings; condemned 'errors and dangerous affirmations' in a French theological book; written to the bishops of the United States drawing their attention to a book on sex and inviting the (Catholic) authors to correct their 'fundamental' errors; requested the bishops of Holland to explain their attitude towards homosexuality; taken away from Professor Hans Küng the right to be formally designated as a Catholic theologian.

Catholics, including very occasionally lay people, are still from time to time 'delated' to Rome for immoral teaching or behaviour, and the Sacred Congregation will instigate thorough questioning where it feels this appropriate. More positively, the Sacred Congregation frequently speaks its mind to the bishops of the world on contemporary religious priorities, as when in 1979 it sent a letter, approved by the Pope, rehearsing traditional Catholic teaching about life after death. And it is the Holy Office's positive role in teaching rather than its traditional inquisitorial function that Archbishop Hamer stresses in discussion.

He is a bolster of a man, with a large handsome head and a booming preacher's voice, accompanied by extravagant gestures. He wears shiny black shoes under a black cassock and gold cross and, as he talks vehemently, his red skullcap falls a little askew. He has the reputation of being a dyed-in-the-wool and aggressive conservative, a hard-liner. He looks like an affable Belgian who likes his food; when he talks, clapping his hands for emphasis every so often, his mind comes over as strong, rational and inflexible.

Archbishop Hamer joined the Dominicans when he was eighteen and studied under Karl Barth for his doctorate in Switzerland. He taught in Belgium and was a director of studies in Paris for seven years. After becoming a consultor in Rome in 1962, he joined the Secretariat for Christian Unity as secretary under Cardinal Willebrands and then moved to the Congregation of the Doctrine of the Faith, like, one feels, a man coming home. Here, the secretary's post brought the mitre of archbishop with it.

Hamer, and the gentle white-robed secretary who shows you in to see him, both live in the old Holy Office building. His office is on the second floor, his living quarters are on the fourth floor, with dining room, library and private chapel. He travels often: to Russia as the Curia's representative to the Orthodox Church in 1977, to the United States the year before, to Mexico with the Pope in 1978. He takes his holidays in Italy or Belgium. In the antechamber to his large marble-floored office hangs a wooden carving of a bearded helmsman steering a ship. It was presented to Archbishop Hamer by Canadian Catholics in 1974, when he attended an episcopal conference in Quebec.

The metaphor he has used to me to describe the Sacred Congregation for the Doctrine of the Faith, however, is of 'a guide in the mountains. . . .' The role of the Sacred Congregation is to 'make sure that the Creed is the rule for all actions in the Church. . . .'

The word 'Inquisition' disappeared from the title of the Holy Office in 1908. In 1965, the congregation was given new directions by Pope Paul VI in the *motu proprio* '*Integrae servandae*' which stressed 'the promotion of sound doctrine', rather than the rooting out of error. Archbishop Hamer believes there is still a need for 'vigilance' against the spread of falsehood but says the role of the congregation is now more positive. The process of investigation of error (until 1966 the task of a special commissary) is less dominant in the congregation's work, and the index of prohibited books which Catholics might neither read nor possess no longer has the force of ecclesiastical law, though it can be argued that it still preserves its moral value.

The Sacred Congregation, headed by eleven cardinals and the statutory seven diocesan bishops, has thirty-five permanent employees, and thirty consultors of many nationalities. Some of the latter are the secretaries of other Roman congregations; most are based in Rome. They are all of 'legitimate' theological tendencies, the archbishop says.

There are four main sections in the congregation: doctrinal, sacerdotal (dealing with, for example, dispensations from vows to the priesthood), matrimonial (dealing with, for example, the abstruse matter of the petrine privilege by which even 'valid' marriages can be annulled for the sake of the faith), and discipline (for example, safeguarding the 'dignity' of the sacraments of confession and the eucharist).

The full-time superiors of the congregation meet every Saturday (in congress) to decide whether the issues before it are major or minor. A minor issue may be decided at the same meeting. A major issue is put before at least one of the congregation's experts for study; the subsequent comment is sent to the consultors, who meet every Monday. After their study of the memoranda and documentation, a week or more later each consultor gives his opinion in the Monday *Consulta*. The conclusions (majority and minority), the earlier memoranda and the documentation are then sent to the nine cardinals of the congregation, meeting on Wednesdays. Subsequently, the decisions which they adopt are taken to the Pope (who has already received the complete dossier) on Friday, for presentation at the audience given to the cardinal prefect or secretary of the congregation. The Pope may adopt, modify or return the decision for further examination.

Archbishop Hamer has outlined these carefully followed procedures to me in loving detail. He is as proud of their thoroughness and exactitude as of the role of the new Holy Office in its promulgation of orthodoxy and defence of the faith. He once bridled slightly when I asked him if he was 'still a Thomist'. 'Why *still* a Thomist?' he exclaimed.

For the Dominican Jerome Hamer, the philosophy of the Dominican St Thomas Aquinas is part of the perennial philosophy, which still has 'great richness for the future'. Significantly, he believes that the true theologian accepts pluralism – the existence of various theological and philosophical schools – as 'a consequence of the human condition', but he does not give up hope of reaching the unity of knowledge, and knows that theological research 'prepares him for the vision of God, where the patch-quilt of pluralism will have no further purpose'. This certitude of aim is at the heart of what has been called the curial mentality. It shows why within the Sacred Congregation, to the resentment of many Catholic intellectuals, condemnation of error remains the obverse of the teaching of the faith and is still, though in milder ways than in the past, vigorously carried out.

When Pope Paul VI started to bring fresh blood into the

Curia, Jerome Hamer was asked to join the Secretariat for Christian Unity, and another Belgian Dominican, Mgr Charles Moeller, was invited to the Holy Office as under-secretary. The latter felt unhappy in his post, one is told, but then the two men changed departments, and each is now in his element. This episode is a warning against generalizing about the Curia, especially since to the age-old congregations and offices have been added new secretariats and commissions with their complements of international staff. Mgr Moeller is now the secretary of the Secretariat for Christian Unity, a member of the Pontifical Justice and Peace Commission and a consultor to several other departments of the Curia. He is a shy, erudite priest with an unusually wide band of intellectual interests, including the study of Proust and Kafka.

The Secretariat for Christian Unity is figuratively on one of the most exposed frontiers of the Curia, likely to be shot at as fiercely from within as from without the walls of the Vatican. It is also in fact just outside the border of the city state, at 1 Via dell'Erba, in crowded offices which have an air of harassed informality. The most important of the secretariats, it was first established under the leadership of the extraordinary German Jesuit Cardinal Bea in 1960, by Pope John XXIII. Today it has two sections: one for Eastern and Orthodox Christians, the other for the different confessions of Western Christianity. Pursuing dialogue and union among Christians, the secretariat includes a Commission for Judaism, and is linked to the Secretariat for Non-Christians, the Commission for Islam and the Secretariat for Non-Believers (all established by Pope Paul VI). Its first secretary is now its cardinal president, Johannes Willebrands, Archbishop of Utrecht, and it has twenty-seven members, including seven cardinals, a staff of nearly twenty and over thirty consultors.

The secretariat is inspired by the noble vision of Christian unity. Its energies sometimes seem diverted to skirmishes with more conservative departments of the Curia. Its officials, though still enthusiastic, have learned patience, circumspection, realism. They say that, in ecumenical matters, the German bishops will go ahead anyway; the French tend to consult Rome. They take care to consult other departments, such as the Congregation for the Doctrine of the Faith, for theological opinions to accompany their own initiatives, when these may be deemed relevant. They typify the newer style of curial bureaucracy in their flexibility, mixed origins and general informality.

An American Jesuit working there describes his day: 'We have a daily staff meeting of all the secretariat at 8.45 a.m. Our general secretary puts everything on the table. Perhaps the items will include a letter from the Archbishop of Canterbury to the Pope, on which the Pope wants advice. We always discuss everything as a group – that was how Cardinal Bea started it all. Or there may be a letter from the United Bible Societies asking us to start a group in Italy. As it happened, in this case we said we were interested but that it was a matter for the Italian bishops. . . . At eleven o'clock we have a coffee break and cookies – that was Bea's idea too – and the cardinal hears about what decisions are being taken and may want to change them. We deal with other urgent matters before 12.30 or one o'clock. We have a very good system for getting things done, and it's very democratic. Bea assembled a marvellous group of men and Willebrands has kept it like this. We're a very happy team.'

On the ground floor of the same building are the offices of the Secretariat for Non-Christians, where I have met various officials through the offices of its late cardinal president, Sergio Pignedoli. Pignedoli was among the list of *papabili* – possible Popes – in the last two elections. He was among the most engaging of the old-style curial cardinals; born in Reggio Emilia, where he entered the seminary, he was a chaplain with the Italian Navy during the Second World War, and then pursued a buoyant career with the Secretariat of State. He headed the Secretariat for Non-Christians from 1973 to 1980 and was a member of five other departments of the Curia.*

Cardinal Pignedoli, when we first met, apologized for being dressed formally (he was on his way to see the Austrian Ambassador) in his black, red-buttoned cassock and wearing a big cross, chequered like a chessboard. He had dark-brown eyes, thin cropped hair and a habit of rubbing his hands together as he talked. He described his hobby as 'young people', whom he liked to receive at his home in the Vatican, whose photographs he collected to jog his memory, and to

---

* The successor to Cardinal Pignedoli at the secretariat is Archbishop Jean Jadot, previously apostolic delegate in Washington.

whom he wrote in their thousands – actually about 6000 – all over the world. He had 12,000 colour slides in his photo collection.

The cardinal emphasized that the work of his department was one of dialogue; it did not aim to proselytize. There were three sections of the Secretariat dealing with: the Moslems (a commission under an Arab priest from Egypt); the great religions of Asia (such as Buddhism); and local religions (of Africa, of the Pacific, of the Indians of America). 'We look for points in common. We have discussions about the state of religion in the world today. About the bases of morality. Here we try to understand the great books of other religions, such as the Koran, the Vedha. We suggest teaching in each other's schools and universities.'

Pignedoli was always a wide-eyed and inexhaustible traveller. One of his earlier journeys as cardinal was across Russia on the Trans-Siberian railway. In recent years he had spent most of his time in Rome, but when I last saw him he had been to visit the Parsees in Bombay ('where there are a hundred thousand of them', he said, 'and another ten thousand in Iran. They are monotheistic. They have fire as a symbol of God: they believe in a principle of evil. I read their holy books before I went . . . especially the Avesta.') He had also been recently to the Gulf States, Hong Kong and Japan, and hoped to travel to China. But he died in the summer of 1980. Archbishop (now Cardinal) Jadot was appointed the new president of the secretariat.

The Secretariat for Non-Christians has twenty-two members, including Cardinal William Baum, over forty consultors and a modest staff of eight. The secretary, Mgr Pietro Rossano from Turin, says that the secretariat is a symbol of the Holy See's will to communicate with non-Christians, including those not touched by the great traditional religions. It searches for common religious elements. It wants to emphasize the need throughout the world for freedom of religious expression, which is still sorely missing in the Islamic world, for example, where there are great social pressures at work. It wants people to discover the rich elements in other religions that may be missing in their own.

Mgr Rossano lectures at the Gregorian University. He first joined the secretariat as a consultor. He travels about two months in the year to explore other religions on their own ground. The image of Christianity is poor throughout the world, he says. It is too tied to colonialism. It must find new approaches. The secretariat is finding its own role, though its work is very recent compared with fifty years of Christian ecumenism.

Mgr Rossano reads Sanskrit and Arabic, and is anxious to visit China. He was offered a flat in the Vatican when he first joined the Curia, but preferred to find his own. His colleague, the secretariat's under-secretary, Fr. John Bosco Masayuki Shirieda, lives in Rome in the house of the Salesians, his own order. He is a plump, smiling Japanese priest, who talks a lot in images and confesses that he had never dreamed he would one day be in the Vatican. This is an understatement. Fr. Shirieda grew up as a Buddhist. He was a *kamikaze* cadet during the Second World War. When he returned home he found his family house devastated. He was caught stealing nails by a tall Salesian missionary priest who then, when he said how deep his shame would be, gave him more nails than he could carry. When he returned again to the mission, the priest asked him if he wanted still more nails, but Shirieda said he wanted simply to follow him, without becoming a Christian. Later, the priest died in a fire in an attempt to save the life of one of Shirieda's friends. 'He had said he wanted his body to mingle with Japanese soil. It was then that I turned Christian. . . .' Shirieda became a professor in Tokyo and used to be very critical of the Curia. He wants to stay Japanese: 'a Christian can and should be Japanese; a Japanese can and should be a Christian'. He reflects that there are only 400,000 Catholics in Japan – but perhaps it was better that they should stay in the minority: 'Christ proposed, he did not impose. . . . The minority are less in danger of *hubris* than the majority.'

Shirieda uses an image from Goethe when he remarks that being in the Vatican is like looking at stained glass from inside a church, with the sunlight streaming through: from the outside you see only the ugly leads with the sun playing on them. 'And you must be long-sighted for the future of the Church; otherwise you see only your own eyelashes.' He himself sees the Holy See as the vital centre and guarantee of the unity of the Universal Church. Korea is near Japan, he says, but there is no communication directly between the Catholic

117

Churches of Korea and Japan. This was through Rome, the new Jerusalem.

Fr. Shirieda carries visiting cards in Japanese and English. His view of the unifying role of the Holy See is close to that taken by Archbishop Deskur, at the Commission for Social Communications, and also to that of Cardinal Gantin, at another of the 'new' departments, the Pontifical Commission for Justice and Peace.

Housed in the Palazzo San Calisto, the Justice and Peace Commission has had a rather stormy passage since it was set up as a result of recommendations made at the Second Vatican Council, in January 1967. Its first-year experimental period was extended by another five years. It was given its definitive structure in Pope Paul VI's *motu proprio 'Iustitiam et Pacem'* of 10 December 1967. This document tugged the commission back firmly under the influence of the Secretariat of State. It was defined as 'the Holy See's organization for examining and studying (from the point of view of doctrine, pastoral practice and the apostolate) problems connected with justice and peace, with the aim of awakening God's people to full understanding of these questions and awareness of the part they play and of the duties that fall to them in the fields of justice, the development of peoples, human advancement, peace and human rights. . . .'

The Justice and Peace Commission has twenty-four members under its president, six of whom are women, including, till her death, the economist, Barbara Ward. It has a staff of fifteen (six of them women) under its Jesuit secretary, Fr. Roger Heckel. There are twelve consultors.

Cardinal Bernardin Gantin (who succeeded the Canadian Cardinal Maurice Roy) is a tall, handsome black African, born in Dahomey (now the People's Republic of Benin) in 1922. His African name means 'tree of iron in African soil'. His father was a railway worker, educated by Catholic missionaries. After seminary training, he went to Rome to study in 1953 at the Urbanian and Lateran Universities. Pope John XXIII made him Archbishop of Cotonou. He was called to Rome in 1970 to be Assistant Secretary (then a joint secretary) of the Congregation for the Evangelization of Peoples. He moved on to the Justice and Peace Commission and was there when it 'upgraded' to have a cardinal at its head. There was some mild speculation in the second Conclave of 1978 that he could be the second black African Pope (if St Victor I is accepted as the first).

Cardinal Gantin appears in his office in a cassock, wearing a silver cross hanging from a gold chain. His white collar gleams against the black of his face and clothes. When he gets excited, speaking French or Italian very fast, he stutters a little.

The routine of his work is like that of most other conscientious curial cardinals: he starts at 9.00 a.m., when he looks at his incoming mail and the messages from the Secretariat of State; at 9.15 a.m. there is a staff meeting. He works with his officials till 1.30 p.m. In the afternoon, he retires to his own apartment, over the office. During the week he attends the meetings of the several other curial departments, such as *Cor Unum*. He reports every week on the affairs of his department to the Secretary of State and sees the Pope 'when the need is there'. Most of his work seems to involve listening to people who come from churches all over the world to tell him their needs and to help if he can. A group of Catholic cardinals and bishops tried to force the needs of the poor and hungry of the developing countries to the forefront of the discussions of the Second Vatican Council. The council produced a document, *The Pastoral Constitution on the Church in the World Today*, which laid down general principles on international social and economic justice. It also led to the establishment of the Pontifical Commission, intended above all, in the minds of the original enthusiasts for a more positive role by the Catholic Church in the world, to promote international economic development. Cardinal Gantin says that his commission is unique because it was born out of the Vatican Council and the initiative of Pope Paul VI (chiefly expressed in the encyclical *Populorum Progressio*).

The Commission for Justice and Peace gave most attention in its early years to the question of aid from the developed to the developing nations. How far it should tackle matters of 'peace' was always a problem; so were the controversial matters of disarmament and population. Cardinal Gantin has tended to deal more and more with 'human dignity', a phrase that opens up extremely wide areas of interest and concern. The commission is liable to create confusion and even resistance on the part of some Catholic bishops throughout the world. Nearly all non-Communist countries have their own justice and peace commissions, answerable to national hierarchies and loosely linked to the parent department in the Curia. Some of them, for example in Rhodesia (now Zimbabwe) in the 1970s, have shown themselves politically forceful, even heroic.

Officials at the Pontifical Commission in Rome ponder on its future role and influence. The emphasis on aid has lessened in international dealings. There is an impasse in world development. The commission is fully part of the Roman system. But – with its aid and peace work more or less taken from it by other curial departments and by the actions of the Pope himself – its explorations of the areas of human rights and dignity could prove increasingly controversial.

Cardinal Gantin, however, says simply that the first concern of his commission is with the reality of the hungry people of the world and the challenge their misery represents. He sees the role of the commission as essentially conciliatory. '*Populorum Progressio* is our Magna Carta. There are the two key words – *peoples*, meaning all people, rich and poor, white and black, who share fundamental rights, and *progress*, re-emphasizing the idea of development for all, so that it is the rich as well as the poor who must realize themselves. Those who are rich must share their gifts, whatever they are, with the sick, the illiterate, the starving. But there is no dividing the world into camps. There is confusion in the very division of rich and poor – in America, where there are gross extremes within the same city. The world is a fraternity of human beings.'

Amidst the obvious possibilities for confusion and controversy at the commission – 'our work is delicate, difficult; we are on a *lunga strada*' – Gantin finds his unifying principle in the visible symbol of the Pope. 'If Rome were destroyed, the Pope might go to New York. Perhaps one day the Pope may go elsewhere,' he says without much interest. In truth, in Rome and in the Vatican, the cardinal finds a deep sense of correspondence between his belief in the universality of the Church and his experience of the Holy See. 'I feel a great sense of family here. We live together as brothers and sisters. There is more regalism and triumphalism in many African states than there is in the Vatican. The Pope is the Pastor, serving the

Church, and the Curia is here to serve him. If it is sometimes secretive, this is out of respect for people. The Curia rests on a foundation of trust, of *fiducia*.'

The criticism that the Roman Curia is still too Italian and theologically too partisan has already been mentioned. One hears stories such as that of the middle-range official, or *minutante*, at Propaganda Fide, tearing up the notes he had taken from an archbishop's impassioned declarations (and promised to pass on to the cardinal prefect) in the full view of the archbishop when he returned unexpectedly to collect his umbrella. The Curia is accused of making slanderous assaults on the good faith of priests whose views diverge from the curial 'line' on particular moral or theological matters. Individuals strongly entrenched at several levels of many curial departments are seen as working constantly to hinder change within the government of the Church in order to sustain their own influence. Its adversary might say that the Curia defends its version of the truth at any cost; whereas the Curia claims to defend the real truth at all cost.

The Curia is a very human as well as a very ancient institution and historically yields rich varieties of human behaviour; individuals and groups are separately capable of the faults and qualities sometimes ascribed to the whole organization. A representative number of them speak for themselves in the interviews reported in this book. As in all human organizations, the importance of a particular post or department in the Curia is closely connected with the experience and personality of the man involved, though some positions bring with them far greater potential than others.

At the Secretariat of State the position of *Sostituto*, or deputy, illustrates these points very fruitfully. The effect of the Second Vatican Council and Pope Paul VI's reform of the Curia in 1967 was to centralize the highest level of administration of the Holy See in the Secretariat of State, directly under the Pope. The two former sections of the secretariat were re-cast into two offices; the newly entitled Council for the Public Affairs of the Church became virtually a Ministry for Foreign Affairs; the Secretariat of State itself became responsible for assisting the Pope directly in the government of the whole Church and the direction of the departments of the Curia and carrying out all the tasks entrusted to it by the Pope. The Papal Secretariat, as it is also called, thus acts as a channel between the Pope and the Curia, and between the Pope and the bishops, cardinals and Vatican representatives throughout the world. Little of the activity of the Vatican escapes it. Its responsibilities include the 'ordinary affairs' of the Holy See through various offices looking after the cipher, the mailing of correspondence and apostolic briefs, Vatican ceremonial and the honours system. Perhaps its greatest long-term influence has been effected through its role as collaborator with the Pope since the Second Vatican Council in drawing up all the pontifical documentation, notably the papal encyclicals.

The Secretariat of State, crammed into part of the third floor of the Apostolic Palace, headed by the Cardinal Secretary of State and the *Sostituto* and his *Assessore* (assistant), employs a staff of about a hundred, including a dozen diplomatic personnel and about twenty members of religious orders. Since it works so closely with the Pope, and its constitutional position is so strong in the government of the Church and the Holy See, the choice of the Cardinal Secretary of State and *Sostituto* is one of the Pope's critically important political decisions.

The functions of the *Sostituto* are neither codified nor laid down in any departmental brief but depend on the wishes of the Pope himself and, subordinately, the Cardinal Secretary of State. They are chiefly executive: the *Sostituto* organizes the work of the staff of the Secretariat of State and is responsible for carrying out efficiently the decisions of his superiors, namely the Pope and the Cardinal Secretary of State. However, he also influences the decisions of the Pope and the Cardinal Secretary of State simply because he is there to give his opinion on their decisions and, in practice, his advice is sought in all their important deliberations.

The influence of the *Sostituto* has been one of the most controversial topics in recent years, partly because of the forceful personality and actions of Mgr Giovanni Benelli who held the post from 1967 till he became Cardinal Archbishop of Florence in 1978. Benelli began his curial career as private secretary to Mgr Montini, later Pope Paul VI, when Montini himself was *Sostituto*, at a time when Pope Pius XII was acting as his own Secretary of State. When Cardinal Villot was Secretary of State and Mgr Benelli was *Sostituto*, the latter was often accused of drawing too many of the threads of power into his own very capable and conservative hands. When Benelli left for Florence and Mgr Caprio took over, tensions relaxed and the Secretariat of State became a less active organization. Benelli's role during the pontificate of Pope Paul VI is now a matter of significant history. Looking back on his period of office, Cardinal Benelli wrote a memorandum for me including these reflections on the role of the *Sostituto*:

> He is the first collaborator of the Secretary of State, but because of the fact that he has immediate contacts with the Holy Father he is also the direct collaborator of His Holiness. His function therefore is particularly large and, although it can never be competitive or discordant with that of the Cardinal Secretary of State, it can sometimes not be subject to it, in the sense that it can lead directly to the Supreme Pontiff. The wider the opportunity in this respect, the more his authority and function become important and influential in the general politics of the Holy See (but that depends entirely on the will of the Holy Father).

Cardinal Benelli recalls a day in the life of the *Sostituto* as beginning with a meeting with the Cardinal Secretary of State to settle and discuss the important questions and receive instructions. After that, there would be meetings with the personnel of the Secretary of State, to receive directives and clarifications; with senior officials of the Curia; with important visitors to the Holy See from the worlds of politics or culture or from international Catholic organizations; with ambassadors accredited to the Holy See and so forth.

In the afternoon, the *Sostituto* would chiefly study and revise the work of his office, and sign the necessary correspondence. (The Cardinal Secretary of State signs the letters to papal representatives and to the bishops; the assistant those of lesser importance, say answers to private individuals.) In the evening the *Sostituto* would normally have a meeting with the Pope:

> These working meetings are not official audiences, such as those regularly conceded to the Cardinal Secretary of State. They therefore do not happen regularly at a fixed time, but only when the Holy Father finds it opportune. They can happen once, twice or more times a week, and are held, generally of an evening, in the private apartment of His Holiness. Contacts between the Holy Father and the *Sostituto*

can also take place by means of a special telephone which connects the Pope's study with that of the *Sostituto*.

Official contact between the office of the Secretariat of State and the Pope is also maintained through a constant flow of written material: the Pope must be informed of all important matters, all the decisions that need his approval, and all the items that he wants to follow personally. Beyond this, in practice, the Cardinal Secretary of State and the *Sostituto* select the questions they feel must be submitted for his consideration.

The inter-relationships of Pope, Cardinal Secretary of State and *Sostituto* as Benelli saw them are still constitutionally significant and still indicate more or less how the system works. But the men have changed, and with them the style and tempo of the management. When he was at home in the Vatican, Pope Paul hardly ever left his desk; the lights of his study stayed on till the small hours. Pope John Paul II is restless, always on the move, no lover of office routines. Among the first appointments made by John Paul II in May 1979, that of Mgr Casaroli to the most influential curial post – head of the Secretariat of State – might have been expected. So too might that of Casaroli's collaborator in implementation of the Vatican's policy of international détente, Mgr Achille Silvestrini, to Casaroli's former post, head of the Public (or Foreign) Affairs Ministry. The choice of Cardinal Paolo Bertoli as *camerlengo* or chamberlain of the Church was both popular among Vatican officials and disturbing to no one.

However, when the Pope put Archbishop Eduardo Martinez Somalo in the post of *Sostituto* (and promoted the Lithuanian Audrys Backis from third position at the Public Affairs Ministry to that of under-secretary) there was speculation about the influence of his personal policy aims and possible new courses in the Holy See's diplomacy. The Spanish archbishop had worked with Mgr Benelli at the Secretariat of State and been a career diplomat, sent as Nuncio to Colombia in 1975: a key post in an area vital to the Catholic Church. His appointment was interpreted as a sign that the Tiber was growing wider – or, in other words, the Holy See was distancing itself still more from Italian politics, with which Mgr Benelli had been closely concerned.

Another of Pope John Paul's important curial appointments, some months later, also seemed to carry some special significance. After the death of Cardinal Wright, Prefect of the Congregation for the Clergy, his post was given to the very conservative Cardinal Silvio Oddi, to the astonishment of some Vatican watchers in Rome and perhaps not a few bishops abroad. It appeared to be a reliable presage, however, of the way the Pope was heading in matters of discipline and belief.

Another of the Pope's early appointments seemed to depart fairly radically from the previous structure of the Curia. When Casaroli became Secretary of State, the man who had succeeded Mgr Benelli as *Sostituto* under Pope Paul VI – Mgr Giuseppe Caprio – was made Cardinal President of the Administration of the Patrimony of the Holy See. Thus, control over APSA, the main financial department of the Vatican, was moved away from the Secretariat of State: this in effect once again divided the main political from the main economic direction of the Holy See. It was even thought that the Pope might on advice have parted the Secretariat of State from a few more of its responsibilities – such as control of the government of the city state – had not the frail but formidable Mgr Casaroli swiftly shown himself quite ready for the duties entailed.

However, early in 1981, the Secretary of State once again became President of APSA, on the transfer of Cardinal Caprio to another financial post, the *Prefettura degli Affari Economici.* What had happened previously was a 'temporary derogation' to the rule established by Pope Paul VI, remarked a Vatican official. Whatever the reasons for these moves, Cardinal Casaroli's responsibilities and influence appeared more formidable than ever. Most of the important positions in the Curia, those of the prefects and secretaries of the powerful congregations, remained in the same hands.

The Pope's wish to widen the processes of consultation in the Church, and to draw more often for his own benefit on sources of advice outside the circle of curial officials in Rome, was expressed in November 1979, when he summoned a full meeting of the Sacred College of Cardinals, which was attended by 130 in the Synod Hall. The over-eighties were there as well. John Paul II confirmed that he wanted all the cardinals to meet together from time to time in Rome, outside the Conclaves, because they had the task of 'sustaining' the Pontiff, in a special way, 'in his pastoral solicitude for the

Church in her universal dimensions'. The idea of a regular consistory sprang from discussions among some of the cardinals during the second Conclave of 1978.

The meeting of cardinals late in 1979 seemed intended as the first of many, designed to give the Pope an international sounding-board of those particularly close to him. The actual deliberations that took place were mostly in private, and the cardinals were afterwards rather secretive. But, on the financial problems of the Holy See, they were given by the end of the meeting a far clearer account than had ever been made available before, and a very worrisome one.

However, the real importance of the meeting or consistory of cardinals lay in the way it demonstrated the Pope's willingness to be modestly experimental in his government of the Church. It associated all the cardinals as a corporate body more intimately than had for centuries been the case with the day-to-day problems of the Holy See. And it highlighted the Pope's own sternly expounded priorities for the Papacy, which he expected the cardinals to approve and pursue: the need for a spiritual reawakening; the need for solidarity within the Church.

5
Foreign Policy and the Pope's Men

In a terse chapter of *The Prince*, dealing bitingly with ecclesiastical principalities, Machiavelli remarked that, since such states were 'sustained by higher powers which the human mind cannot comprehend', he would not argue about them: 'They are exalted and maintained by God, and so only a rash and presumptuous man would take it on himself to discuss them.'

Writing at a time when the Medici Pope Leo X ruled large, recently consolidated territories slung like a broad sash across the centre of Italy, Machiavelli was both circumspect and sarcastic about the relationship between the Holy See and the temporal power. Today, the temporal power has shrunk to the lace-handkerchief dimensions of the Vatican City State. Some of the forms and ceremonies of Vatican diplomacy still emphasize the worldly claims of the Papacy in terms of prestige and precedence and recall the historical development of the papal entourage as a princely household and a royal court. But the diplomatic activities of the Pope are wider ranging and more ambitious than ever before, and they are based on a unique form of sovereignty claimed by the Apostolic See independently of any temporal power.

The nature and function of the sovereignty of the Apostolic See were cogently summarized by Pope John Paul II when he addressed the General Assembly of the United Nations on 2 October 1979: 'The territorial extent of that sovereignty is limited to the small state of Vatican City, but the sovereignty itself is warranted by the need of the Papacy to exercise its mission in full freedom, and to be able to deal with any interlocutor, whether a government or an international organization, without dependence on other sovereignties. . . .'

The sovereignty of the Apostolic See, the Pope added, stood out in contrast with that of states which were linked with territory and people; the sovereignty of the Apostolic See and the Catholic Church belonged to a kingdom 'not of this world'. The Apostolic See can talk to any state on equal terms, as it did even at the time between 1870 and 1929 when it lacked territory and subjects completely. As the See has gained increasing confidence in its ability to exist among other states on equal terms with them, the Vatican City State has become progressively more shadowy, a wisp of temporal power.

In international law and convention, the vital component of the Vatican is the sovereignty of the Pope as head of the Apostolic See. The Pope is also sovereign ruler of the Vatican City State, but, with the exception of a few technical missions to specialized agencies of the United Nations, the state sends no diplomatic missions to other states (not even Italy), nor does it have a foreign office or similar institution. Thus, Vatican diplomats, so called, hold passports of the Holy See, not of the Vatican City State. As mentioned in Chapter 2, Vatican City State passports, though rare, do exist. They have been issued, for example, to enable priests of St Peter's who possess East European nationality to travel abroad. Most Vatican residents travel on their own national passports. Officials in the service of the Holy See travelling on official business are issued with Holy See passports, either 'diplomatic' or 'service'.

During the Middle Ages and the Renaissance, the Papacy played a very creative role in the evolution of diplomacy, through the reception first of special envoys and eventually of resident ambassadors. Mostly formed by priests until 1870, but nowadays with the Catholic states among them in a minority, the diplomatic missions to the Apostolic See today total ninety-seven. The first Protestant country to establish permanent representation was Prussia in 1806, and the first non-Christian country was Japan in 1942. A growing number of non-Christian Asian and African states sought representation after the Second World War.

An important distinction within the Holy See's representational structure is between apostolic delegations, which have no official diplomatic function, and nunciatures, which do.

Pope John Paul II celebrates mass in the Sistine Chapel with the cardinals
who have just elected him

The Pope among his people: *(above)* at an audience and *(below)* walking in St Peter's Square. The papal apartments are in the building behind him

Cardinal Wojtyla, the future John Paul II, at the meeting of the Synod of Bishops in 1977

Four of the Pope's men: *(top left)* his private secretary, Fr. John Magee; the
Cardinal Secretary of State, Agostino Casaroli; the Secretary of the Council
for the Public Affairs of the Church, Archbishop Achille Silvestrini; the
President of the Social Communications Commission, Archbishop Andrzei
Maria Deskur

The everyday Vatican: *(top)* Swiss Guards on duty, and *(above)* a chance
clerical meeting

(above) switchboard duty *(below)* restoration and building work never ceases

The endless corridors of the Vatican Museums *(above)* are safeguarded by a
modern security system *(below)*

The Pope looks out from the balcony of St Peter's on Easter Day to bless the City and the World: *Urbe et Orbi*

The nunciature is headed by a nuncio, if he takes automatic precedence at the head of the diplomatic corps, or a pro-nuncio if he takes precedence among the ambassadors in accordance with his seniority of arrival. Double accreditation is a common feature, and the same man can be both the Holy See's local apostolic delegate (whose legation is only to local churches) and its pro-nuncio elsewhere (with a legation to a state or government), and may hold the personal rank of nuncio. Thus the Holy See's man in Copenhagen is apostolic delegate to Denmark, Norway and Sweden, and Pro-Nuncio to Finland and Iceland, both of which reciprocate with non-resident ambassadors to the Holy See.

Traditions, tactfulness and religious susceptibilities provide some fascinating diplomatic diversions. The Holy See never accepts as an ambassador a man who has been divorced or whose wife has been divorced, and since 1870 has always refused to accept as an ambassador (save on a 'one-day' mission to, say, a funeral) a man also accredited to Italy. So, unless a country's relationship with the Holy See is important enough to justify a mission resident in Rome and entirely separate from its embassy to Italy, ambassadors to the Holy See are found elsewhere in Europe, in Bonn, Berne, Paris or London, for example. There have even been cases of foreign ministers accrediting themselves as non-resident ambassadors to the Holy See.

The differences between the Swiss cantons make relations between Berne and the Holy See somewhat delicate, but the Swiss Ambassador to Italy is a visitor to the Vatican once a year for the annual swearing-in of new recruits to the Swiss Guards. After centuries of non-recognition, again for religious reasons, the Greek government moved in 1979 towards full diplomatic relations with the Holy See, and an ambassador was received in 1980; but it was carefully stressed on the Greek side that these relations indicated only governmental recognition, not recognition by religious bodies.

Diplomatic relations between the United Kingdom and the Holy See are exceptional for many reasons, of which the foremost is lack of accreditation to the government for the representative in London. As apostolic delegate, he is appointed to represent the Holy See to the hierarchies of England and Wales, of Scotland, and to the Archbishop of

Canterbury, at Lambeth Palace. His post is important as a vantage-point for observation of the Anglican Church and English views on Northern Ireland and, to some extent, as a sounding-board for developments in former British colonial territories. The roots of the problem go back to the English Act of Supremacy in 1559, which severed diplomatic relations with Rome, 'restoring to the Crown the ancient jurisdiction over the state ecclesiastical and spiritual, and abolishing all foreign power repugnant to the same'. In the seventeenth century, the Catholic King James II sent a formal embassy to the Holy See, chiefly remembered for the banquet it gave in the long gallery of the Pamphilj Palace on Piazza Navona (now the Brazilian embassy to Italy). Various British agents, based in Florence, visited Rome officially during the nineteenth century. Tentative diplomatic approaches during the pontificate of Pope Leo XIII spurred the Irish bishops to protest at the very possibility of a nunciature in London, which might give the British government some influence over nominations to Irish bishoprics. The Catholic hierarchy in Ireland, like the Irish Trade Union Congress, covers both the Republic and Northern Ireland. So diplomatic communications in this sensitive area are especially convoluted.

The British Legation to the Holy See was effectively founded in 1914, in response to the danger of German and Austrian influence on the Pope. It began as a 'temporary' mission under a Catholic, Sir Henry Howard, who had the rank of minister. Count de Salis, who succeeded Howard, was also a Catholic (and wrote his final report from the Travellers' Club in London). Since the mission became permanent in 1923, the minister appointed has always been a non-Catholic and his deputy a Catholic. (Until recently, the latter was the felicitously named Michael Angelo Cafferty, now UK Ambassador to Santo Domingo; he was succeeded by James Callan.)

The working contacts of the British Envoy Extraordinary and Minister Plenipotentiary, Mark Heath, are in the main with the Council for the Public Affairs of the Church, usually at a high level, and the Secretariat of State. For very special reasons, he may see the Cardinal Secretary of State himself. More often, he is in touch with the *Sostituto*, who has open house for heads of missions every Thursday and Saturday afternoon. The envoy also calls from time to time on the heads and members of the Roman congregations, perhaps to hear the impressions of a cardinal returning from a special mission. He also has working contacts with colleagues in the diplomatic corps accredited to the Holy See, especially those of the EEC countries, with whom he has frequent working lunches or breakfasts.

The minister emphasizes the enjoyable importance of the social side of an envoy's occupation. He maintains cordial relations with the Anglican Centre in Rome. Membership of the *Circolo di Roma* (a club founded to enable diplomats and clerics to meet for a lecture or discussion, followed by a drink) helps him maintain personal contact with Vatican officials, other members of the diplomatic corps and interested outsiders. Back at the office, he finds his staff often busy securing tickets for Britons wanting to attend a papal audience or according diplomatic or service visas on Vatican passports. Much of his time is taken up with papers and correspondence sent by the Foreign and Commonwealth Office and other British diplomatic posts to keep him informed on subjects relevant to the Vatican, those on which the British government is anxious that its policies and activites should be clearly understood by the Vatican, and those on which it is profitable for it and the Vatican to exchange views.

The British envoy, like the other diplomats accredited to the Holy See, finds a considerable ceremonial element in his work, especially attendance in uniform or in tails at Masses celebrated by the Pope or a cardinal, most often at St Peter's. Mark Heath followed the British Foreign Secretary in the Queen's suite on her visit to the Pope in 1980, and was knighted by her almost immediately afterwards.

Pope Paul VI clarified the functions of the representatives of the Vatican in a document issued in June 1969:

> The primary and specific purpose of the mission of a papal representative is to render ever closer and more operative the ties that bind the Apostolic See and the local churches.
> The ordinary function of a pontifical representative is to keep the Holy See regularly and objectively informed about the conditions of the ecclesiastical community to which he has been sent, and about what may affect the life of the Church and the good of souls.

On the one hand, he makes known to the religious and faithful of the territory where he carries out his mandate, and forwards to Rome their proposals and their requests; on the other hand, he makes himself the interpreter, with those concerned, of the acts, documents, information and instructions emanating from the Holy See.

Pope Paul stressed that representatives were bound to respect the autonomy of the local churches and bishops. In regard to the state where they served, the general aim was to establish sound relations with civil government and to work for peace. The representative was to act

... under the guidance and according to the instructions of the Cardinal Secretary of State and Prefect of the Council for Public Affairs of the Church, to whom he is directly responsible for the mandate entrusted to him by the Supreme Pontiff.

Papal representatives normally have to retire at seventy-five.* Their long and varied experience, and their contacts with official Catholic and high-level non-Catholic circles, make them an intelligence network – open but discreet – which can provide unique information and insights for collation in the Vatican and study by the Pope, adding additional streams of knowledge to what he learns from constant contacts with thousands of bishops throughout the world.

The Holy See's representative can sometimes also be observed in the guise of trouble-shooter. Mgr Angelo Felici, for example, an old colleague of Cardinal Casaroli's at the Secretariat of State, used his influence to ensure 'conservative' appointments to bishoprics of the troubled and divided Dutch Church when he was pro-nuncio in the Low Countries. In 1979, his appointment as Papal Nuncio to France was seen as fitting the pattern of Pope John Paul II's strong reassertion of central discipline over the Catholic Church, including the independent-minded French.

Distinguished laymen such as Baldesar Castiglione have been papal envoys in the past. Virtually all high-level Vatican diplomatic representatives are priests today. Despite efforts made in recent years to 'internationalize' the Roman Curia, only a handful of the hundred and more heads of missions are

---

*Cardinal Casaroli urged them to retire at seventy, and return home rather than to Rome.

non-Italian, but there is a steady increase in the number of non-Italians entering the service, and this will eventually affect its composition at the top.

The Holy See's diplomats usually start their careers – which will traditionally take them to the highest positions in the Roman Catholic Church, and even to the papal throne itself – at the Pontifical Ecclesiastical Academy in Piazza della Minerva. It used to be known as the Pontifical Academy of Noble Ecclesiastics, and was founded at the beginning of the eighteenth century by Pope Clement XI, himself generally considered to have been diplomatically rather inept.

The patron (*protettore*) of the academy is nowadays always the Cardinal Secretary of State. The president is Archbishop Cesare Zacchi, originally from Arezzo, whose own diplomatic experience has included a spell as counsellor in Cuba. They keep careful watch over the thirty or so students at the academy, which is a charming sixteenth-century palace facing the Roman Pantheon, a stately reminder of times past and past gods. The students, mostly Italian, work harder than at any other ecclesiastical college, it is said, and attend three or four hours of lectures in the mornings, and the same in the afternoons. They mix pastoral work around Rome with their studies, which end with a probational appointment.

Occasionally there have been brushes between the carefully selected young priests of the Pontifical Ecclesiastical Academy and the authorities. In 1968, for example, in the wake of the Vatican Council, the students wrote a collective letter to Archbishop Benelli, then the Secretary of State's deputy, complaining about the rules of residence (the door closed at 10.00 p.m. and they had no keys) and the inadequate teaching of languages. More relaxed regulations and a language laboratory followed, but the academy is still a place for rigorous training in discipline and hard work. The Pope receives a visit and report from the president twice a year.

Budding diplomats must already be priests possessing a doctorate in canon law, or its equivalent; their two-year course covers diplomatic methods, Latin, ecclesiastical history, international law, sociology, economics and three modern languages. The course leads to a diploma and is followed by a year's training either in the Vatican at the Secretariat of State (where opening the Pope's mail might be one of the duties) or a posting as an attaché to a mission abroad. After the training period, the diplomat enters the service as a secretary of the second class. Promotion proceeds through a series of ranks from secretary of the first class, auditor of the second and then first class, and then counsellor. The head of mission is usually chosen from the diplomatic staff of the Secretariat of State and the Council for the Public Affairs of the Church.

Among Popes living in the twentieth century, Leo XIII had studied at the Pontifical Academy of Noble Ecclesiastics; Benedict XV had served in the papal diplomatic corps; Pius XI had been an apostolic nuncio; Pius XII had early on entered the Secretariat of State and had been a professor of ecclesiastical diplomacy at the Pontifical Academy; John XXIII had entered the diplomatic service in middle age as apostolic visitor to Bulgaria; Paul VI had attended the Academy of Noble Ecclesiastics before entering the Secretariat of State. Neither John Paul I, however, nor John Paul II, had served in the diplomatic service.

The Vatican diplomat can bring the influence of the Papacy to bear directly or indirectly on national and international politics. In Spain, during the period of Franco's government, the apostolic nuncio, Archbishop Luigi Dadaglio, outsmarted General Franco and brought about an episcopacy of a distinctly liberal nature. In Dublin, the apostolic nuncio, Archbishop Gaetano Alibrandi, was a key figure in the advice given to Cardinal Baggio at the Holy See concerning the choice of Archbishop (now Cardinal) O'Fiaich as Primate of Ireland. In London, with fewer, if any, political implications, the apostolic delegate, Archbishop Bruno Heim, took and interpreted for Rome the 'soundings' that led to the appointment of George Basil Hume as Cardinal of Westminster in 1976.

Archbishop Heim was born in Basle, Switzerland, in 1911, and was ordained a priest in 1938. He spent five formative years as secretary in the nunciature in Paris, under the inspiring influence of the nuncio Angelo Roncalli, the future Patriarch of Venice and Pope John XXIII. He served as First Secretary at the nunciature in Vienna, *chargé d'affaires* at the nunciature in Bonn, apostolic delegate in Scandinavia (also becoming apostolic pro-nuncio in Finland) and, his last appointment before London, apostolic pro-nuncio in Cairo from 1969 to 1973. In Egypt especially, he won a reputation for private generosity and charitable concern, and for sharply directing his public energies towards Orthodox–Catholic reconciliation and Christian ecumenism. While he was pro-nuncio in Cairo, the Egyptian government restored tracts of nationalized farm land to the Holy See, and he was associated with pleasing cultural gestures such as the financial contribution from European Catholics towards marble paving for the new Coptic cathedral at Al-Morcos-sia.

As apostolic delegate in London, Bruno Heim lives and plainly relishes a life studded with social engagements: an embassy evening reception; lunch with the editor of a Catholic newspaper; an evening Mass in Southwark Cathedral where a Knight of the Order of St Gregory receives the brief of his appointment; a dinner with civil servants in Whitehall; the bishops' Low Week reception at Archbishop's House, West-minster; an informal discussion at Lambeth Palace; dinner at his own house in Wimbledon with England's Queen Mother as principal guest. He pops up, figuratively, in less expected places such as the pages of Roger Peyrefitte's scandalous *Knights of Malta*, where he appears in the nunciature on the Avenue du Président Wilson dressed like an English clergyman, smoking a pipe, and wearing the badge of a sports club. 'I don't even smoke a pipe,' Archbishop Heim comments ruefully.

Archbishop Heim also walks into the pages of Matthew Manning's book on parapsychology *In the Minds of Millions* as a very interested observer of the author's psychic experiments. Certainly, he is an idiosyncratic prelate, whose approach mingles humour and even eccentricity with sound bureaucratic steadfastness and suavity.

In conversation in his own living room, he tells his rosary and talks eagerly. In public, he can seem shy and brusque, withdrawn and yet observant, a plump fleeting figure, with a smile that comes and goes. He is a wise and experienced diplomat, an authority – *the* Vatican authority – on heraldry, about which he has published several books. His advice is to hand for the design of the coats-of-arms of Vatican cardinals, and the Popes themselves. (Pope John Paul II disturbed him by insisting on the heraldic solecism of the incorporation of a large M – for Mary – in his own insignia in black on blue. In the event, they settled for gold on blue – heraldically acceptable as metal on colour, not colour on colour.)

When you visit him at home opposite Wimbledon Common (a roomy old stone house, full of icons, chandeliers, silver, glowing oil paintings and highly polished furniture) the apostolic delegate, though he does not give interviews, talks in an unbuttoned manner over biscuits and cocktails of his own mix about the characters of the Popes he has known personally. (Pope Paul VI was 'a reader rather than an intellectual'; Pope Pius XI 'was probably the greatest of the recent Popes . . .') and about the delays that Vatican diplomats may have to put up with from the 'centre' in Rome.

His functions are often ceremonial and symbolic. At a reception in honour of the Pope where he receives Coptic, Orthodox, Anglican and Roman Catholic bishops, the Chief Rabbi, strings of ambassadors and papal knights, British cabinet ministers and Catholic dignitaries, some of the last kneel to kiss the ring on his hand. He has a few nuns to cook and clean for him and his small staff, including an Italian secretary, Mgr Mario Oliveri, who was formerly with Mgr Benelli at the Secretariat of State; quite often he cooks himself. He is in frequent communication with the local hierarchy officially, and with individual bishops over one private matter or another, less often with British government officials, from whom he waits for approaches rather than taking initiatives. You feel that his own pastoral work is always on his mind, but he, like all but a very few of the Vatican's diplomats, will stay in the service till retirement or death.

Archbishop Heim's career and duties may stand as a model for Vatican diplomats in the field. It is dedicated, wide-ranging in its interests and influence, a careful balance of the priestly, in the sense of pastoral, and the political. The delegation in London, like the Vatican nunciatures, works more or less onthe lines of a secular embassy, but with no commercial or military involvements. It is considered a 'prestige' post, like the other leading capitals of Europe, and Washington, Buenos Aires and Rio de Janeiro. The concerns of the delegate, in broad terms, are religion, charity, peace and culture. More practically, he watches what is happening in the national Catholic Church and reports to the Vatican; the information he provides is mostly routine, but it includes his assessment of people and pressures.

The 'pouch' goes to Rome by Alitalia once a week, supplemented when need be with coded cables to the Cardinal Secretary of State. The sender is a shrewd man, a vigorous defender of the Vatican's role in the modern world, of course, but not uncritical of its bureaucracy's amateurism in public communications, and a lover of ceremonial splendours, which it has shed too blunderingly under the pressure of fashion.

The Catholic Church in the United States, with its fifty million baptized members and extremely diverse problems and composition, has passed through what might almost be called mutual love-hate relations with the Vatican. It is among the largest of all Catholic Churches. Although the Holy See's diplomatic relations with the United States are anomalous, they have usually been amicable. They originated in contacts of a commercial kind, in 1784, when the Papacy announced it was willing to open the ports of Civitavecchia and Ancona to the new republic. A few years later, the United States sent its first consul, the Roman-born John B. Sartori, to the Papal States. A series of consular officials served the Papacy in the USA until 1895. (The last of them, Louis Binese, still held the title of Consul for the Papal States, in New York, after their annexation by the kingdom of Italy.)

Encouraged by the first flush of apparent liberalism from Pope Pius IX, the United States maintained a diplomatic post in Rome from 1848 to 1867. It was headed first by a *chargé d'affaires* and then by five successive ministers, after which it was left to wilt for lack of funds. Of the ministers, one died within a month of presenting his credentials (Jacob L. Martin); another later became a senator from New Jersey (John P. Stockton); another, instead of going to Rome, took up a commission as a brigadier general in the US Army (Rufus King). During this time there was no serious attempt to establish reciprocal diplomatic facilities.

In 1893, the Holy See established an apostolic delegation in Washington, but the diplomatic results were meagre. The ice was broken during the Second World War by President

Roosevelt, who responded to the peace moves of Pope Pius XII on the eve of the conflict and felt the need for more direct influence and closer consultation. He sent Myron C. Taylor as his 'personal representative' to Rome in 1940. At the time, the German Ambassador to the Holy See was doyen of the diplomatic corps. The Taylor mission lasted till 1950, into the period of Harry Truman's presidency. When Taylor was away from Rome, Harold H. Tittman, a career diplomat, maintained contact with the Vatican, from the entry of the USA into the war till 1944.

The greatest American influence in the Vatican was evident in the time of Cardinal Spellman (1889–1967). For seven years, from 1925 to 1932, he served in the Vatican Secretariat of State, where he first met Mgr Eugenio Pacelli, the future Pope Pius XII and soon a firm friend. During the Second World War, Cardinal Spellman ensured generous political and financial support for many of the initiatives of the Vatican. His influence dwindled after the death of Pius XII. During the Vietnam war, the diplomatic peacemaking moves of Pope Paul actually opened a rift between the cardinal and the Holy See. But, within the American Catholic Church, Spellman's influence continued for a while through his domination of the bishops, many of whom he had in effect selected himself. He handpicked Cardinal Cooke as his successor. At the Second Vatican Council, the influence of America's basically tradition-alist and cautious hierarchy was demonstrated through the strong roles played by Cardinals Spellman and Ritter during the debates, especially on the subjects of Catholic relations with the Jews and attitudes to religious freedom. But, in recent years, the US influence over the Vatican's policies has seeped away. Partly this has to do with shifts in international politics. Partly, it can be traced to the Holy See's suspicion of liberal trends in the Catholic Church in America, from the growth of the 'underground' Church with its evidently unorthodox practices and beliefs, to the support manifested among many American Catholics for married clergy, the ordination of women and the acceptance of birth control. Too influential an American position at the centre and in the missions of the Church might lead to the export of these ideas, traditionalists in the Vatican have feared.

On their part, US Catholics have traditionally followed their bishops in displaying affection for the person of the Pope and distant respect for the Holy See as an institution. Generally, there was a welcoming response to the reforms of Vatican II including the updating of papal ceremonies and practices. However, Pope Paul VI's encyclical *Humanae Vitae* (concerned with married life and procreation) was, to quote Bishop Thomas Kelly of the National Conference of Catholic Bishops, 'misunderstood and under-appreciated in the United States, and this in turn undermined to a certain extent respect for the Papacy as an institution – there was no rejection of the Papacy but a shift in the weight that American Catholics gave to it'.

Since the Second World War successive Presidents of the USA have visited the Vatican. President Nixon appointed Henry Cabot Lodge as his personal envoy to the Pope, and regular meetings were held between him and Pope Paul VI. President Ford also exchanged views with Pope Paul through his Secretary of State, Henry Kissinger. In October 1978, President Carter asked Robert F. Wagner, a New York lawyer, one-time US Ambassador to Spain and Mayor of New York, 'to visit the Vatican from time to time to exchange views on international and humanitarian subjects of interest and concern to the Vatican and to the US government'. In 1981, President Reagan appointed an old friend, Californian businessman William Wilson, as his personal representative to the Holy See.

The future of diplomatic relations between the US government and the Holy See remains open at this modest and informal level. Not the Act of Settlement but the First Amendment to the Constitution is held by some to forbid any change. Protestant opinion in the United States still presents strong, highly charged, emotional opposition to closer ties. Since the formal initiatives must come from Washington, the Vatican has to wait patiently, a keen but passive suitor.

In Washington, as in London, the Papacy's representative (living on Massachusetts Avenue) is an apostolic delegate and not a nuncio. Archbishop Jean Jadot, a Belgian with experience of diplomatic service in the Far East and Africa, was the Pope's envoy to the Catholic bishops in America until 1980 and the first non-Italian to hold that position. His eight predecessors included Cardinal Vagnozzi, who returned to Rome to supervise the Vatican's financial books, and Cardinal

Cicognani, who, after twenty-five years in the USA, was Papal Secretary of State under Pope John XXIII and Pope Paul VI from 1961 to 1969. (Apostolic delegates become cardinals only on leaving Washington.)

Mgr Jadot is in his mid-seventies, Belgian-born and French-speaking, educated at Louvain University and the major seminary of Malines–Brussels. He started his Vatican career as a member of the Sacred Congregation for the Evangelization of Peoples. He served the Holy See in Thailand (as pro-nuncio) and simultaneously in Laos, Malaysia and Singapore (as apostolic delegate); then in Cameroon and Gabon (pro-nuncio) and Equatorial Guinea (apostolic delegate), before taking up the post of apostolic delegate in the United States in 1973. In 1978, he was also appointed the Holy See's Permanent Observer to the Organization of American States.

He is a thin, lively man, sharp and quick. After he arrived in the United States, he was credited – through his assessment for Rome of the candidates put forward by the American hierarchy – with encouraging the choice by Pope Paul of pastoral, liberal-minded bishops rather than old-style, rather authoritarian administrators. He himself dislikes this emotionally charged language, but there is no gainsaying the immense popularity he won, and retained, as a very human and unpedantic prelate.

In America, the archbishop was loaded with very wide responsibilities, which meant, he once mildly complained, that he was always busy, with little time for private work. He travelled constantly and got to know the United States well, partly because of his wish to interpret for a sometimes critical Rome the diverse cultures of the Catholic Church in the New World. The year 1979 brought him the exceptional if welcome burden of Pope John Paul II's American tour. Mgr Jadot needed to make the arrangements for the programme; accompany the visitor; face the repercussions, often emotional and disruptive, of the Pope's gravely important policy speeches. In 1980, Archbishop Jadot was appointed Cardinal Pignedoli's successor at the Secretariat for Non-Christians. As apostolic delegate, he was succeeded by Archbishop Pio Laghi, formerly apostolic nuncio in Argentina, with long experience in the Near East.

For the mission of the apostolic delegate in America,

140

meanwhile, the Pope's visit had signified a decisive re-orientation: the implementation of a firmer line from the Holy See on doctrinal orthodoxy than had been expected; the exploration, with limited resources, of the long vistas of potential religious renewal brought into view by the impact of the personal presence and words of an extraordinarily appealing Pope on American soil.

Vatican diplomacy seems at its most subtle when illustrated by the relations of the Papacy with Communist countries. After Pope John Paul II visited Poland in the early summer of 1979, one British newspaper (the *Observer*) heavily criticized Vatican Radio for exploiting the Pope's initiative in order to foster rebellious attitudes in Eastern European countries; the *New Statesman* argued that the visit marked the fostering of an alliance between the Kremlin and the Vatican that suited both allegedly oppressive systems. Whatever the motive, the Vatican has been increasingly ready to sup with the Communist devil since 1958, the year of the death of Pope Pius XII, during whose pontificate fifteen countries fell under Communist rule and who decreed the excommunication of all Catholics adhering willingly to the Communist Party and its policies.

Some tentative overtures to the Kremlin were made by Pius XII towards the end of his reign. The log-jam was loosened, however, by Pope John XXIII's encyclical *Pacem in Terris (Peace on Earth)*, published in 1963, which provided the intellectual justification for diplomatic *rapprochement*. The encyclical distinguished neatly between false ideas and the historical movements based on them, which could change their nature over time, and might contain good and positive elements. In the 1960s, bishops' delegations from Communist countries were allowed to attend the Second Vatican Council, and President Khrushchev exchanged encouraging messages with Pope John, to whom he sent various intermediaries including his son-in-law.

Pope Paul VI shifted the exchanges to a more practical level when he twice met the Soviet Foreign Minister, Andrei Gromyko (at the United Nations in New York in 1965, and at the Vatican in 1966); received the Chairman of the Presidium of the Supreme Soviet, Nikolai Podgorny, in 1967; and, seizing the chance, sent Archbishop (now Cardinal) Agostino Casaroli, then Secretary of the Council for Public Affairs, to Moscow to deposit the Holy See's adherence to the treaty against the proliferation of nuclear weapons.

This last opportune move arose from the anxiety that every state in the world should sign the 'non-proliferation' treaty, copies of which were deposited in the United States, the USSR and the United Kingdom, who between them have diplomatic connections with all governments. Pope Paul wanted to sign the treaty as an important moral gesture, and as a neutral state the Holy See needed to sign all three texts. So the apostolic delegates in London and Washington signed the Foreign Office and White House copies respectively (enjoying technical diplomatic status while doing so), and Casaroli had a good reason to go to Moscow. The Swiss Guards, as a consequence of the Holy See's adherence to the treaty, are now regularly inspected for illegal nuclear warheads.

There are no permanent diplomatic relations between the Soviet Union and the Vatican, but the less chilly atmosphere of the 1970s did help the Vatican prise open slightly the grip of Communism on the freedom of religion and education in several Eastern European countries. The Vatican's official yearbook, the *Annuario Pontificio*, in the lists of its embassies and delegations throughout the world, and of permanent missions at the Vatican, prints nearly all the names of Eastern European countries with blank spaces following.

Yugoslavia, however, exchanges representatives with the Vatican. Ambassador Zdenko Svete has his chancery, run by himself and a first secretary, very appropriately in Via Gramsci (named after the Marxist writer and martyr); Archbishop Michele Cecchini with his councillor serves as apostolic pronuncio in Belgrade. Diplomatic relations between Yugoslavia and the Vatican were ruptured in 1952 when Pius XII made Archbishop Stepinac a cardinal, soon after his release from imprisonment by Tito's government. The Yugoslav bishops were allowed to attend the Second Vatican Council. The thaw continued slowly. In 1970 Yugoslavia became the first Communist country to conclude an agreement with the Holy See for mutual diplomatic ties, and in 1971 the octogenarian President Tito called officially on Pope Paul.

After Castro's seizure of power, Cuba maintained the diplomatic relations that had been established (in 1935) both with the Vatican and, more surprisingly, with the Knights of Malta. Relations are handled rather gingerly by a Vatican pro-nuncio in Havana and a Cuban ambassador in Rome. A Communist Cuban ambassador has actually served as Dean of the Diplomatic Corps accredited to the Holy See.

Towards these Communist countries, the interest from the Vatican is primarily motivated by the existence of large Catholic populations within their borders, in some cases the majority of the people.

Communist China challenges Rome for other reasons as well as the existence there of a small Christian minority, including perhaps up to three million Catholics. The tradition of Christian missions to China goes back to the thirteenth century. The Jesuits were brilliantly successful in their work in China between the mission of Matteo Ricci to the Ming Emperor Wan-li in 1583 and the condemnation of Chinese ancestral rites by Pope Benedict XIV in 1742. Pope Leo XIII tried hard to establish diplomatic contacts with the Chinese but was opposed by the French government, which claimed special status as the protector of Catholic missions in China. Eventually an apostolic delegate was accepted in Peking in 1922. In 1943 a permanent minister from China was greeted by Pius XII, and in 1946 a papal internuncio went to Nanking. After the People's Republic of China was proclaimed, the internuncio, Archbishop Antonio Riberi, was expelled and through a 'Patriotic Association of Chinese Catholics' the government formed a 'National Church', with forty-five bishops of its own, which surfaces from time to time. In 1979, it announced the appointment (unacceptable to the Holy See) of the first new Catholic bishop in China for fifteen years. Pope Paul attempted to re-open diplomatic negotiations with China on several occasions, though hindered by the Vatican's recognition of the nationalist government in Taiwan. In the Vatican, the diplomatic corps includes a very self-aware embassy from Taiwan.

Bishop John Baptist Cheng-Chung Wu of Hong Kong is a refugee from Communist China, as are most of Hong Kong's Catholic population of over 260,000, constantly swollen by new arrivals from China and Vietnam. In the Far East, fidelity to the Holy See is staunch among the bishops, but the possibilities of dramatically more relaxed Chinese attitudes to an official Vatican presence will impose great strains on different loyalties.

At dinner in Kensington Palace Gardens, with the Soviet Ambassador, Nikolai Lunkov, not long before the election of Pope John Paul I, I was discussing the Vatican's contacts with Communist China. With the Sino-Soviet split well established and feelings running high, the subject called for tact. The young Soviet official to whom I talked over coffee agreed that the Vatican must know a great deal about what was happening politically in Peking. I recalled the conversation a few months later, on the election not just of a non-Italian Pope, but of a Pope who would have tremendous influence inside the Communist world itself, since he came from the over-whelmingly Catholic country of Poland. Pope John Paul II expressed hopes for 'a new contact with Chinese Catholics' in August 1979, when responding critically to the news of the appointment of Michael Fu-T'ieh-Shan as Bishop of Peking. Cautiously, the feeling grew during 1979–80 that the Chinese authorities were ready to encourage such contacts, including the restoration of educational ties with the Jesuits. On the other side, the Papal visit to the Far East in 1981 provided an occasion for clearer though still cautious overtures from the Vatican, notably via Cardinal Casaroli, for dialogue with Chinese Christians and the Chinese authorities.

The diplomats of the Holy See are also found sparingly scattered throughout many of the international organizations of modern times. Their entry into this field is religious in its motivation, interestingly technical in its origins. To most of the organizations, accreditation is for the Holy See rather than for the Vatican City State. But it is the Vatican City State which belongs to the Universal Postal Union and the International Telecommunications Union, and through its membership is asked to conferences of the United Nations. Embarrassed by the possibly extended emphasis on the Pope's position as sovereign of a state, the Vatican negotiated with the then Secretary General of the United Nations, Dag Hammarskjold, and in an exchange of notes (October 1957) it was agreed that 'it is the Holy See which is represented by the delegations accredited by the Secretariat of State to the different sessions of the various organs of the United Nations'.

In consequence of the UN attitude, the Papacy decides whether the Pope will be represented through the Holy See or through the Vatican City State at the United Nations and its specialized agencies. The Vatican's interest in the affairs of the UN – covering, for example, social and cultural activities touching on population and religion – is obviously acute. The organizations to which the Holy See and the city state are linked constitute a weird catalogue, painstakingly listed in the *Annuario Pontificio*. 'Excellent though the Holy See is at traditional diplomacy', a British diplomat explained to me, 'it is still very inexperienced in the modern United Nations-type multinational diplomacy. Observer status at the UN, which the Holy See possesses, doesn't yield anything like the experience that even junior diplomats get from their membership of key bodies such as the Security Council, the Economic and Social Council, the Human Rights Commission and so on.'

The Holy See has participated in the preparation of the Vienna Conventions, including in recent years those on Diplomatic Relations, the Law of the Sea, the Law of Treaties, and Consular Relations. It participated in the Conference for Security and Cooperation in Europe in Helsinki and Geneva, in 1973 and 1974. Its attitude to the chance of joining in diplomatic happenings of all kinds has been positive, indeed highly enthusiastic, and Pope John Paul II has maintained the same eager stance as his recent predecessors.

Some Vatican diplomats (for example, Archbishop Igino Cardinale in his book on *The Holy See and International Order*) argue that, if the Holy See had membership instead of observer rank at the United Nations, this would put it at risk of being party to actions such as international coercion running counter to its own mission. Therefore it should shun UN membership. However, recent Popes have shown an instinctive attachment to the organization. Pope Paul VI, in particular, made an enthusiastic appearance and speech there in 1965. Pope John Paul II followed in 1979. The Vatican feels sympathy with the internationalism of the United Nations, with its large component of developing nations, with its avowed mission for peace. It also sees the importance of a presence in a global forum where weighty matters of ethical and religious practice – birth control, religious freedom – must come up for influential debate. There is no chance that the world will see the Swiss Guards on active duty overseas, but the Holy See did sign the Non-Proliferation Treaty, did leap at the chance of attending the Helsinki Conference, and would surely not refuse membership of the United Nations if it were possible to obtain it.

The Vatican's Permanent Observer to the United Nations at New York is Mgr Giovanni Cheli, a 'career' diplomat who was born in Turin and made an archbishop by Pope Paul VI in the summer of 1978. The elevation belatedly confirmed his personal worthiness and the importance attached by the Vatican to its links with the United Nations. Archbishop Cheli's career has been that of an enthusiast, close to the very heart of Vatican diplomacy through his friendship with Casaroli over many years. His *curriculum vitae* reads like an excerpt from a play on the glittering prizes to be harvested by those educated in the Vatican's Oxbridge of the Pontifical Academies. He was born in 1918 and ordained in 1942. He took his master's degree in theology and then his doctorate in canon law at the Lateran University, Rome, before studying for his diploma at the Pontifical Academy for Diplomacy. He spent three years as a second secretary in Guatemala, seven years as a first secretary in Madrid, five years as a counsellor in Rome, and six years at the Secretariat of State and Council of Public Affairs in the Vatican, dealing with the Communist countries of Eastern Europe, before being appointed the Holy See's Permanent Observer to the United Nations in New York. He is a Knight Commander of Spain's Order of Isobel the Catholic, of Italy's Order of Merit and of Germany's Green Cross. For recreation he likes to listen to classical music, play tennis, or go mountain climbing. He designed his own coat-of-arms as archbishop.

Archbishop Cheli's office is at 20 East 72nd Street, New York, where there is a small permanent staff working day to day on the study of UN documents, attending UN meetings and preparing reports for the Secretariat of State and the Council of Public Affairs of the Church. The main topics in which the Holy See and therefore the mission are interested, the Archbishop says, are human rights, religious intolerance, disarmament, social issues, youth, the advancement of women, economic issues . . . and matters before the Security Council. The UN proceedings are fully reported to Rome; in the other direction, the mission's task is to convey to the permanent staff and the delegates to the United Nations both general religious attitudes and the particular concerns of the Holy See. 'We are often asked our opinion on topics with which the Holy See has had long experience or where delegates know we have a particular concern, such as human rights and religious freedom.'

With its status as a permanent observer (like Switzerland, Monaco and the two Korean states), the Holy See cannot vote and its representative can only speak in the committees of the General Assembly when authorized by the chairman; but this has never been refused.

Archbishop Cheli sees the Holy See 'as spiritual collaborator in the ideals of the United Nations Charter'. Pope John Paul II, he recalls, early in his pontificate recorded that the Holy See 'consistent with its own identity and at various levels has always sought to be a faithful collaborator with the United Nations . . .'.

In 1978, Archbishop Cheli's predecessor, Mgr Alberto Giovannetti, who first opened the permanent observer's office, published a novel called *Requiem for a Spy*, which involved the impersonation of the Vatican observer by a KGB agent. The spy went on to experience the triumphs of conversion and martyrdom, but the impressions the novel conveyed about the UN were decidedly cynical. The fact that such attitudes are shared by many Catholic bishops adds its particular stresses to this area of Vatican diplomacy.

The Permanent Observer of the Vatican at UNESCO is Mgr Renzo Frana, and his predecessors in the post have included the future Pope John XXIII, who added the job to his other duties in Paris. Like Pope John, Mgr Frana was born in Bergamo; but he has followed so far a more conventional diplomatic career, starting when he left the Lateran University with his degree in canon law for the Pontifical Academy. He entered the diplomatic service at the prompting of the president of the academy. At first, his local bishop refused to release him but, he recalls, he relented after the election of Pope John – who came from Bergamo. ('You do not *ask* to be a papal diplomat,' Mgr Frana explains. 'Your bishop will usually be approached by the Pontifical Academy after your name has been suggested by the university where you are studying. . . .')

The office and residence of the Permanent Observer to UNESCO is a tall brick house approached through an iron gate at 10, Avenue du Président Wilson, Paris, where Pope John Paul II stayed in 1980. There is another office in the centre of Paris. At Number 10, on the corner of Rue Freycinet, the house faces a busy street market, crammed with stalls loaded with vegetables and fruit, meat and cheeses.

The Holy See keeps an interested eye on the multifarious activities of UNESCO. The cultural interest expressed and documented by the Roman Catholic bishops at the Second Vatican Council sharpened this curiosity. In the fields of education, information, culture, human rights, the Vatican wants to know what UNESCO is up to, and to collaborate 'in making its own ideas known in areas of common interest, always respecting the liberty of others'.

The Vatican regards UNESCO as especially useful for its mission in the Third World countries, often ready to accept ideas and initiatives from UNESCO more readily than from Western countries. Mgr Frana reflects on the danger of materialism in culture and education, and the aggressive influence of the materialists both of East and West. 'We are here to assert moral principle. People are ready to talk about God.'

In a delicately decorated and panelled blue reception room, Mgr Frana (who was appointed Vatican Observer to UNESCO in 1975) agrees that the residence is very grand and adds that it was bought to confer status on the delegation. 'This is a good house to receive in. . . .' Relaxed, short, good-looking, with thinning black hair, he talks with somewhat unusual openness about his personal career and the strengths and weaknesses of the Vatican diplomatic service. Before his appointment to the Paris post, he served in Nicaragua, in Brazil, in Rome under Mgr Benelli, and in London and Washington. It was a fairly swift climb up the ladder of promotion in the Vatican's service, where each rung is clearly marked and defined.

Mgr Frana suggests that the composition of the service is getting 'healthier' as it involves more nationalities, especially lower down the line. It is good to see quite a few Irish, but there are no English at all. At the centre, there should be less secrecy, though men like Mgr Casaroli are both fair-minded and accessible. 'Happily, he is not an exception.' However, the diplomats in the field feel the need for a more formal personnel policy. There is one experimental bureau for relations between the diplomatic personnel. The Holy See's diplomatic service does have an inspector, Archbishop Enrici, who was Heim's predecessor in England. The diplomats of the Vatican, however prudent and priestly they may be, are likely to disagree with their superiors from time to time (and indeed vice versa) and the consolidation and improvement of personnel relations, Mgr Frana feels, would make decisions visibly fairer.

The vocations of men like Renzo Frana from Bergamo (which has a strong tradition of papal diplomatic service) place at the disposal of the Pope an international information service unique for its dedication, continuity and level of education and intelligence. His sources are supplemented by the frequent visits of political leaders and heads of state to the Vatican; the regular visits of Catholic bishops from all over the world; the international headquarters of the many Catholic orders and organizations in Rome; and the day-to-day contacts of the Curia with the many diplomatic representatives accredited to the Holy See.

There was a remarkable increase during the pontificate of Pope Paul VI in the number of countries establishing some form of diplomatic relations with the Holy See. The Pope used to claim proudly that diplomatic representation had doubled. The countries included now number nearly a hundred, swelling the diplomatic corps at the Vatican to several hundreds. Some diplomats fly in for their regular visits. Chancelleries in Rome, scattered all over the city, range from a room or two, through the medium-sized apartment of the British at 91 via Condotti, to Spain's magnificent Palazzo di Spagna on the Piazza di Spagna, run by Ambassador Dom Angel Sanz Briz, which was used as a refuge for Spanish princes of the blood during the Napoleonic Wars. Despite modernization and reform, Vatican protocol still offers

149

diplomats the experience of ancient ceremonial, re-enacted history, magic.

After his arrival in Rome, the head of mission pays an official visit to the Secretary of State, Cardinal Agostino Casaroli, to hand him a copy of his letters of credence. He also calls on the Substitute Secretary of State, Archbishop Eduardo Martinez Somalo, and the Minister of Foreign Affairs (Secretary of the Council for the Public Affairs of the Church), Archbishop Achille Silvestrini. The Prefect of the Apostolic Palace, Bishop Jacques Martin, arranges the date and time for the Pope's reception of the new envoy.

He is met by the two Attachés of the Antechamber and two Gentlemen of His Holiness and escorted to the courtyard of San Damaso, where he is saluted by a little formation of Swiss Guards. The lift takes the ambassador to the second loggia of the Apostolic Palace, where he and his party are received by two Attachés of the Antechamber and the *Sediari* (the chair-carriers). They walk to the Papal Apartments, where with the Prefect of the Apostolic Palace and the Consultant of the Vatican City State they proceed through the *Sala del Papi* to the *Sala del Trono* to meet the Pope. By the throne are grouped various Vatican dignitaries: the Almoner of His Holiness, the Vicar General of His Holiness for the Vatican City, the Prelates of the Antechamber.

The ambassador reads his address, presents his letters of credence, hears a brief response from the Pope, and goes into the Pope's library for a private conversation, followed by the introduction of his own suite. Sometimes, Pope John Paul II leads an ambassador in arm-in-arm. After the audience, the ambassador, moving from the *Sala Clementina*, where the prefect says his goodbyes, visits the Cardinal Secretary of State for a conversation before (if a Catholic) praying in front of the Chapel of the Blessed Sacrament in St Peter's Basilica, and visiting the tomb of St Peter, or (if not a Catholic) leaving through the courtyard of San Damaso. The same day, the many Vatican officials whom the ambassador has met sign the visitors' book at his embassy. The ambassador writes to the Cardinal Dean of the Sacred College requesting an audience. His formal visit is returned by the cardinal dean on the same day, and over the following days the ambassador visits all the curial cardinals in residence in Rome.

Diplomatic memoirs and literary recollections have left a rich store of anecdotes and descriptions of papal audiences through the ages – always colourful, sometimes bizarre. Sir Odo Russell, British Minister to the Holy See from 1922, wrote some vivid impressions of Pope Pius XI and the extraordinary Vatican diplomat Cardinal Pietro Gasparri, Secretary of State to two Popes:

> On February 6, 1923, accompanied by Cecil Dormer, my Secretary and invaluable adviser, I repaired to the Vatican to present my credentials. The ceremony was extremely impressive. Military honours were rendered as we were escorted by Swiss Guards across the Clementine Hall to the entrance of the Papal apartment where we were received by members of the Papal Court. The solemn audience took place in the hall of the Throne. After delivering a short speech and presenting my credentials [sic] the Pope replied in felicitous terms expressing his admiration for the British nation. He then descended from his throne and asked me to enter his private library. There the conversation continued on less official lines with great benevolence on the part of His Holiness.
>
> The Cardinal Secretary of State [who has since moved] occupies an apartment in the Vatican Palace just below the Papal apartments, and I called there for the first time as is customary, after presenting my letters of credence to Pope Pius XI. It was with very special interest that I first entered the Cardinal's presence as it was with His Eminence that I would have to conduct all business during my mission. He was then about seventy – somewhat rugged but of a distinctly picturesque aspect, which was greatly enhanced by his dress – a black cassock edged and buttoned with crimson, with a crimson skull cap and a pectoral cross of gold. . . . Every Wednesday he received the Heads of Missions separately and in turn to discuss current affairs. I rarely omitted to attend these receptions but as the time at his disposal with so many visitors was of necessity brief, I occasionally sought him out in the evening when his ante-room was empty and when he seemed more disposed for a talk . . . he once said with that whimsical smile of his – that the Devil could not be so clever as he was supposed to be since the war had resulted in the deliverance of the Church from its three worst enemies, the Tsar, the Kaiser, and the Caliph. . . .

Sir Alec Randall was appointed Second Secretary to the British Legation to the Holy See when this was established under Russell in 1925. In his *Vatican Assignment* (London, 1957), he recalled the luncheon offered by Cardinal Gasparri to all the members of the diplomatic corps accredited to the Pope in 1929, after the Vatican's historic agreement with the Italian government.

> In our uniforms, wearing decorations, we all assembled for sherry and aperitifs in the Borgia Apartments . . . there was still a sufficient aura of exciting historical imagination about the name to give an especial interest to the occasion and to the speculations of some of the older diplomats, as they sipped their sherry, as to whether on this occasion the Borgia gold plate would be used, as they said it had been when, to mark the end of the First World War, Benedict XV had arranged a similar function. But this time it was not brought out; the table was decorated with candelabra in the Empire style and the various courses served on Sèvres porcelain, the whole a gift from Napoleon to Pius VII, who crowned the Emperor in 1804 but was arrested by him in 1809 and kept prisoner until 1814.

The Vatican's diplomats throughout the world and the foreign representatives accredited to the Holy See – respectively embodying the Papacy's rights to 'active' and 'passive' diplomacy – rarely meet. The information they generate, however, flows to the Pope through the single key organization of the Curia and, indeed, of the institutional Roman Catholic Church, the Secretariat of State, which is linked to the Council for the Public Affairs of the Church.

The Cardinal Secretary of State can be compared with a prime minister or head of a government where foreign affairs are of overwhelming importance. He is entitled to call meetings of the heads of all curial departments; and the activities of these departments, of course, contain a substantial diplomatic and international element. His is the prime responsibility for the Pope's relations with the representatives of the Holy See abroad and those of civil governments at the Vatican. He is the highest official representative of the Pope, as both ruler of the Vatican City State and the head of the Holy See, in dealing with outside powers. The office carries such authority that, even under a strong-willed and exceptionally intelligent Pope, the policies of its holder exert a most powerful influence on the destiny of the Catholic Church, provided his personality is strong. (He can come unstuck. One eighteenth-century forerunner of today's Secretary of State, Cardinal Niccolò Coscia, spent nine years in Castel Sant'Angelo as punishment for graft.)

Essentially, however, the Secretary of State is influential as the 'creature' of the Pope. Appointments to bishoprics are normally dealt with by the Secretariat of State if in a country where a concordat gives the state rights of presentation; otherwise the appointment is normally through the Congregation of Bishops, Propaganda Fide for missionary countries, or the Oriental Congregation for Uniate Churches. To these, the Secretariat of State is rather like the Cabinet Office is to Whitehall. It is relatively small and (certainly under Mgr Benelli) has shown itself very efficient.

The Secretary of State, unlike most Vatican departmental heads, need not offer his resignation after five years, but the appointment is terminated by a vacancy of the Holy See. The *Sostituto* remains in office even after the death of a Pope (when he answers to the College of Cardinals) and he too is free of the five-year rule. (As well as the *Sostituto*, the Secretary of the Council for the Public Affairs of the Church remains in office after the death of a Pope, to continue to deal with foreign governments; so does a third man of importance, the Prefect of the Pontifical Household.)

The rights of all these three to approach a newly elected Pope are spelled out in *Romano Pontifici Eligendo*. The moment the new Pope has assented to his election, it states:

> . . . he may be approached by the Substitute of the Secretariat of State or Papal Secretariat, the Secretary of the Council for the Public Affairs of the Church, the Prefect of the Papal Household and whoever else needs to consult the elected Pontiff on matters of immediate necessity.

This specific provision arises from an incident following the election of Pope John XXIII. To the irritation of some of the cardinals, anxious to be back in their own beds, the new Pope decreed that the Conclave should continue for another night so that he could seek the cardinals' advice. Unaware of this but knowing a new Pope had been elected, several senior officials of the Curia entered the Sistine Chapel, as they usually do to greet the new Pope. At the door, they were met by a furious Cardinal Tisserant who told them they were guilty of breaking into the Conclave enclosure and had incurred automatic excommunication and the direct ecclesiastical penalties. On his distant throne, receiving the homage of the cardinals, Pope John was stirred to turn and make the sign of the cross over those concerned with the words 'I absolve you . . .'. Pope Paul VI, with his usual caution, legislated to allow admission to the Conclave after the election to be without deprivation 'of every honour, rank, office and ecclesiastical benefice'.

The Secretary of State is also the prefect at the head of the cardinals nominally running the Council for the Public Affairs of the Church, which focuses on certain areas of foreign affairs with a decidedly political content: the nomination of bishops, where governments are interested; papal representation throughout the world; concordats and agreements with different states. The Public Affairs Council, along with the Secretariat of State, oversees the work of the Pontifical Commission for Social Communications, and it tucks under its wing the Pontifical Commission for Russia.

This last body (with liturgical and religious rather than political antecedents) comprises three archbishops. The Public Affairs Council has a commission of sixteen cardinals and a secretary and an under-secretary, both of whom live in the Vatican. At their offices, adjoining those of the Secretariat of State in the Apostolic Palace (on the third floor near the Pope's apartments), they are served by a staff of about thirty, divided into diplomatic and administrative staff. The former include thirteen counsellors and auditors, equivalent to first secretaries in the world of civil diplomacy. Theirs is the business of travel and negotiation for regulated periods within the Vatican and throughout the world. The administrative staff, confined to head office, include four with secretarial rank (*minutanti*), one technical and eight secretarial assistants (*addetti di secretaria*) and five clerical assistants (*scrittori*), with two laymen among them to help with office work and typing. There are two special pontifical representatives.

The foreign affairs work of the Secretariat of State and the Public Affairs Council ranges from the routine translation and transmission of the Pope's messages to the bishops to vital negotiations with heads of state. The choice of the men responsible for the latter, and for running the affairs of the two departments, is enormously significant in every pontificate. It indicates the likely direction of affairs, the aims of the Pope, and the practical interpretation that will be given to his broad statements of objective and principle.

One of the key jobs is held by the good-looking, French-educated, Lithuanian born Mgr Audrys Juozas Backis, who spoke to me in the Apostolic Palace (and later drove me in a fast Fiat across the back of St Peter's to the Palazzo San Carlo for an appointment there) about working life and conditions as a Vatican diplomat at base.

Mgr Backis's family moved to France from Kaunas in Lithuania in 1937 when he was one year old. His father was a diplomat at the Lithuanian Legation in Paris. After studying at a French seminary, Backis went to the Pontifical Lithuanian College of St Casimir in Rome to follow a theology course at the Pontifical Gregorian University. He was ordained in 1961, worked briefly among Lithuanians in the United States, then returned to Rome to the Pontifical Lateran University (for a canon law degree) and to the Pontifical Ecclesiastical Academy. He joined the diplomatic service in 1964 and gained experience successively at apostolic nunciatures in the Philippines, Costa Rica, and Turkey, and at the delegation in Lagos, Nigeria.

When I saw him in 1978, Mgr Backis had been for three years with the Council for the Public Affairs of the Church, living inside the Vatican. Of the thirteen diplomats at the Public Affairs Council, one was a Spaniard, one German, one American and one Indian. For these career diplomats, a good knowledge of languages is important. They mostly live in a hostel near the huge audience hall, though some seek their own private accommodation in Rome. They have all had experience abroad (Mgr Backis had chalked up nine years). They tend to stay for a few years working on the council before being sent away, perhaps as nuncios, on another tour of duty, and they can be sent abroad at any time. Some diplomats may transfer to the administrative staff and stay permanently in Rome. They specialize in different areas of the Vatican's foreign policy concerns: Mgr Backis, for example, was concentrating on international relations, and British and Irish affairs.

The administrative staff at the council make their own arrangements for accommodation, the several members of religious orders among them usually being attached to a 'house'. They include some priests with very long service, such as the Jesuit Fr. Fiorelli Cavalli, who has been in the service for over twenty years. They, too, specialize in concordats, say, or in certain international areas. They are all Italian save two, and they include a nun, from the sisters of the Sacred Heart.

The atmosphere in the offices, away from the corridors and waiting rooms full of ticking clocks and endless time, is bustling and sometimes tense. The system and working routines are hierarchical – 'straight up,' says Backis, 'to the prefect and then to the Pope, a vertical line'.

The Public Affairs Council has no budget of its own. Bills are handed to the Secretariat of State, most of whose services, the diplomatic pouch and the translation facilities for instance, are available to the council. But it has a definite character of its own, shaped, in recent years, by one of the most subtle and experienced personalities in the Vatican, Mgr Casaroli.

The way for a reshuffle of the 'cabinet' of Pope John Paul II was opened by the death of Cardinal Jean Villot in March 1979. Villot had been Secretary of State and Prefect of the Public Affairs Council of the Church since 1969, when he was appointed by Paul VI. As Villot's successor Pope John Paul II appointed Archbishop (now Cardinal) Agostino Casaroli. First he was made Acting or Pro-Secretary of State; the appointment was made permanent after Casaroli received his cardinal's hat in June. (Certain Vatican jobs – the prefects of the congregations, the Secretary of State – are held only by cardinals. A man without a hat is therefore designated as, say, pro-prefect until the impending consistory, when he can become a cardinal.)

Archbishop Martinez Somalo was appointed the new *Sostituto* to the Secretary of State, as Archbishop (now Cardinal) Giuseppe Caprio moved from that post to the position of Pro-President of the Administration of the Patrimony of the Holy See. The now Archbishop Achille Silvestrini was appointed in place of Casaroli as Secretary of the Public Affairs Council, with Audrys Backis moving up to become his under-secretary.

These and previous appointments gave the Pope a comparatively young and more international team in the foreign affairs hierarchy. They seemed to emphasize the Pope's interest in diplomacy and international affairs, spanning the *ostpolitik* of his predecessors and future bridgehead campaigns on human rights.

When I talked at length to Agostino Casaroli, shortly before he became Pope John Paul's Secretary of State and Prefect of the Council for Public Affairs, he said that the 'real chief' was the prefect (at that time, Cardinal Villot). He himself had a place as 'chief collaborator. . . . I send the cardinal all the papers. He sees everything. He will discuss matters with the Pope. Everything I do is with his knowledge. He gives me wide-ranging scope. . . .' Casaroli's personal role in the diplomatic activities of the Holy See, even before his promotion to the right hand of the Pope, has been remarkable. Casaroli was born in 1914, in Castel S. Giovanni, Piacenza. Two uncles were priests; one became a bishop, the other the rector of a seminary. In the 1930s he read canon law at the Lateran University, then entered the Pontifical Ecclesiastical Academy, and was ordained in 1937. He joined the First Section of the Sacred Congregation for Extraordinary Ecclesiastical Affairs (now the Public Affairs Council) in 1940, to work first in the archives, then on administration as a *minutante*. After some foreign experience in the 1950s through visits to Rio de Janeiro and Madrid, he spent three years as Professor of Diplomatic Procedure at the Pontifical Academy, until Pope John XXIII appointed him an Under-Secretary of the Sacred Congregation in 1961.

The flexible cast of Casaroli's mind, and his developing talents as a negotiator, suited his task of building an unprecedented structure of understandings and agreements on the new Vatican attitudes to Communism laid down by Pope John XXIII and Pope Paul VI. From the middle 1960s Mgr Casaroli has frequently travelled to Eastern European countries, and has represented the Holy See at international meetings of consequence. The journeys to the East started from Austria in 1963, after he had led a delegation to the UN Conference on Consular Relations in Vienna. In 1964, he signed a limited agreement in Budapest between the Holy See and the Hungarian government. In 1964–5, he reached a series of agreements in Prague affecting Church–State relations, including the position of Archbishop Beran who was made a cardinal by the Pope and released from prison into exile.

In 1966, in Belgrade, he signed a 'protocol' on behalf of the Holy See. This was the Vatican's first comprehensive pact with a Communist government since the Second World War and led to the exchange of non-diplomatic envoys after a rupture of fourteen years. In August 1970 he paid an official visit to Yugoslavia for new discussions and a meeting with President Tito. In February 1971 he was in the Soviet Union to deposit the instrument of the Holy See's adherence to the treaty on the non-proliferation of nuclear arms, and while there made history by holding talks with the Ministry for Foreign Affairs and the Commission for Religious Affairs of the USSR. In 1973 and 1975, Mgr Casaroli was the Representative of the Holy See at the Helsinki Conference on Security and Co-operation, whose final declaration he signed for the Pope.

The Helsinki Conference was another important first. It was *not* a United Nations conference, nor a conference of 'States Members of the United Nations and Specialised Agencies'. Under the Lateran Treaty, the Holy See could attend only if specifically invited by each single one of the participants. There was a general expectation that the Holy See would attend, but specific invitations of the type mentioned in the Lateran Treaty were not forthcoming from a great many of the participants. When the time came, the Holy See just went.

Contacts with the Communist countries pushed forward by Casaroli during the 1970s – through visits to Cuba, Czechoslovakia and East Germany. In 1979, before the Pope's return home to Poland, he visited Warsaw to discuss the arrangements with government officials.

The image of Mgr Casaroli flitting through the corridors of Communist power on delicate missions from the Vatican in the 1960s and 1970s is not inappropriate. His thin grey hair is wispy over a sensitive and sharp-featured bespectacled face; he is short and slight, and moves as quickly and lightly as a bird. In a black soutane, he wears an aquamarine ring on his right hand, a red skullcap on his head. In his own reception room in the Secretariat of State, with marble floors, bronze plaques, plush chairs, stone fireplaces and beige silk-covered walls, he spoke almost chirpily about his visits to the Communist countries and the Vatican initiatives that were proving so momentous for the Catholics in that part of Europe, and perhaps, indeed, for the future of the world. Mgr Backis had said to me in fluent English, 'It's amazing how he's picked up so many languages, without going to all the places: French, Russian, German, English. . . .' But Mgr Casaroli said, 'I am sorry for my English. I have only been to England once. Cardinal Hume tells me I have to return. . . .'

He explained the overlap between the work of the Secretariat of State and the Council for the Public Affairs of the Church. The latter's earlier title – the Sacred Congregation for Extraordinary Ecclesiastical Affairs – went back to the French Revolution and Napoleon 'when there was an extraordinary situation in France. But then, there began to be extraordinary situations for the Church everywhere.'

Until he became Secretary of State, Casaroli's tasks included work on the revision of the concordats with Spain, Portugal and Italy, which also took him outside the Vatican. His unifying responsibility is to settle and improve through diplomacy the relations between the Catholic Church and the State, allowing maximum freedom to Catholics who practise and teach their religion, with all that implies.

Since 1940, Mgr Casaroli has been living in the Vatican, most of the time in the Palazzina della Zecca, close to successive Popes. Under Pius XII, he saw the making of several treaties or concordats – notably those between the Holy See and Spain and Portugal, and later with Haiti and Peru. He said with a smile, 'In this department, concordats are our bread and butter. But the Holy See does not officially like them all that much. It's said, *storia di concordi, storia di dolori*. . . . In countries such as the United States, the UK and Brazil, there is no interference by legislation with the life of the Church; so the Church is completely free and there is no room for an official relationship through a concordat. In many countries, the Church is impeded in its life, but Catholics can live freely as citizens, and then agreements have to be sought. In non-democratic countries, we have to seek for the possibility of life for the Church, a *modus vivendi* (or, as they say in the Communist countries, a *modus non moriendi*, a way of not dying).'

Casaroli regarded his work as head of the Public Affairs Council as 'diplomatic and political in substance; always a work of the Church. The Pope and the Cardinal Secretary of State have important contacts with states and governments. I have been called the Foreign Minister of the Holy See, but the Prefect of the Council is really that. . . .' Now, Casaroli is the Cardinal Secretary of State and Prefect of the Council, bringing to the affairs of the Church mature, first-hand experience of the international world of diplomacy, especially in relation to the Communist countries, and serving a Pope whose experience marvellously complements his.

Through his recommendation, his place at the Public Affairs Council was filled by another career diplomat with high academic achievements, the Italian Mgr Achille Silvestrini. Born at Faenza in the Romagna, Silvestrini worked in the 1960s under the bluntly traditionalist and narrow-visioned Cardinal Domenico Tardini and the aged Cardinal Amleto Cicognani, former Apostolic Delegate to the United States, who first combined the offices of Secretary of State and Prefect or Chairman of the Public Affairs Council.

Mgr Silvestrini's diplomatic flair began to show itself in the period of Pope Paul's cautious *rapprochement* with Communist countries and assertion of the Holy See's interest in U N affairs. He led the Holy See's team at the U N Geneva Conference in 1971 on the peaceful uses of atomic energy; and took part in the Helsinki Conference and its aftermath.

Silvestrini is the type of pure papal diplomat, appreciated by his staff, impatient of detail, fairly out-going and most of the time very cheerful. When I met him in the Vatican in 1980, he gladly took me for a fresh look at the bathroom painted by Raphael for Cardinal Bibbiena and reflected that it was finished just a year before Luther nailed his theses against indulgences to the door of the castle church of Wittenberg. He is skilled in international negotiations and extremely positive in his approach. He knows the stresses and strengths of the Vatican system intimately, and will have his own say in the new relationship with Cardinal Casaroli as it develops in the 1980s. And the voice of the diplomats working for the Vatican in Rome and abroad has a powerful effect on the mind of the Pope, whose formal and informal meetings with the Cardinal Secretary of State are regular, intimate and comprehensive. The straight line mentioned by Mgr Backis goes through his office to the private apartments of the Pontiff, on the same floor.

* * *

The theoretical basis for papal diplomacy was modified considerably during the reign of Pope John XXIII, as is shown by the changed perspectives of the Catholic Church in Pope Paul VI's *Ecclesiam Suam* and Pope Pius XII's *Mystici Corporis*, and the modulation of the idea of the Church as a perfect society to the idea of the Church as a pilgrim people. The thinking behind the exercise of diplomacy by the Vatican will continue to change.

The professed ideological purpose of Vatican diplomacy is to further the cause of international peace and the creation of conditions which foster the full development of the human personality. This has been stressed in encyclicals with increasing emphasis since the Second World War. The first encyclical issued by Pope John Paul II under the title *Redemptor Hominis* (The Redeemer of Man) talked of the Church's mission to safeguard and teach the truth of religious freedom in the context of its commitment to human rights. Vatican diplomacy works on a timescale different from that of most governments: a generation or more ahead.

The practical purpose of Vatican diplomacy, which the Papacy claims is vital to the religious purpose, is to ensure the continued independence and influence of the Holy See and to encourage collaboration between states and local churches for the sake of the well-being of Catholic communities. Allied to this is the use of diplomacy for two-way communications between the Holy See and local Catholic churches, primarily between the Curia and the bishops.

The Vatican diplomatic system has had, and still has, its enemies on political grounds; some English and American bishops in the past have seen papal envoys as Roman spies, likely to spoil their personal relationships with their own faithful and their own governments. Critics of the system today argue that the Church should enhance the independence of the local Catholic churches, while strengthening the authority of the bishops, both nationally and in the central government of the Church. They see the powerful envoys and the strong Curia as undermining the progress of 'collegiality'. Certainly, papal envoys are from time to time at odds with the opinion of local Catholic communities and bishops; though some argue that this is often just as well. Nuncios often safeguard the independence of the local hierarchies or churches against oppression by providing channels of communications or appeal to the morally powerful centre in Rome. Delegates can often mediate between conflicting sections or opinions within the local churches. Both can extend the effectiveness of the Papacy's services as a mediating organization in international disputes.

Power in the relatively small diplomatic establishment of the Holy See is the most centralized in the world. Moreover, it is centralized in a single individual, the Pope, who shapes its exercise not only by the sense of his inheritance, which is profound, but also by his own religious and political experiences and by his emotional and intellectual make-up.

During the early stages of his pontificate, Karol Wojtyla, Pope John Paul II, showed how responsive is the entire apparatus of Vatican diplomacy to the will of the Pontiff. His ground plan for the development of Vatican influence, after an open-ended international début at the conference of Latin American bishops in Puebla, had the key features of Polish nationalism, 'Europeanism', religious freedom and human rights placed in the context of a humanist but conservative theology. The Pope believes that it is among the most vital needs of the Catholic Church in the modern world to seek accommodation with its greatest, because atheistic, enemy, Communism – but this will be done on the Church's own terms.

The assessment of the value to the cause of world peace and human dignity of the Vatican's energetic diplomacy has to be made in broad terms. Its explosive potential for the assertion of human rights in some parts of the world, especially where Catholics are numerically strong, was dramatically shown by the industrial and political upsurge of free trade unionism in Poland in 1980–81. In the cause of peace between nations, the Vatican offers its services as intermediary more often than they are sought after, but its ceaseless preaching of peace is at the least a constant reminder and reproach to the nations.

6
Speaking from Rome

The late Archbishop Roberts SJ, an *enfant terrible* of the Catholic Church in his ripe old age, once told me that he voted at the Second Vatican Council in favour of the document on the *Means of Social Communication* because it was so dreadful and the chances of improvement during the debates so slight that he simply hoped it would quickly pass into oblivion. The decree was in fact passed at the second session of the council by a vote of 1960 to 164. Its thinking was certainly simplistic and its language very tired. In 1971 it was supplemented by a more thoughtful and down-to-earth *Pastoral Instruction on the Means of Social Communication*, which confirmed the official approval and encouragement of the Catholic Church's own enthusiastic use of the mass media – television, radio, cinema and the press.

Throughout history, the attitude of the Papacy towards the freedom of communication has sometimes been ambivalent; but towards the means of communication it has usually been very positive. The essence of the purpose of the Catholic Church, and of the Papacy, armed with the Gospel – the Good News – is to communicate. Before literacy was widespread, the medieval Church used wall paintings to teach the dogmas of the faith. Bulls, briefs and encyclicals have poured out of the Vatican over the centuries. The Papacy's cultural interests have themselves been a means of communication, often accurately reflecting developments in theology and shifts in moral and political attitudes.

Raphael's paintings in the *Stanze* communicated the self-glorification of the Renaissance Papacy and its belief in the compatibility of classical humanism and Christianity. Pope Paul IV felt that Michelangelo's nudes in the Sistine were

163

communicating the wrong message altogether and, though he was dissuaded from having the *Last Judgement* destroyed, he commissioned Daniele da Volterra to paint draperies over the offending parts. (Daniele earned the nickname of *il braghettone*, the breeches-maker.) Not long after the rise of printing, the Polyglot Press in Rome was producing religious teaching material in many languages including Japanese. Among recent Popes, Pius XI was quick to welcome and use the technical possibilities of radio, and enlisted the help of Marconi himself. But modern means of communication have presented the Vatican with serious psychological problems as well as gratifying technical opportunities.

The Second Vatican Council debated the subject of the means or media of communication just a hundred years after Pope Pius IX published the *Syllabus of Errors*, which refused to contemplate the loss of the temporal power of the Popes, the separation of Church and State, religious toleration, or freedom of the press. The council's subsequent decisions and especially the largely American-inspired *Declaration of Religious Freedom*, revolutionized the formal intellectual position of the Church. But, as well as straining physical resources, the new attitudes can create emotional stresses in both the broad divisions of the communications activities of the Vatican. communications within the organizational structures of the Catholic Church, and communications with the outside world. The division is not clear-cut, and as usual in the Vatican various individuals and organizations cut across the boundaries.

The decree on the *Means [or Media] of Social Communication* (*Inter mirifica*) did not disappear like Orwellian Oldspeak. It recommended that Catholic bishops throughout the world should try to strengthen the Church's use of the media, partly through an annual fund-raising exercise, and that since the Pope had at hand 'a special office of the Holy See' dealing with social communication he should extend its competence to include all the media, including the press. The special office which suddenly and willingly found its horizons widened was a Vatican commission first started by the inexhaustible Pope Pius XII as the Pontifical Commission for Education and Religious Films. In 1964, Pope Paul VI re-styled it the Pontifical Commission for Social Communications and set it to tackle problems that concerned the Catholic faith in regard to cinema, radio, television, and the daily and periodical press. It has responsibility for the Vatican Film Library (first set up in 1959) and,the Vatican Press Office (established in 1968).

The Pontifical Commission is a permanent office of the Holy See formally attached to the Secretariat of State. Its non-executive members are selected by the Secretariat of State to serve for five years from among the cardinals and bishops, and include three presidents of official Catholic international communication organizations. A permanent staff of ten officials, headed by the Secretary, Fr. Romeo Panciroli, and including a friendly American, Dr Marjorie Weeke, is supported by thirty-six lay and clerical consultors from various parts of the world. The press office (*Sala Stampa della Santa Sede*) has a small staff, which is increased during special events.

The offices of the Pontifical Commission are inside the Vatican, in the Palazzo San Carlo, near the city's petrol pumps. Here the lovely, quiet little square by the side of St Peter's, with the Canons of St Peter's and the Palazzo San Carlo forming two of the other sides, shows Michelangelo at his best. On important ceremonial days, the square is full of life and bustle, as personalities of the Holy See, dressed gorgeously in purple or scarlet, arrive to greet and meet each other before going into the Basilica through the side entrance leading from the square.

The president of the commission, Archbishop Andrzej Maria Deskur, is a Pole in his late fifties and a close friend of the present Pope. On my first visit he suggested that we spoke in French, as English is only his seventh language. His family is French, and migrated to Poland.

A typical working day for the head of the commission includes meeting staff and colleagues; getting on top of the 'documentation' by reading newspapers and agency reports, and watching films and television; meeting bishops, communications experts of one kind or another, and other officials of the Curia; corresponding all over the world, chiefly with the hundred or so episcopal conferences of the Catholic Church and with Catholic professional organizations. Travel is essential, and during the twelve months before his illness Deskur visited the United States, West Germany, Australia and New Zealand.

In 1980, these duties were inherited by the likeable Scottish priest and broadcaster, Agnellus Andrew. He was appointed

165

vice-president of the commission with full executive authority. The title of president stayed with Deskur, as a matter of courtesy and affection, despite his incapacity, and he was created an archbishop.

Pope John Paul II pursued the new man for the job in his own way by inviting him first to celebrate Mass with him at 6.30 in the morning, and then to breakfast. The appointment came a few months later. Bishop Agnellus Andrew not only took over Deskur's arduous duties in a very sensitive area, but also inherited Deskur's profoundly elaborated philosophy of communications, which is very near to the Pope's own approach.

The problems of the Pontifical Commission for Social Communications are partly linguistic: Cardinal Gray, its senior member, once said it had a twenty-ninth language all of its own. But its real, as against technical, problems are those of the Papacy itself: how to communicate an essentially religious message to a world which finds religion, especially the institutional religion of Catholicism, difficult to comprehend.

The Holy See enjoys a unique double character for which there is no analogy. It is the central institution of the Church, and yet it has a national and cultural incarnation in all countries and civilizations. So over 700 million people live in the world with a sense of their own local identity and laws, and also with an international identity as Catholics. This latter is sometimes a great source of support; sometimes it provokes difficult confrontations.

Reflecting on this, Deskur cited Communist countries where the authorities cannot understand how people can have another juridical life, as well as that within the state. 'No other Church possesses the same unity and hierarchy as the Catholic Church. The Lutherans of Germany are in a federation with those of Poland; whereas the Catholic Church in Germany is co-responsible with that in Poland, and vice versa.'

The problems caused by this double vision among Catholics are compounded by the lack of correspondence between 'the modest bureaucratic structure of the Holy See and the expectations that people have of its active universal moral influence. Concerning all the "wrongs" in the world – the sufferings of the Jews under the Nazis, the blacks in South Africa, the Indians in America – the Holy See is expected to be ready to intervene. This is new. In the nineteenth century, the Pope was there for Catholics. . . . Now there is the idea of the Pope as a unique moral authority.'

Deskur complained to me with some asperity that, when the Popes have made pronouncements in their role of moral leaders to the world, their words have often been ignored. He cited Pius XI's encyclicals against Nazism (*Mit brennender Sorge*) and against Fascism (*Non abbiamo bisogno*) both in the vernacular languages of those to whom they were addressed, not in the usual Latin. None the less the disproportion between the means at the Pope's disposal and the tasks he was set was enormous. And that was especially so in the realm of communications.

Deskur saw his own personal concern as President of the Pontifical Commission for Social Communications as fostering a religious motivation in the world. 'Religion has lost its place in public interest and opinion compared with political and economic issues. It has access to the front pages of the newspapers only when political or economic matters are involved. The mission of the Holy See which we have to communicate is to recall that there is a life after death. This life makes sense only in relation to another life. The Church must work for social improvement, but we need to transmit our motivation. Otherwise we shall fail.

'I am optimistic because I am from an Eastern European country where it is evident that the attempt to limit a man in his religious needs always provokes a tremendous reaction. In the West, this is all difficult to explain.'

The 'other-worldliness' of the Church is basic to understanding the Holy See and the Curia. The degree to which it is emphasized or played down relates to some of the tensions in modern Catholicism, especially in Latin America. In May 1979, over the signatures of the Prefect and Secretary of the Sacred Congregation for the Doctrine of the Faith, a letter approved by the Pope was sent to all the Catholic bishops of the world summarizing the 'essentials' of the Church's faith in the matter of life after death.

The bewildering complex of organizations surrounding the Pope can be resolved by the functional implications of Deskur's analysis into a simple logical pattern.

The aim of the central bodies of the Holy See is to enable the

Pope to communicate with the world: hence the Secretariat of State, along with the Council for Public Affairs, and the office for papal audiences, and the collegial mechanism of the Pontifical Commission for Social Communications. The choice and collaboration of the bishops is vital to the mission of the Holy See: hence the Congregation for Bishops, the Congregation for the Evangelization of Peoples and the Congregation for the Eastern Churches (all collegial bodies). The structure must be braced with intellectual rigour: hence the Congregation for the Doctrine of the Faith.

The Communications Commission, chiefly a channel for the Holy See to the outside world, is also a spur to Catholic initiatives. The Secretary, Fr. Panciroli, a rather withdrawn, precise man, says that it is 'a matter of aiding the Catholic Church on national, continental and international levels to gain access to the modern means of communication and to profit from this access in a professional manner. We assist the organizations of the Holy See and the Catholic bishops of the entire world to adapt the organization of their dioceses to a world dominated by information.'

It was the patient Fr. Panciroli who drily carried out the dramatic task of announcing at a routine press conference in December 1979 that the Sacred Congregation of the Doctrine of the Faith had declared that, 'Professor Hans Küng, in his writings, has departed from the integral truth of Roman Catholic faith, and therefore he can no longer be considered a Catholic theologian or function as such in a teaching role.'

The commission's consultors represent nineteen, and its permanent staff nine, different nationalities. The commission's activities – covering the press office, audiovisual projects, the film library and the work of international coordination – incur annual expenses of about £100,000. Three times this is distributed by the various Catholic aid agencies for social communications projects in developing countries, on the recommendation of the commission.

The press office is on the edge of Vatican territory, between St Peter's Square and the Via della Conciliazione. Over 300 journalists are accredited to it, and the numbers have been rising steeply since the election of Pope John Paul II. It provides a weekly press conference, usually taken by Fr. Panciroli, and a daily news bulletin. Its publications include the various speeches of the Pope and the Acts of the Curial Congregations.

The atmosphere is relaxed most of the time, but hectic when the press and television descend in great numbers on the Vatican for, say, a meeting of the Bishops' Synod, or, as happened six times in the memorable year of the three Popes, for funerals, Conclaves and inauguration ceremonies.

'The aim of all of us is to be the voice of the Pope.' The sentiments of Fr. Tucci echo those of the staff at the Pontifical Commission for Social Communications, but the atmosphere is very different. In the Palazzo S. Carlo, the *monsignori* who glide through beautifully furnished and polished offices are neatly attired and smoothly decorous. Fr. Roberto Tucci's rather cramped office in the Palazzina of Leo XIII, in green and wooded surroundings at the top of the Vatican Hill, is cluttered with papers and the air is thick with tobacco smoke. Tucci is an intense but unbuttoned sort of man, originally from Naples, and with Scottish blood in his veins; he is grey-haired and his nut-brown face is very lined. He is the Director General of Vatican Radio, where he has worked since 1973. He used to be the editor of the Jesuit fortnightly *La Civiltà Cattolica*, and is clearly an intellectual to the core, though he loves talking technical jargon about the radio.

Most of the thirty Jesuits working full-time for Vatican Radio live close to the Vatican in a Jesuit community, together with other Jesuits mainly occupied with historical research on the order. 'There is a contrast between the serious scholars and the irregulars,' Fr. Tucci jokes. 'They say, "You are merely journalists." We say, "You are still living in the sixteenth and seventeenth centuries." ' Five of the Jesuits working for Vatican Radio live in a little house in the Vatican grounds, looked after by a Jesuit brother.

Vatican Radio has always been under Jesuit direction. By statute, its four directors (the director general, the technical, programmes and news bulletin directors) are Jesuits. At present, all are Italian, but among the rest of the staff there is that rare phenomenon a Swedish Jesuit, and the central editorial office of Vatican Radio is the responsibility of a Spanish Jesuit. The Pope himself approves the choice of the director general; the Holy See appoints the other three directors from names put forward by the father general.

All the Jesuits working in Rome for the Holy See are covered by a 'convention' between the Secretariat of State and the order itself, not by service contracts. They have no pension rights, no entitlement to severance pay, and their salaries are meagre – 'about the same as an usher's', Fr. Tucci says. However, like most Italians, the Jesuits enjoy an annual bonus of pay for the 'thirteenth' month – *il tredecesimo*. 'We live in the spirit of the order,' Fr. Tucci comments, 'with a special vow of fidelity to the Pope. We live in a community and, as we want to serve the Holy See, we are proud to do so, no matter if it's for so little.' This system may play havoc with differentials for Vatican Radio employees who are not Jesuits, but it is another bolt securing the centralization of Vatican communications policies.

Vatican Radio's administrative offices are mostly inside the Vatican or adjoining the main studios in the Palazzo Pio in the Via della Conciliazione, a modern marbled building in white stone. The technical control centre is where Roberto Tucci has his office, in the Palazzina, a converted and extended medieval tower which once housed the Vatican Observatory, and where the radio's first studios were built. Near the tower (where there are also studios, a chapel, and connections with the city's public address system) is the Vatican City's radio transmitter, planned by Marconi and today, after successive improvements, used in conjunction with transmitters at Santa Maria di Galeria. Here, about eleven miles from Rome in tranquil grounds that enjoy diplomatic immunity and are ten times the area of Vatican City itself, is the rather bleak main transmitting centre opened in 1957 by Pope Pius XII.

Vatican Radio broadcasts in short bursts of programmes rarely lasting over fifteen minutes each, chiefly to Europe (ranging from the USSR to Ireland), then (in order of number of programmes) to Africa, America, Asia and Australasia. The international broadcasts in one or more languages (chiefly English followed by French and Spanish) include news bulletins, religious programmes, music and commentaries and of course the Mass, which is broadcast every day live in Latin from inside the Vatican, with the lessons in different European languages, especially Slav languages.

Thirty-six regional language programmes are broadcast in thirty-two languages, sixteen in programmes for East and Central Europe. The non-European languages are Amharic,

Tigrina, Arabic, Chinese, Japanese, Hindi, Malayalam and Tamil. Most of the languages relate to areas where there is little or no religious freedom. A half-hour programme of varied feature material is broadcast to China every day in Mandarin, and a complete weekly Mass in Mandarin was started in 1980. However, according to Fr. Tucci, Vatican Radio is not obsessed simply with reaching Communist countries. 'If the Church refuses to be docile under a Fascist regime, then it will be put under censorship. This applies to many countries in Latin America, for instance. Often, the bishops there cannot reach their own people. So we try to inform the local churches about what is happening in their own area, as well as what is happening in the Vatican.'

The general aim of Vatican Radio is to provide a strong bond between the Pope and the Holy See and local Catholic churches throughout the world. This means more than straightforward religious coverage because of the Holy See's growing determination to involve itself in all areas of human rights. Other 'targets' of the radio are encouraging communication within the Catholic Church, as it tends towards increasing decentralization, and providing for Christian communities of some robust, even old-style, 'apologetics' – 'to help those poor people,' Fr. Tucci says, 'who are being attacked by atheists all the time, especially in the name of science'.

The feedback from listeners is fascinating. Nuns in Yugoslavia distribute the Eucharist with their radio set on the altar, tuned to the Vatican. When Dubcek was in power in Czechoslovakia, 14 per cent of the population regularly listened to Vatican Radio; presumably more do so today. Letters arrive constantly from Eastern Europe, usually sent to box numbers in Italy, 'as a letter addressed to the Vatican invites censorship or the wastebin'. Letters may be signed 'from a Christian living in Carpathia'; but the Poles are never anonymous. The Japanese, to whom Vatican Radio broadcasts three times a week, respond very eagerly in five or six hundred letters a month. Another feedback comes in the shape of gifts from the faithful – a Philips transmitter from the Dutch in 1950, a Telefunken transmitter from Cardinal Frings of Cologne in 1961, and, as gifts from the late Cardinal Spellman, the American Knights of Columbus and other American

benefactors respectively, three RCA transmitters in 1966.
Vatican Radio has a full-time staff of 260 people from thirty-
five different countries. Over sixty of them, including ten
nuns, are in religious orders, twenty-eight are secular priests,
thirty-five are laymen and thirty lay women.

Finance for expansion is one of Fr. Tucci's headaches.
Vatican Radio, like the BBC, which it resembles in many ways,
is non-commercial but claims to be economical. 'We are
worried by inflation and high technical costs. Since 1972 we
have more than doubled our hours of transmission, however,
and we employ only thirty-five more people. In fact, we are
very economical: a minute of Vatican transmission costs about
four or six times less than a minute of Swiss or Canadian
transmission, though they use far fewer languages than us. . . .'

The Vatican Radio budget (which is large in Vatican terms,
but small for an international broadcasting centre) is the
responsibility of the *Governatorato*, the administration of the
Vatican City State. The Secretariat of State also oversees Fr.
Tucci as its delegate responsible for the programmes. News
about the Holy See can be censored, if 'delicate negotiations'
are in progress, for example; otherwise, Vatican Radio is
allowed discretion, and of course discretion means that the
staff are carefully selected. Fr. Tucci recalls that a few years ago
some of the East Europeans working for the radio were
unhappy about the Vatican's *ostpolitik* – the *rapprochement* with
Communist régimes. 'When this sort of disagreement happens,
we discuss the problem. In this case we tried to convince them
of the need to be more prudent, to take a softer line.'

The Director General of Vatican Radio is answerable to two
Vatican authorities. The governing board – *Direzione Generale* –
comes under the aegis of the Vatican City State, whereas Fr.
Tucci is personally a delegate of the Holy See's Secretariat of
State. He serves on several international organizations as the
representative of the city state. As Vatican Radio is also the
radio for the Holy See, he can be given directives by the
Secretariat for State – for example, to extend a particular
programme.

Vatican Radio is a professional organization run by men and
women whose vocations are deeply religious, which makes
them exceptionally sensitive to criticism from within as well as
from outside the Vatican. They work at the centre of a highly

stretched communications system, where the tensions can mount very sharply. However, they share feelings of intense loyalty to the person of the Pope in the Vatican, and this sentiment is an effective lightning conductor for flashes of exasperation caused by sometimes conflicting responsibilities, loyalties and emotions. Fr. Tucci believes that the Vatican's own internal communications have improved during recent years. There is better access to the curial departments, he says; there is more coordination and less conflict: the Vatican Press Office, Vatican Radio and the *Osservatore Romano* are in his experience working together more happily than they did.

The offices and printing works of the Vatican's group of newspapers and publications have been since 1929 in a long, squat brick building in the Via del Pellegrino, a few hundred yards from the Porta Sant'Anna. The most important publication, the *Osservatore Romano*, is a daily newspaper founded in 1861. It is owned by the Holy See and, like the press office and Vatican Radio, is directly answerable to a department of the Secretariat of State – the Office of Information and Documentation – on policy matters, and to the Administration of the Patrimony of the Holy See with regard to finance and administration. It is a thoroughly 'official' publication, administered like the Vatican Polyglot Press by a religious order, the Salesian Congregation of Saint John Bosco.

In collaboration with the Secretariat of State, the Salesians appoint the director of the newspaper, who combines the roles of chief executive and editor-in-chief. The present director is an academic, Professor Valerio Volpini, who has two priests as assistant director and editorial secretary respectively, and an editorial board of ten, of whom three are priests. Since 1971, the management has been split between the editorial and the technical and printing sides of the enterprise.

Professor Volpini runs a sizeable press and publicity empire: the *Osservatore Romano* is published daily at 3.00 p.m., and there are weekly editions in English, French, Spanish, Portuguese, German, Italian and Polish. Each of these has its own editor. Two are laymen and four are priests, including a Portuguese Jesuit and an Irish Dominican. The group employs

173

no overseas correspondents but for special coverage can call on the Church's episcopal conferences throughout the world, and on informal collaborators.

The *Osservatore Romano* is a good-looking, rather staid, publication. It carries very little advertising in the weekly editions, some in the daily, and with a circulation of about 50,000 for the daily edition in Italian has had a rough time financially.

Editorially, the newspaper has always been a most loyal and pugnacious defender of the Papacy, even at times *plus papiste que le Pape*, if one credits, for example, the story that Pope John Paul I's use of 'I' as his personal pronoun was regularly changed to 'we' in its columns. At any rate, its approach is signified by the two mottoes on the masthead referring to the rupture with Italy in 1870: *'Unicuique suam'* ('To each his own') and *'non praevalebunt'* ('They shall not prevail'). The paper is valuable as a record of nearly everything the Pope says and does; it prints, for example, the packed lists of his daily engagements, his appointments of bishops and officials, and full texts of his speeches. On the whole, despite its conservative and pietistic bias, it is a good barometer of Vatican political weather, and occasionally it carries an article of serious political significance or historical importance.

With its semi-official status, the *Osservatore Romano* often needs subtle interpretation. It is obviously useful for publishing the Court Circular and the official texts of papal speeches. (In this regard, it was said at the beginning of Pope Paul VI's reign that the newspaper would print speeches as drafted for the Pope without checking against delivery, so everything Pope Paul actually wrote himself for his speeches was automatically excluded; the editor then had to attend with the galley proofs of all papal speeches for them to be passed by the Pope before they were printed.)

Editorials are especially important if they are unsigned, when they are usually 'inspired' at a high level, and often by the Pope. One is told to interpret three asterisks as denoting an 'inspired' text, rather like a starred brandy.

The Vatican Polyglot Press, which used to be the parent organization of the *Osservatore Romano*, is officially classified, along with the newspapers, the board of St Peter's (the Reverenda Fabbrica di San Pietro), the Secret Archives, the

Vatican Library, and the Vatican Publishing House (*Libreria Editrice Vaticana*) as part of the *Amministrazioni Palatine*. The press and the publishing house's publications, invariably finely printed, in a large number of languages, range from liturgical books to official news-sheets.

A large quantity of printed matter emanates from the Sacred Congregation for the Evangelization of Peoples –Propaganda Fide – almost a Vatican within the Vatican, situated on the piazza at the bottom of the Spanish Steps; it includes missionary publications and documentation and, in French, German, English, Italian and Spanish, the publications of the Fides International News Agency printed on its own premises. For the Secretariat of State, the Vatican Publishing House produces the *Acta Apostolicae Sedis*, a monthly bulletin which contains the Pope's encyclicals and the acts, or laws, of the Holy See, which come into force three months after publication. The *Annuario Pontificio*, also printed and published for the Secretariat of State, is a compendious and essential yearbook in a bright red cover. A good half of its 1000 or so pages is a complete list of all the Catholic bishops throughout the world. The index of names at the back includes all the *monsignori* (the mode of address for clerical office bearers of all sorts). Vatican officials and the diplomatic representatives account for a fairly small part of the book. Its hierarchical arrangement and detail make it a perfect introduction to the traditional mentality and sociology of the Vatican. A separate and more detailed diplomatic list is published annually.

The *Annuario Pontificio* is complemented by the yearly publication *L'Attività* della Santa Sede, a comprehensive, illustrated account of the activities of the Holy See and the city state.

Despite the power and initiatives of the congregations, the development of 'collegiality', the gradual internationalization of the Curia, and the decentralization of the Church, the animating principle of the Vatican's communications system is still the presence of 'the Holy Father'. The words of the traditional papal blessing – *urbi et orbi* (to the city and the world) – derive from a legal context, the affixing of papal rescripts to the gates of the Vatican. The Pope is Bishop of Rome, Vicar of Christ, Successor of the Prince of the Apostles, Supreme Pontiff of the Universal Church, Patriarch in the West, Primate of Italy, Metropolitan of the Roman Province and Sovereign of the State of Vatican City. He has to use innumerable channels of communication, for an immense variety of purposes.

Everyone within the Vatican itself is within walking distance, though a car takes the Pope to the audience hall and the helicopter pad, or a visitor up the hill to Vatican Radio. The Holy See telephone directory is a magnificent work, with a bizarre list of extensions, including sundry tombs and altars in St Peter's. The Swiss Guards have special problems in answering the ubiquitous telephone when they are wearing helmets and starched neck-ruffs. In the days of Pius XII, it is said, devout nuns would kneel to carry on a telephone conversation with His Holiness. Certainly, a large measure of informal consultation between the Pope and his closest advisers takes place on the phone. It is impossible to assess the relative importance and the frequency of the Pope's contacts with various high officials simply from the published records (in the *Osservatore Romano*) of his formal meetings. These meetings, none the less, given the hierarchical structure of the Vatican City State and the Holy See, are essential if the system is to function efficiently. As a matter of routine, the cardinals at the head of the congregations, sometimes with their secretaries, meet the Pope at least once a month for at least an hour. The Cardinal Secretary of State, the *Sostituto* and the Secretary of the Council for the Public Affairs of the Church see him almost daily, though these continual meetings are not listed. Ceremonial occasions apart, there are regular meetings of all the curial cardinals in the Apostolic Palace over which the Cardinal Secretary of State presides and which Pope John Paul II has been in the habit of attending. Apart from informal contacts, there is, as we have seen, a high degree of cross-fertilization within the Curia through the 'multiple director-ships' held by most senior Vatican officials.

Towards the Pope himself, there is a dogged protective tendency on the part of those close to him. The flexibility and openness of the Vatican's internal system of communications depends on the Pope's own character and strength of purpose, and there are occasional conflicts. I remember being told by an exasperated American bishop in the Curia, when John XXIII was Pope, that His Holiness spent too long talking to ordinary people and not signing his papers. Pope John Paul II has tended to let the bureaucratic machine function in its traditional way, while concentrating on his international pastoral and political role.

Most of the visits paid to the Pope are formal, but through the force and spontaneity of his character the Pope can turn these into sources of useful information or occasions for imparting significant decisions, advice or warnings. One of the most regular and important of the Pope's engagements is the reception of bishops making their *ad limina* visit to Rome. Bishop Jacques Martin, the Prefect of the Pontifical Household, calls these visits the essential '*métier du Pape . . .*' – the Pope's real business. They derive from the ancient practice of the *Visitatio ad Limina Apostolorum*, the duty that grew in the early days of the Church for the bishops to visit the tombs of the Apostles SS. Peter and Paul in Rome. In the sixteenth century it was made a positive law, and today each bishop of a diocese sends in a report every five years and presents himself in person every ten years. The report is sent round the relevant congregations on whom the bishop must also call, and their comments are ready for the actual *ad limina* discussion at the end of the bishop's visit. Traditionally, each bishop received a private interview. Pope Paul VI started to group the bishops, and to use group meetings for formal messages or speeches about their countries. In some cases, such as Ireland and Poland (from both of which the bishops were due for their *ad limina* in the year when Pope John Paul II was elected), discussions can be held with all the bishops of a single country at once.

During the last years of the pontificate of Paul VI, because of the Pope's state of health and age, the bishops would be seated round him in a semicircle to conduct their dialogue. The present Pope walks freely among them, but always makes a formal address, generally of an exhortatory nature, after receiving an address of homage. The meetings give the Pope an opportunity to show how his own thinking and that of the Curia may be developing on particular problems, such as the need for more vocations to the priesthood. The visiting bishops may also seize the opportunity to ask for a visit from the Pope, as the Irish did in 1977.

An important development in the communications system of the Vatican and the Catholic Church has been the launching of the Synod of Bishops by Pope Paul VI as a central ecclesiastical institution for the 3000 bishops. It comes under the authority of the Pope, who has the right to set its agenda and fix its sessions. According to the document in which Pope Paul established the synod (*Apostolica Sollicitudo*), it is to encourage:

> . . . close union and valued assistance between the Sovereign Pontiff and the bishops of the entire world; to ensure that direct and real information is provided on questions and situations touching upon the internal action of the Church and its necessary activity in the world of today; to facilitate agreement on essential points of doctrine and on methods of procedure in the life of the Church.

The synod meets every three years, and the bishops are able to forward suggestions for the agenda.

The Pope is the president of the synod. Its first secretary general was Bishop (now Cardinal) Wladyslaw Rubin, Rector of the Polish Hospice for priests at Rome in Via della Botteghe Oscure, who became Prefect of the Congregation for the Eastern Churches in 1980. The permanent staff is tiny, and the secretary general's Council of Advisers (with twelve members elected by the bishops in their assembly and three nominated by the Pope) has a mandate that lasts from one assembly of the synod to the next. The present Pope was an elected member of the Inter-Synod Committee of Bishops and chose Cardinal Hume as his successor.

The number of bishops attending the synod depends on the size of the hierarchy. Thus Italy and the United States send four delegates each – the maximum possible. So, surprisingly, does Britain, the four being made up of two from England and Wales, one from Scotland and a half-share in the two from Ireland.

Meetings of the synod since the first in 1967, attended usually by about two hundred bishops, have discussed theological research and canon law; the nature of 'collegiality'; the priesthood, and justice in the world; evangelization in the modern world; catechesis or religious education; and, in 1980,

Christian family life. 'Particular' synods are held from time to time, such as the assembly held in January 1980 to tackle the vexed problems of the divided Dutch Church.

The synod, so far, has not caught the imagination of ordinary Catholics. Its debates on evangelization in 1974 lasted three weeks, at the end of which papers were left with the Pope, who eventually produced his own impressive documentation on the subject. The 1977 Synod on Catechesis did produce the assembly's first publicly issued statement (*A Message to the People of God*), as well as two documents presented to the Pope. The 1980 Synod on the Christian Family produced 168 set speeches by the bishops and a set of 'propositions' reserved for the consideration of the Pope. It was a useful meeting of minds; it prompted several thoughtful 'interventions'. But it largely evaded the tension within parts of the Church on subjects such as birth control; and it ignored the theological tug-of-war between those who would foster its role in 'collegiality', the sharing of powers of decision.

The synod arouses strong views across a wide spectrum of thought. One curial cardinal, when I asked him his opinion, reminded me, perhaps teasingly, that when King Henry VIII broke with Rome only one bishop stayed loyal to the Pope. Less ultramontane Catholics would like the synod to become more formally responsible with the Pope in the government of the Church, and, incidentally, to be served more directly by the Roman Curia.

The Pope never misses the opportunity, in his many audiences and discussions, not only to hear what the world may want to say to him, but to reiterate the themes of his pontificate in speeches that are subsequently released to the press and gain a wide circulation. One of the grand occasions in the Pope's calendar, for example, is the regular New Year meeting in the Consistory Hall of the Apostolic Palace with all the members of the diplomatic corps accredited to the Holy See. The Pope's response to an address of homage from the doyen of the corps invariably touches on the Vatican's campaign for human rights and religious freedom, its horror of the violence in specific areas of the world, and perhaps some of his own plans for travel for the forthcoming year.

The most important set occasion, usually just before the

diplomats' meeting, is when the College of Cardinals calls to pay its collective Christmas and New Year greetings. At this, Pope Paul would make a general review of church activities during the previous year, usually covering everything systematically.

Following his example in many ways, Pope John Paul II has shown from the first days of his pontificate, when he returned to Poland, a determination to extend the influence of the Holy See through personal visits abroad: in 1978–9 alone, Latin America, Poland, Ireland, the United States and Turkey. The purpose of this unprecedented form of personal communication on the part of two of the most recent Popes is to inform themselves, to confirm faith and loyalty among Catholics, and, one senses, to fulfil an inner compulsion to pay witness personally to the universality of the Holy See. As he flew over their air space on his way to Zaire in 1980, the Pope sent telegrams to the heads of state of all the countries on his route.

The general audiences the Pope gives to large crowds in the Vatican every Wednesday and at which he delivers impromptu greetings and a formal address which is subsequently printed and distributed are also aimed, with a mixture of calculation and simplicity, at securing worldwide hearing. It is a unique form of communication: the personality and mystique of the white-robed figure of the Pope; the emotional response of the crowd, in which patriotic or nationalistic fervour is invariably demonstrated in conjunction with Catholic faith; the repetition by the Pope week after week of the fundamental teachings of the Gospel and their application to contemporary events; the diffusion of the message, or the recounting of the experience, by thousands on their return home.

The Pope's Wednesday speeches provide eloquent testaments to the spiritual leadership asserted by the Vatican. They are drafted by the Curia to the Pope's brief, as are the addresses he delivers at international conferences and indeed all of the formal statements he makes. But though their curial style (an abstract language based on the norms of Latin rhetoric) can betray their origins, the formal communications of the Pope are utterly his responsibility, checked and amended by him, sometimes rejected in their first draft. A significant example of papal changes in a draft is Pope Paul's sermon at the Canonization of the Forty Martyrs. The passage about the

Church of England as a 'sister church' was a very late insertion by Pope Paul himself.

The same holds true for the Pope's encyclicals, among the oldest form of papal communication, which command the highest historical and theological status of all pronouncements from the Vatican. They originated when the Papacy was young as circular letters sent to those in communion with the Holy See to clarify doctrine, for example, or to commend their bearers. They are the most formidable of the Pope's battery of 'Letters Apostolic' which also include papal constitutions (about discipline or doctrine); bulls (nowadays, usually about appointments or canonizations and including one from John Paul II naming St Francis the patron of ecology); briefs (about ecclesiastical grants and concessions); rescripts (responses to requests for favour); decrees (from the Curia, approved by the Pope); *motu proprio* (the Pope's personal acts); and *chirographi* (messages in the Pope's own handwriting).

The encyclicals are the richest source for establishing the authoritative beliefs of the Roman Catholic Church through the *magisterium* or teaching authority of the Popes. During the past century, they have covered an increasingly wide field of human thought, particularly the concern of the Catholic Church to clarify its own nature and its relationship with the international community of nations and peoples. Pope Paul VI issued seven encyclicals, ending with *Humanae Vitae*, after which he preferred other forms, such as apostolic exhortations, of which *Evangelii Nuntiandi* – 'Evangelization in the Modern World' – is the most important.

John Paul II's first encyclical was published five months after he became Pope.* *Redemptor Hominis* (the first two words of the message – 'The Redeemer of Mankind' – are the title of the encyclical) is a lengthy discourse on the role of the Church in the modern world, confirming the universal dimension of the Papacy's communications and mission. It was addressed as from the Supreme Pontiff to 'his Venerable Brothers in the Episcopate, the Priests, the Religious Families, the Sons and Daughters of the Church and to all Men and Women of good will. . . .'

---

* The second encyclical of John Paul's pontificate – a sequel to the first – appeared in December 1980 entitled *Dives in Misericordia* (rich in mercy).

Throughout the Catholic Church the Pope's office guarantees him an almost automatic reverence and hearing. The present Pope has raised the popularity of the Pontiff and his power to communicate to higher levels than ever before. The readiness to enhance the position of the Pope and the Holy See through the harnessing of exceptional personal qualitites attracts criticism. Sometimes this springs from emotional distaste at hearing, for example, excited cries of '*È Jesu Cristo rivenuto*' – 'It is Jesus Christ come back' – around the new Pope not long after his election; more fairly and seriously, it comes from the conviction that the healthy progress of decentralization in the Catholic Church is being dangerously hampered.

If they criticize, the fellow bishops of the Pope tend to murmur about the policies of the Curia rather than the Pope. I have heard several papal diplomats complaining that their own ministry in the Vatican is slack in keeping them up-to-date with important developments relevant to their local responsibilities. But most bishops, as Cardinal Heenan once said, want to keep out of the engine room.

7
In the Service of the Church

Rome is packed with centres of teaching and administration for the whole of the Catholic Church. As well as the Pontifical Academies, the nearly thirty ecclesiastical colleges of different nationalities and about twenty colleges for advanced studies for priests, there are over fifty colleges of the religious orders, scores of convents, and headquarters of many of the religious orders.

The Sacred Congregation for Religious and for Secular Institutes, the Sacred Congregation for the Clergy, the Sacred Congregation for the Propagation of the Faith, and the Sacred Congregation for Catholic Education are among the curial departments supervising and coordinating the massive international activities these institutions represent. Their formal and informal relationships with the Holy See and the Supreme Pontiff are complex, subtle and highly differentiated.

At 5 Borgo San Spirito, a narrow road parallel to the Via della Conciliazione and a few minutes' walk from the Apostolic Palace, is the headquarters of the most highly centralized of all the religious orders, the Society of Jesus. Here in a bare reception room adorned only with one religious picture and a crucifix, I have discussed the mission of the Jesuits and their links with the Papacy with the Superior General of the Order, Fr. Pedro Arrupe. The surroundings show a characteristic Jesuit disregard for appearances and comfort.

Fr. Arrupe, always dressed in black, is a tiny, slightly hunched, white-faced Spaniard from the Basque country, delicate in appearance, but bursting with nervous intellectual and physical energy, and with a most captivating smile. He was

183

in Japan during the Second World War and witnessed the atomic explosion in Hiroshima. He loves music, especially Wagner and Verdi. He himself used to sing in concerts, in a tenor or baritone. But he is 'rusty' now, he says; too busy to sing or even to see much of Rome where he lives. 'I have to relax with Heaven. . . .' Keeping him busy are heavy duties of world travel and consultation, which have grown ever more stressful in times of unprecedented change and pressures on the society. Fr. Arrupe spends about ten and a half months a year with his 'Curia' in Rome, the rest of the time travelling among the 28,000 Jesuits in 107 countries. He is Vice-Chancellor of the Jesuits' Gregorian University and President of the Union of Superior Generals, serving on the General Council of the Pontifical Commission for Latin America, and on Propaganda Fide.

As Superior General of the Jesuits, head of the day-to-day government of the entire order, Fr. Arrupe was elected for life in 1965 by a general congregation of the order. General congregations, which have supreme legislative power, subject to the Pope, meet irregularly and at long intervals. The last one was called by Fr. Arrupe in 1974. He is the twenty-eighth superior general since the Society of Jesus was founded by another Basque, the ex-soldier and saint Ignatius Loyola. His four assistants are elected by the general congregation, and he appoints a dozen territorial counsellors for different areas of the work. But, he says, 'I am no autocrat.'

The fourth vow of the Jesuits is one of special obedience to the Pope, in which the promise is made to undertake any mission required. The religious and juridical closeness of the society to the Papacy creates an emotional and sometimes tense relationship. In the eighteenth century it was for many years actually suppressed by a Pope. A zealous papal eye is kept on its conduct and discipline – including censorship – often exercised in regard to its affairs. In Rome, many of the hundred or so Jesuits, of twenty or more different nationalities, work in key positions in the Vatican, running Vatican Radio and the observatory, for instance, or the Gregorian University, or as consultors to many of the curial departments and publishers of the important *Civiltà Cattolica*.

Problems arise not so much at the centre as out in the field of the Jesuits' activities, where their motto *ad majorem dei gloriam* –

to the greater glory of God – propels the invariably well-educated, highly trained members of the society into wide-ranging activities in education, in parish and social work, in the areas of so-called charismatic renewal, in missions in developing countries, in fresh contacts with China, in revolutionary atmospheres in Latin America. They are often on the dangerous edge of events and processes: intellectually in theology and education, for example, as well as physically in unstable or repressive parts of the world that have included Zimbabwe–Rhodesia, the Philippines, Chile and Guyana. From the centre, and from their own intellectual formation, comes the pressure to move swiftly in adapting their methods and behaviour to keep abreast of the times. Fr. Arrupe says, 'The whole world is in a ferment and sometimes we must take calculated risks.' On the other hand, the Jesuit is especially dedicated to the service of Popes who tend to move with conservative circumspection. So the strains occur.

Several times in recent years, Pope Paul VI admonished the Society of Jesus for lack of balance among some of its members, and Fr. Arrupe has had to face some icy-cold winds blowing from the Vatican. In 1979, Pope John Paul II saw Fr. Arrupe and all the society's assistant generals and regional superiors, and told them that the Jesuits had not been spared from the crises which had troubled religious life 'causing disorientation among the Christian people and worry to the Church, to the hierarchy and also personally. . . .'

In 1980, Fr. Arrupe began the process which would have led to his resignation, but was asked by the Pope to remain in office for the time being. In resigning, the Superior General of the Jesuits would summon a general congregation of the society, and the Pope felt that this would be inopportune. The Pope's request may have pointed to his wish to demonstrate confidence in Fr. Arrupe, but it underlined the delicacy of their relationship and the difference in their styles of religious government.

When we met, before the news of his intended resignation, Fr. Arrupe gently waved away any question of serious rifts between himself and Paul VI or John Paul II. The pattern of his routine relations with Pope John Paul II was still to be established, but he stressed the important role the Jesuits traditionally played, and would still play, as close advisers to

185

the Popes on special matters. This was a 'service', springing from the society's deep-rooted allegiance to the Papacy, that was too little known and appreciated. 'We are so different from the Machiavellian image we wear in history. Our fulfilment is work, the whole gamut of work, for the Church, and therefore for the whole of mankind.'

Through the Jesuits (whose numbers are falling, though recruitment has been rising after a decade of sharp decline), the Catholic Church can ensure a presence among new movements throughout the world. They muster religious troops who can be swiftly dispatched to different fronts. They are neither homogeneous nor monolithic, despite their carefully structured hierarchy; but the eagerness of many of them to be theologically or politically daring often gets them into trouble with governments, with local bishops, with the Roman Curia itself. So, from time to time – through pressure on the publication *Civiltà Cattolica*, for example, or through stern orders from the Pope – the reins are tugged in.

Pope John Paul II gave a sharp twitch in the reins, in fact, in the autumn of 1979. After a meeting with the Pope, Fr. Arrupe wrote to Jesuit superiors throughout the world noting that the past two Popes and now the present one were calling for their attention. The matters needing special concern were secularizing tendencies, austerity and discipline in religious and community life, fidelity to the *magisterium* (the teaching authority of the Papacy) in doctrine, and the priestly character of a Jesuit's apostolic work, as well as the formation of young Jesuits.

There are about 7000 Dominican friars (fathers and unordained 'cooperator brothers') throughout the world – what, in less democratic times, used to be called the 'First Order' – and over 4000 contemplative nuns of the former 'Second Order'. In addition, the former 'Third Order', organized in very diverse fraternities, regular and lay, includes as many as 42,000 sisters (distributed in over 150 congregations) and at least 70,000 diocesan priests and lay people.

In Rome, Dominicans are most noticeable in the Congregation for the Doctrine of the Faith (the former Holy Office, along with the Index of Prohibited Books, was once virtually a Dominican preserve); in the membership of many of the other curial departments; in the theological college, the Angelicum (the Pontifical University of St Thomas Aquinas); and at the headquarters of the order, in the convent of Santa Sabina, Piazza Pietro d'Illiria, on the Aventine Hill. The church there was given by Pope Honorius III to St Dominic for a convent in the thirteenth century, shortly after he had founded the order. The Master of the Dominican Order, Fr. Vincent de Couesnongle, hurried into a rather musty, whitewashed reception room to welcome me to Santa Sabina, as soon as he had finished watching the Pope on television, delivering his 1979 speech to the United Nations. Even the French find it difficult to pronounce his name. He is a Breton, with a strong provincial accent. He wears the white habit of a Dominican, with scapula and capuce, a leather belt with a fifteen-decade rosary fastened to it, and shiny black shoes. He is a short man, with closely cut hair, brown-rimmed glasses and small features on a broad face, reticent for the first few moments, and then, like a preacher getting into his stride, voluble, emphatic, declamatory, explosive, as he talked about the Dominicans and the part they play.

A former professor of moral theology at Lyons. Fr. de Couesnongle was elected master of the order in 1974, for a nine-year term of office. He oversees the order with the help of several assistants dealing with individual regions of the world and two dealing with general apostolic and educational work respectively. He spends about five months a year visiting Dominican communities around the world.

The constitution of the Dominicans is as loaded with checks and balances as that of the USA. The mendicant friars take one single vow to obey their superiors and the master according to the rule and constitutions of the order. This puts the emphasis on both obedience and flexibility. There are three tiers of authority: the master, in charge of the whole order; the provincials, responsible for the provinces; and the priors, at the head of their houses, called priories. There are also Congregations of Dominicans, under vicars, sometimes with no territorial identity. Except for the vicars, all the superiors at each level are elected by the chapters of the relevant jurisdiction: provincials for four years and priors for three. The choice of prior has to be approved by the provincial.

There is a meeting of the order every three years. The

process is intricate and politically ingenious. The provincials and the *diffinitori* (*elected* representatives from the provinces) meet together in an elective chapter; three years later, there is a chapter only of the representatives; three years later, a general chapter only of the provincials. This last, it is scandalously said, being made up of practical men, usually unscrambles the work of the dreamy 'difinitors'. However that may be, the nine-year cycle – the next elective chapter is in 1983 – sustains the balance between specially elected representatives and constitutionally strong though elected provincials.

Rigid control of the Dominicans by the master or the Pope is clearly impossible. When the master does need to act in important matters, he must have the support of the provincials. The Popes, whenever there have been problems with the order – and its history has been stormy and brilliant – have scarcely known which way to turn: in the eighteenth century, Benedict XIV, rummaging for a solution, made himself personally its protector to ensure that it remained loyal to its constitutions.

The Pope remains the 'protector' of the Dominicans. But on a day-to-day basis papal authority is exercised through the master of the order (not through the bishops, as the Dominicans are an exempt order), most Vatican business with the order being done through the Congregation for Religious or through the Congregation for the Doctrine of the Faith. The dispensations granted from the vow of celibacy, which Pope John Paul stopped granting, went through the latter.

There have been several squalls at Rome over Dominican behaviour in recent years. During the 'worker priest' movement in France in the 1950s, which the Curia feared had become dangerously radical, the French provincials of the order resigned *en bloc* to forestall the threat of suppression. Pope Pius XII insisted that the very conservative Irish theologian Fr. (later Cardinal) Michael Browne should be elected master of the order; otherwise he might change its constitution. The French Dominican theologian Yves Congar then gave it as his opinion that such an event would release the Dominicans from their vows, because the rules would have been altered without the consent of the brethren. More recently, the Congregation for the Doctrine of the Faith, after lengthy negotiations through the master, condemned a theological book by a French Dominican priest, Fr. Jacques Pohier, and applied sanctions against his teaching in public because of his views on the nature of the Resurrection of Christ. This was the first intervention of such a kind in the Church since the Second Vatican Council.

'We are the dustbin of the order,' said one Dominican friar, commenting on the work of the order's headquarters on the Aventine. But most of the liaison with the Vatican is routine and untroubled, carried out through one of the master's thirty-strong staff, the procurator general, Fr. Rafael Moya.

The chief concern of the master of the order is with 'looking after the brethren in our forty-two provinces throughout the world'. Like Fr. Arrupe, the master is eloquent on the staggering pace of change in the modern world, no longer a religious but an atheistic world. He hammers the need for the education of all Dominicans to be adaptable and flexible in their minds and emotions to constantly shifting human realities. He has no mean sense of the importance of the order to and beyond the boundaries of the Catholic Church. In terms of numbers alone, he says, think of the importance of all those tens of thousands of Dominican sisters, teaching and bearing witness to God. 'Of every 250 Catholic women in the world, one is a religious.'

Vocations to the former 'First Order' are running at the rate of about two hundred a year, a third the level of twenty years ago. Since then, there has been a dramatic 24 per cent slump in the numbers of Dominican friars, caused by a combination of the fall in vocations, the dying-off of the men who entered during the 'vocations boom' before the First World War, the departures, and the fact that numbers entering in the 1950s were unusually high. Fr. de Couesnongle fears a 'crisis of hope' among the young entrants to the order, arising from the difficulties of making their traditional religious beliefs and attitudes relevant to the modern world: how to make sense of long-term commitment, how to find, and then effectively communicate, spiritual relevance in poverty, chastity, obedience. His own job, he comments, is to be a 'presence' for his brother Dominicans and to communicate what they are discovering in the world to the Vatican. 'We are concerned with the basic problems of life; at the top, everything becomes too abstract. The superiors general know more of the world than the bishops: they deal more closely with personal, human problems.'

The claim is echoed a few hundred yards distant from the convent of Santa Sabina, when you walk by the gardens which give a serene, panoramic view of Rome, and by the villa of the Grand Master of the Knights of Malta, to the Priory of Sant'Anselmo and the headquarters of the Benedictines.

Throughout the world there are over 10,000 Benedictine monks, about 9000 Benedictine nuns who have taken solemn vows, and about 12,000 Benedictine sisters and oblates, or lay associates. The Benedictine way of life is still based on St Benedict's Rule for his monks written at Monte Cassino in the sixth century. It gives instructions on how to form, govern and administer a monastery and on how the monks should conduct their day-to-day life, fusing spiritual and practical advice with astute and sensitive psychological insight. Through its insistence that monasteries should accept people of any age or class sprang the intimate and influential Benedictine association with education.

The Rule stresses the independence and autonomy of the single monastery; the monastic concept pre-dates the concept of an order of monks. Throughout their history, the Benedictines have tended to swarm away like bees to found new independent houses. But there has also been a centralizing tendency, partly through periodical pressures for reform and partly through the zealous interference of the Papacy.

In the thirteenth century, at the Lateran Council, the Benedictines were advised to set up provincial chapters following the example of the Dominicans and the Franciscans. These eventually produced national congregations, of which there are now twenty-one, covering 372 abbeys, priories and dependent houses. Another important centralizing move was made in the nineteenth century by Pope Leo XIII when he directed the Benedictines to set up an Abbots' Congress, under an abbot primate, to meet regularly in Rome, on the lines of the congresses of the other orders.

The Abbot Primate of the Benedictines is elected to the primacy of honour (not, it is stressed, of power or authority) by his fellow abbots and conventual priors throughout the world. He lives at Sant'Anselmo. The present abbot primate, Dom Viktor Dammertz, is a German from the Rhineland, elected for his term of office in 1977 after two years in charge of the missionary Congregation of St Ottilien. He came to the job with a reputation as an excellent canon lawyer, but with a pastoral rather than legalistic cast of mind. He shares Fr. de Couesnongle's vision of a Catholic Church that adapts its spirit and structures to the future, and he regards the Benedictine Rule as essentially flexible and adaptable to the complex problems of monasticism in the modern world. An efficient and straightforward negotiator, he has perhaps the least clearly defined, yet none the less important, role of all the heads of the religious orders in dealing with the Vatican.

The somewhat nebulous status of the abbot primate's position *vis à vis* the order and the Roman Curia springs from the fierce spirit of Benedictine independence, observable in tensions not only over organization but even over liturgical matters – for instance, how strong should be the insistence on a common breviary? For the Benedictines, as for the Catholic Church as a whole, the cycles of history bring now centralization, now an emphasis on autonomy. The Benedictines' instinct for the latter makes them stress that the abbot primate should communicate but not rule. An abbot primate and a centralized headquarters in Rome are against the Benedictine instinct.

The present abbot primate and his predecessor, Dom Rembert Weakland (now Archbishop of Milwaukee), have worked, against this background, to represent the Confederation of Benedictines in Rome and also to act as a bridge of communication between the various monasteries and national congregations, and have travelled extensively to keep in touch with local communities: Rembert Weakland visited over five hundred different monastic houses during ten years. Some of his fellow monks may have been surprised to see him. The former Prior of Sant'Anselmo, Dominic Milroy (who became headmaster of Ampleforth College in 1979), told me, 'I didn't actually know there was an abbot primate until I had been ten years in a monastery. . . .'

Ordinary contact between the Benedictines and the Vatican is through the priests appointed by each congregation as their procurator in Rome: the procurator approaches the appropriate curial department on matters ranging from, say, an abbot's request for the dispensation of a monk's vows to the prioress's suit for the Holy Father's blessing on the occasion of a nun's golden jubilee. Each congregation has the right to its own procurator to deal with matters that fall within the jurisdiction of the curial departments; in practice, procurators are often shared.

The job of the abbot primate is what he makes of it. Depending on the needs of the moment, he can concentrate either on the confederation's affairs in Rome (for example, the current revision of the code of canon law insofar as it concerns the monastic life) or in travelling to individual monasteries. Recent primates have made a point of visiting the more isolated or 'underprivileged' monasteries (for example in Communist countries of East Europe, or in the Third World) which are most in need of encouragement and of a sense of solidarity with the rest of the order. There is a loose and limited interface between the Vatican and the confederation as a whole. The monastic orders are anomalous to the structure of the Roman Curia: the Vatican has a monarchical structure, and the monastic system predates it. Cardinal Eduardo Pironio, the greatly respected Prefect of the Congregation for Religious and Secular Institutes, regards it as being at the service of the orders rather than the other way round (as does the one Benedictine cardinal, Basil Hume). For this and other reasons, he is popular with the various superiors, who believe that he respects and reinforces their special autonomies.

Abbot Dammertz serves on the Congregation for Religious and Secular Institutes, and is a consultor to the Congregation for Catholic Education. Most important, like Fr. Arrupe and Fr. de Couesnongle, he is a member of the Council for Relations between the Congregation for Religious and Secular Institutes and the two International Unions of Superiors General. The council includes sixteen priests and nuns, all heads of religious orders, who meet every month to discuss problems of religious life with representatives of the Sacred Congregation.

Fr. de Couesnongle says that the meetings are simple, sincere and open. In 1978 the council published an important document on relations between Catholic bishops and the religious orders (*Mutae Relationes*), looking at often-vexed questions of coordination and collaboration. The Union of Superiors General itself (of which Fr. Arrupe was elected chairman for an unprecedented fifth term in 1979) meets twice a year in a three-day session. His aim as chairman, Fr. Arrupe has said, is to strengthen ties with the Vatican, with the bishops' conferences, and with women's religious and non-Catholic religious groups.

The 1¼ million strong network of Catholic religious organizations, monks, friars and nuns throughout the world is very complex, very alive, very sensitive in every possible human way to the tugs on the threads from the Vatican centre. Under Pope John Paul II, the tugs have been quite fierce. During a Mass in the Sistine Chapel, he told the sisters attending the 1979 General Assembly of the International Union of Women Superiors General (UISC) that 'faithfulness to Christ can never be separated from faithfulness to the Church' – as during his visit to the United States, the Pope warned the women in front of him to keep to the traditional paths of fervent prayer, community life and decorous religious garb (all of which have been modified, sometimes astonishingly, around the world since the Second Vatican Council).

In Rome, members of the religious orders form an indispensable source of talent and energy for the service of the Church. They are present in strength in every department and office of the Curia, ranging from men with the stature and influence of the late Cardinal Bea, the Jesuit who helped to transform the attitude of the Catholic Church towards ecumenism, to the lesser-known Jesuits working for Vatican Radio, the Dominicans with the Congregation for the Doctrine of the Faith, the Salesians dedicated to printing and publishing, and the unobtrusive Franciscans who are internationally perhaps the most pervasive of all. Despite the real tensions between the orders and the Vatican, their members give the Holy See remarkable loyalty and unique dedication. One Dominican, Fr. Lambert Greenan, for example, who edits the English language edition of the *Osservatore Romano*, a silver-haired, drily humorous priest from Newry, Northern Ireland, says, 'We publish the views of the Pope and of the Holy See; not those against. We were attacked at the time of the *Humanae Vitae* for not publishing those of the other side. There would have been complete confusion had we done so. On official matters, we have to be official.'

Loyalty to the Holy See is also an important by-product of the work of the great many educational institutions of Rome. Mostly (in the case of the Pontifical Universities) they award degrees in philosophy and theology to students, handpicked by their bishops, who usually return to important diocesan work in their own country. The North American College (the most important American Catholic centre in Rome) is the largest residential college for students attending courses at the Pontifical Institutes. The likelihood, and partly the intention, is that they should return from the national residential colleges in Rome with a heightened understanding of the Holy See. This is confirmed by the Rector of the North American Pontifical College, Mgr Charles Murphy. (There are, incidentally, sixty-three Murphys listed in the index of the *Annuario Pontificio.*) The main reason for the foundation of his own college (in 1859) was, he told me, that the Holy See wanted American priests 'to have an exposure to Rome'.

The North American College is today housed in a large, airy cluster of buildings on the Janiculum Hill, built on land bought by the American bishops in the 1930s and dedicated by Pope Pius XII in 1953. The direction of the college is shared by the Pope (through a cardinal patron, at present Cardinal Gabriel-Marie Garrone) and a board of American bishops, representing every diocese in the United States. About 170 students at the North American College are spending four to five years preparing for the priesthood and on the study of theology; about sixty are pursuing graduate studies. The college has a teaching staff of ten.

Mgr Murphy is a Harvard man who studied at the North American College himself. Before joining the staff of the college a few years ago (he was made rector in 1979), he had been in charge of a parish in the United States, and then a diocesan director of education. He is a lean, soft-voiced, eager priest with a direct manner of approach that wins immediate confidence. He looks very Irish, and talks with a strong American accent. His personality and opinions are important to the Catholic Church in the United States and to the Holy See. Many of his students will eventually hold high-level positions in the Church, and not a few of them will become bishops and cardinals. Well over a hundred of the college's past students were made bishops, and its alumni have included Cardinals Farley, O'Connell, Dougherty, Mooney, Stritch, Spellman and Meyer, all men with a touch of greatness to them. One of Mgr Murphy's predecessors as rector, Mgr James A. Hickey, left the college to become Bishop of Cleveland and is now Archbishop of Washington in succession to Cardinal Baum.

Weight is given at the college to the pastoral as well as the intellectual training of its students, for the service of the Church in the United States. They are sponsored by their home dioceses. They spend their first year studying European history and culture, and travelling in Europe; during the third year (when as deacons they can baptize, teach and perform marriages) they are sent on fieldwork in the United States or, if they choose, somewhere else, such as Africa.

All but a few of the students return to the United States on completing their courses. A handful stay to work in the Vatican. In the autumn of 1979, one priest from the college's graduate house was going on to the Secretariat of State, a second to work at the Pontifical Ecclesiastical Academy, another to the Congregation for Bishops. How are they chosen? It is bad form in the Church to recommend yourself, I have been told, so they must have been recommended by the college authorities or spotted by curial officials looking for talent.

Vatican links with the college are strong. The rector is nominated by the American bishops, selected by the Sacred Congregation for Catholic Education (which administers the *ratio fundamentalis*, the basic rules, for seminaries) and appointed by the Pope. He is in frequent consultation with the Prefect of the Congregation (Cardinal Garrone). The college is open to inspection by teams of American bishops, especially from the Bishops' Committee on Seminary Education.

Mgr Murphy is as concerned that the priests who return from the college to the United States as future leaders should have respect and even love for Italian culture as much as for the Holy See. 'We do not want, I'm glad to say we do not have, the "ugly American" at the college. . . .' Despite the pressures on the curriculum (one time-consuming aspect of Italian culture is its dedication to three serious meals a day), students of the college start their course with a five-week 'orientation programme'. 'They usually experience the shock of Italy quite deeply; then in most cases they come to love the Italian people and the city of Rome, and all that it offers.'

The outsider's growing appreciation of Italian *mores* helps him to a greater acceptance of the ways of the Curia. At the North American College, staff and students also experience the workings of ecclesiastical Rome at close quarters. All ordinations must be approved by the vicariate of Rome. (Being ordained in Rome used to be an odd affair. The vicariate had ordinations carried out always in Italian, even for students who studied in English at the Beda and had no Italian. No advance date was given for the ceremony, in case interlopers joined the procession and were ordained with the rest. . . .) Students are expected, and are usually anxious, to be involved in papal ceremonies. They do not, Murphy reflects, become greatly involved with the Roman Curia, but 'our priests tend to leave here as apostles not only of Christ but also of the Holy See. . . . They become very papal. In American political terms the analogy would be with going to live in Washington and developing great loyalty to the Presidency and the President himself.'

Mgr Murphy recalls the intense emotional involvement of his students in first the election of John Paul I and then his sudden death, 'which devastated them'. (A permanent, very touching, exhibition in memory of John Paul I was mounted in the college.) But their attachment to the Vatican is not a naive sentiment. 'Being here in Rome,' Mgr Murphy comments, 'gives you a sense of realism about the Church. Here, the institution is everywhere. If you have trained here, you take the institution very seriously. You cannot have an ethereal sense of the Church. This grounds your priesthood on the real nature of things. And then, through studying theology here, you become very fully aware of the teaching role of the bishops and of the Pope.'

Before they join the North American College, all the students are carefully vetted and psychologically tested in the United States. They are not always brilliant, it appears, but they are said to be very stable.

The North American College deserves special prominence as part of the loosely described Vatican 'network'. It trains 'loyalists' for high positions in the powerful, numerically strong but volatile, American Roman Catholic Church. It illustrates the benefits or snags (depending on one's theological stance) of 'exposure' to the Holy See. One of the inner wheels of the Catholic Church came full circle when Pope John Paul II, speaking in Chicago during his first visit to the United States in 1979, emphatically clarified his own position on various questions of (mostly) sexual morality by quoting to the American bishops, with vehement approval, their own pastoral letter, *To Live in Christ Jesus*, of 1976. And he paid 'public homage to a long tradition of fidelity to the Apostolic See on the part of the American hierarchy'. In the spring of 1980, John Paul II planted a Californian redwood sequoia tree in the grounds of the North American College.

All the regional or national ecclesiastical colleges for candidates to the priesthood, of which there are nearly thirty in Rome, cement the loyalties of future Church leaders from all the five continents to the Holy See, as well as providing them with, generally speaking, first-class education at great teaching academies, where philosophical diversity and tolerance flourish despite the conservative vigilance of the Sacred Congregations. The English College, for example, saw its previous rector (the extra-tall and gentle Mgr Cormac Murphy-O'Connor) plucked back to England in 1978 to become Bishop of Brighton and Arundel.

The British relationship with Rome is exceptional, since there are a record number of four colleges involved: the Venerable English, the Beda (for late vocations), the Scots College and a part share in the Irish College. Nowadays, there are also Anglican students living at the English College, an old (sixteenth-century) and famously hospitable institution in a rambling *palazzo* in the narrow, cobbled, workshop-crammed Via di Monserrato. It is proud of its association with the priests martyred in Elizabethan England. Like those at the American College, a selection of its seventy-odd students are likely to become bishops themselves, or at any rate the intellectual supports of the English bishops and seminaries, after their studies in Rome (usually at the Gregorian University) are over.

Institutions such as the Venerable English College, the

Pontifical College of North America, the Pontifical Irish College – to give them their full titles – also play a useful part in communications between the Vatican and the local hierarchies. They make good sounding-boards, and they provide useful feedback to the Vatican, on all sorts of ecclesiastical issues.

About a score or so of English bishops visited the English College in early October 1979, to celebrate its four hundredth anniversary. The Pope had been invited to the college for this special occasion many months before, but in the event was absent in Ireland, to the rather intense disappointment of many of the English. (He paid his visit a few months after and made the rounds of the other colleges in a blaze of warmth and affection). Among the social events at the English College in October 1979 was a reception for the senior staff headed by the rector, Mgr George Hay, and the visiting bishops, given by the then British Minister to the Holy See, Geoffrey Crossley. The chief guest (arriving early, I was asked to leave the first space in the visitors' book blank for him to sign) was Cardinal Bertoli, the Camerlengo, resplendent in red, and representing the Pope. Some genuflected to him; others shook his hand. Among the guests, including Anglican and Methodist clergy-men, I was fascinated to meet a 'professed knight' of the Order of Malta.

In social and indirectly political ways, the Order of Malta, despite its anachronistic name, still helps to sustain and spread the influence of the Holy See. It is a secretive, though not a secret, organization, sensitive to questions about its place in today's Church and troubled about its relevance to the modern world.

The Knights of Malta or Knights Hospitaller (in full, they constitute the Sovereign Military Order of the Hospital of St John of Jerusalem, of Rhodes, and of Malta) were founded in a hospice–infirmary in Jerusalem in the eleventh century. They are, therefore, after the Benedictines and the Augustinians, the third oldest religious order in the West, though with the special character of a religious order of laymen. They grew during the Middle Ages into a powerful military–religious order with extensive territories, including at different times Rhodes and Malta. They were one of the very first religious orders to be 'exempt' from the jurisdiction of the local bishop and brought directly under the Supreme Pontiff.

Today, the order's headquarters are in Rome in the Via Condotti, close to the Piazza di Spagna. But the grand master has his villa on the Aventine near the headquarters of the Benedictines and the Dominicans, high up, overlooking the city, in the piazza named after the knights. This is also the chancery for their envoy to the Holy See (Christophe de Kallay). The order is internationally recognized as sovereign by a growing number of countries, now exceeding forty and including the Holy See. Its aims are the spiritual development of its members – about 8000 laymen and chaplains throughout the world – the service of the Catholic faith and the Holy See, and charitable activities.

These endeavours are helped by its chivalrous traditions and its sovereign status. They include the building and maintenance of hospitals and health centres of various kinds in Africa, Asia, Europe and Latin America; care and first-aid provision for the wounded from European-based centres; and relief work for refugees.

The Order of Malta has three classes of members: the knights of justice and professed chaplains, who take the religious vows of poverty, chastity and obedience, and among whom many full-time administrators are to be found; knights of obedience and donates of justice, who promise to strive towards religious perfection in their lives; lay members and secular chaplains, subdivided into a profusion of medieval-sounding grades such as knights and dames of honour and devotion, and knights and dames of grace and devotion. There are twenty-six national associations.

Proof of 'nobility' is required for admission to several of the higher grades of the order, and there is currently some dispute about whether the emphasis on noble blood might not be shifted still further towards kind hearts.

Knights of Malta have had an occasionally tempestuous relationship with the Holy See. Nowadays, the supreme head of the order, the grand master (at present Fra' Angelo de Mojana di Cologna) governs the order with the help of a council. The order's supreme assembly is a general chapter which is called regularly. As a religious order, the organization comes under the authority of the Vatican's Sacred Congregation of Religious; as a sovereign entity, it deals with the Secretariat of State and maintains diplomatic relations with the Holy See.

The relationship of the Knights of Malta was put on a new footing with the Holy See, after a commission of cardinals (appointed by Pope Pius XII) reported to Pope John XXIII, who approved their new Constitutional Charter in 1961. This resolved a long-running battle for control of the order during the reign of Pius XII which forms the subject of Roger Peyrefitte's facetious novel *The Knights of Malta* and which, knights admit, is only about a quarter false. The real-life Cardinal Canali, represented by Peyrefitte as hungering for power over the order, certainly provoked the struggle to increase the influence of the Curia in its affairs. The dispute was acrimonious but perhaps inevitable in some form or another because of the tension between independent sovereignty and religious obedience. At present the order is on good terms with the Holy See under its new constitution, and its chief worries are about ensuring enough recruits to maintain its impressive charitable record without weakening too much its adherence to the concept of 'nobility' as a form of leadership or maintaining the spirituality of what is essentially a religious order.

The care of the sick has always been central to the religious work of the order. Centuries before Florence Nightingale, 'our Lords the Sick' would be accommodated in the hospital of the order in large airy wards of noble proportions, with fine linen on their beds and dining on chicken breasts served on silver dishes, while the knights themselves made do with goat's meat on pewter platters in small noisome chambers. The body of a dead knight was mutilated with swords and then given to the barber–surgeons of the order to practise their surgical skills.

Today there are four other orders of St John, of which the most important is the Most Venerable Order of the Hospital of St John of Jerusalem, whose first Royal Charter was given to them by Queen Victoria and of whom the Queen is sovereign, and whose St John's Ambulance Brigade is a familiar sight throughout many countries of the world. A particularly warm relationship exists between the Order of Malta in Rome and the Order of St John in Clerkenwell. The grand master, paying his first visit to England since the reign of Henry VIII, called on the Queen at Buckingham Palace, and no major function of the Order of St John in Britain is ever complete without a delegation of Knights of Malta from the British Association.

The Military Order of the Knights of Malta strengthens the Vatican network with an emotional underpinning that affects the climate of opinion throughout the world. The ancient but very different Order of the Knights of the Holy Sepulchre of Jerusalem, which is under the protection of the Holy See and dedicated to support of the Christian Holy Places, also helps foster individual loyalty to the Holy See and the person of the Pope, as does the vast membership of thousands of international and national Catholic special apostolates, youth organizations and societies.

Worth special mention is the organization called *Opus Dei*; it exemplifies, in a controversial way, the perennial surges of new religious movements within the Catholic Church, which the Papacy constantly strives to control and direct. *Opus Dei* is one of the secular institutes that, after a period of rapid growth, were regulated by Pope Pius XII in the late 1940s. The institutes consist of laymen dedicated to works of charity or the apostolate (the spread of the Catholic religion) and their own religious perfection, under the command of superiors, and bound by certain private vows or oaths.

Opus Dei – 'the Work of God' – was founded by a Spanish priest in the late 1920s, with separate divisions for men and women. It was finally approved by the Holy See in 1950 and has spread to most countries of Europe and America as well as to Africa, Asia and Australia. It is governed by a President General (Mgr Alvaro del Portillo) and General Council with headquarters in Rome. It has about 73,000 members in over eighty countries. In the autumn of 1980 a group of members of *Opus Dei* from fourteen different countries were ordained priests in Rome by Cardinal Oddi, Prefect of the Congregation for the Clergy, and about 1500 members of the movement are priests.

Members of *Opus Dei* dedicate themselves to the practice of an intense spiritual life and to the apostolate, without giving up their own profession or social environment. A great deal of their visible work has been educational: founding colleges, student residences and technical schools.

Opus Dei has been linked, as a secular institute, with the Congregation for Religious and Secular Institutes. It is a self-confident, mostly middle-class movement, with strong professional and business ties, an aggressive, missionary drive and staunchly conservative theological instincts. The quiet increase in its membership and influence in recent years, which created resentment and suspicions among many liberal-minded Catholics, prepared it to aim for a constitutionally more important position in the Church on the accession of Pope John Paul II, thought to sympathize with its ideals and to appreciate its zeal in the dedicated service of the Papcy and the Catholic Church.

8

Treasures on Earth:
The Culture of the Vatican

A simple but effective illustration of the Papacy's love of the arts is the story of Giotto's O. A thirteenth-century Pope sent a messenger to Tuscany to ask Giotto for an example of his work. Giotto took a sheet of paper, dipped his brush in the paint, and, keeping his arm closed to his side, with a twist of his hand drew a perfect circle. When the Pope received it, among a sheaf of drawings from other artists, he at once realized the outstanding talent of the draughtsman. The mutilated mosaic of the *Navicella* in St Peter's remains as one of the fruits of this encounter.

It is hard to think of any philistine Popes. The papal tradition of informed patronage of the arts, and of active participation, carries on in the person of Pope John Paul II. Like many Pontiffs before him, including his immediate predecessor as well as Pope Paul VI, who employed a very distinctive style, he is a literary Pope. Among his poems are a handful written in the Basilica of St Peter's in 1962, during the Second Vatican Council.

The whole of the Vatican ranks as a work of art. It is listed in its entirety in the 1960 UN international register of 'cultural works' under special protection in case of war. But, among the riches spread through the city state, the greatest concentration of art treasures, indeed the greatest in the world, is in the Vatican Museums. Since the eighteenth century, they have been under the special patronage of the Popes, who have lavished resources on them.

Pope Paul VI inaugurated a large collection of modern religious art in the Apostolic Palace in 1973. Behind this initiative was the Pope's philosophical vision of art in the service of religion, and his emotional feeling for artists. The impulse came when he met a group of artists in the Sistine Chapel, in the early days of his pontificate. Fortunately for the image of a poor and pilgrim Church, the collection was acquired virtually for nothing, through donations from collectors or gifts from the painters and sculptors themselves. There are oils by Matisse, Chagall and Gauguin; and watercolours or drawings by Klee, Kandinsky, Moore, Dali and Modigliani. Among the Americans on show are Ben Shahn and Lyonel Feininger. The Vatican's modern collection includes over eight hundred signed works by about two hundred and fifty artists. It has been used as another stick with which to beat the Papacy for its worldliness and for competing in an area where its resources are limited. But it can be argued that the support and encouragement of art are fundamental to the spiritual life of the Vatican.

'For since God intends man to develop at both the divine and the natural level, the Church encourages art as being one of the most noble faculties of the human spirit. This is among the profound reasons why in the papal residence itself, in the city of Rome, the Vatican Museums came into being. . . .' The apologia comes from Dr Deoclecio Redig de Campos, who was Director General of the Vatican Museums from 1971 to 1979. His career in the Vatican started in 1933; so he had served six Popes (as a diplomat as well as a scholar) by the time he retired and had daily access to the museums for some fifty years. He has made the bold claim that they constitute an essential part of Western civilization, 'which cannot be conceived without them'.

Dr Redig de Campos is a pan-European by education and commitment. He speaks six European languages. He attended the Hohenzollern Gymnasium in Berlin, the Freies Gymnasium in Berne, and the Lycée Chateaubriand in Rome. At the University of Rome he studied history of art and philosophy. Now director general emeritus, he still comes in to work on the second floor of the administrative block of the Pontifical Museums, approached through the massive entrance made in the northern part of the Vatican walls by order of Pope Pius XI in 1932.

Dr de Campos's successor, Professor Carlo Pietrangeli, creates the same atmosphere of scholarly serenity. If anything, he prefers to stick closer to his books and desk than de Campos. Professor Pietrangeli is Roman born (in 1912) and an archaeologist with a special interest in topography and epigraphy. He has a long, lean, sharp-featured, bespectacled face, full of intelligence and of smiling enthusiasm when he talks about his particular field of work. Over the years, he has written books on the family of Augustus and on the excavations made during the reign of Pope Pius VI, as well as a few hundred articles for learned journals. He represents the Holy See on various non-governmental agencies such as the International Committee for the History of Art. He is on the Council of the Pontifical Academy of Archaeology and is a member of the Order of Malta, *Cavaliere Magistrale*, Knight of Magisterial Grace.*

It was strange, Pietrangeli told me, that he had come to succeed Redig de Campos as director general of the Vatican Museums. His working life had been spent mostly at Madrid's Real Accademia de Bellas Artes, but he had started to study the history of the Vatican Museums, notably the Pio-Clementine, thirty years ago.

Professor Pietrangeli reminded me how amazingly wide were the responsibilities of a director general. They covered all the basilicas of Rome, save St Peter's. All the pictures, dispersed through all the Vatican Palaces, were theirs to trace and catalogue. His own professional pride, he said, was engaged in getting the museum system to function more efficiently; above all, he was keen to improve the museums' catalogues and produce many more detailed and scholarly guides (and there is certainly a long way to go). The museums were for the pleasure and instruction of all the world, but it was his job to make sure that the world's scholars had easy access to them and were well briefed with accurate material.

The director general's job is partly academic, partly practical. He is responsible for coordinating the scientific work of the directors of the various sections of the museums and for supervising the activities of the museums' secretary and treasurer. His correspondence may be the continuance of a long and erudite exchange of letters; it may include a request

*One who has become a knight by the grace of the grand master, formal proof of nobility being absent.

from an art historian for access to a particular Renaissance medal stored in a cupboard, or the proposal of a fascinating art 'swap', as when a Belgium museum pursued the offer of a Barberini tapestry missing from the Vatican series in exchange for some of the antiquities of which the Vatican have so many. (This in the event was effected through a 'permanent deposit' arrangement.) Mornings and evenings take him away from his office desk to his own study and his own papers and books, or to enjoy the social rounds of Rome.

Professor Pietrangeli talks with an unaffectedly loyal devotion to the Holy See and the Popes. He is not sure that he sees many cardinals walking in an absorbed manner along the corridors of the museums; they seem less interested in art nowadays than they were in the past; though would one necessarily recognize them? In his day-to-day work, however, Pietrangeli is acutely conscious of the Pope's presence in the Vatican as head of the Catholic religion rather than, or far more than, as head of the Vatican State. Pietrangeli said to me, brightly, that like Pope John Paul II, he was also 'a bit of an Alpinist'. That was how he kept fit, along with walking around his place of work.

Redig de Campos also liked to wander along the corridors and across the halls of his domain of historical buildings, pacing out their architecture, and contemplating the 'treasures' to which he is attracted. He still does so, to gaze above all on the frescoes of Michelangelo and Raphael, among the exquisite Renaissance wall-paintings in the chapel of Nicholas V, the Borgia Apartments, the Raphael Rooms, the loggia of Raphael and the Sistine Chapel and Pauline Chapel.

The earliest Vatican paintings include frescoes by Fra Angelico in the chapel of Nicholas V, showing scenes from the life of St Stephen and from the life of St Laurence. The paintings are luminous, delicate, all light blues and golds, shot through with a spirit of Christian humanism that portrays the world realistically with its lights and shadows, yet as divinely created and sustained. In the six Tuscan-style halls of the Borgia Apartments is Pinturicchio's brutal, fleshy portrait of Pope Alexander VI, taken from life, which de Campos has compared for its acute psychological insight to a pen-portrait by Tacitus.

The *Stanze*, the suite of four princely rooms painted by

Raphael and his followers, provide a unique gallery of High Renaissance art at its apogee. They were planned as quarters for the Pope. The absolute and serene assurance of the paintings in the first two, whose themes are the triumph of human intellect in the *Stanza della Segnatura* and the divine protection of the Church in the *Stanza d'Eliodoro*, sum up and prefigure all the claims of the Papacy. Dr de Campos sees the strong 'political' influence of Pope Julius II in the subjects of the *Stanza d'Eliodoro*. These are the Mass of Bolsena, the expulsion of Heliodorus, the liberation of St Peter and the meeting of St Leo the Great and Attila, showing the Church protected by God in its faith, its patrimony (in the person of the first Pope) and in the seat of its power at Rome. The painting of the School of Athens in the Room of the *Segnatura* has what may be Raphael's signature in letters of gold on the edge of the portrait of Euclid ('RUSM' – Raphael Urbinas Sua Manu) and a modest self-portrait. The Mass of Bolsena in the *Stanza d'Eliodoro* includes a fragment perfectly preserved in its original state, with sharp outlines and strong red, black and green colours, showing a group of Swiss Guards in the first flush of their service under Julius II.

When the Sistine was built as the new palace chapel, and part fortress, in the fifteenth century, the great walls of the nave were completed as flat surfaces with scarcely any projections. The first painters of the Sistine included Perugino (most of whose work was sacrificed for Michelangelo's *Last Judgement*), Signorelli, Ghirlandaio (of whose efforts mostly repaintings exist), Botticelli and Cosimo Rosselli – all summoned to Rome by Sixtus IV. They left the ceiling with a coating of blue paint and scattered gold stars. Then, in 1508, Michelangelo single-handedly began work on his tremendous sculptural fresco cycle of the story of mankind, from the Creation to the Coming of Christ, the Old Dispensation and the New. The *Last Judgement*, commissioned from Michelangelo nearly a quarter of a century after the ceiling was finished, stupefied Rome when it was unveiled and is still a cause of bafflement, even scandal, to many serious critics as well as the tourists craning their necks in the chapel. Michelangelo's tense balance between art and faith seems to have broken down in old age from the force of his own interior emotional turmoil. The distorted figures (among the 391 painted over the altar) had to violate rules which could not contain the expression of his agonized spiritual vision.

Amidst such turbulence the cardinals cast their votes for a new Pontiff in the Sistine Chapel; in the Pauline Chapel, which is rarely open to visitors, they assemble to say their prayers during the Conclaves. Here I have brooded on Michelangelo's last two great frescoes, two vast rectangular paintings showing the *Conversion of Saul* and the *Martyrdom of St Peter*, executed in the 1540s. The paintings are bleak and troubling, unfinished. In the first, Redig de Campos perceives a parallel to St Thomas Aquinas's *Summa*, the great theological work left unfinished after the angelic doctor's ecstatic glimpse of the glory of God; in the second, which is desolate, nostalgic and dreamlike, he sees an arrested classicism of form which is on the edge of dissolution. The eyes of the naked and tortured St Peter, in the fresco of his martyrdom, appear to follow as you walk along the aisle and stare into them. The trompe l'oeil seems very appropriate to the prayers of cardinals that they make the right choice of Peter's successor. It is slightly unnerving, even for a layman.

The sunnier aspects of the Renaissance and the great frescoes are at their brightest in the loggia of Raphael, on the second storey of the double-arcaded and three-storeyed façade planned originally by Bramante for Pope Julius II. The loggia overlooks the courtyard of San Damaso and faces one wing of the Pope's private apartments. Pope Leo X kept his antique statues there and reserved it for his own relaxation. It was decorated to Raphael's designs and under his supervision by a band of artists including Giulio Romano, Perin del Vaga and Giovanni da Udine. They painted scores of pagan and Christian scenes, grotesques and Gospel incidents, on its walls, arches and domes. The surfaces are a riot of flowers, fruits, copies of statues, mythological and historical incidents and portraits of contemporaries, such as Raphael in his workshop and Michelangelo wearing a hat.

In 1952, the loggia provided one of the thrills of discovery that constantly occur at the Vatican. Among its damaged and faded adornments, two painted half-pillars were found beneath one of the terminal walls, with decorations that had been preserved almost unblemished since the reign of Pope Paul III (1534–49). Such discoveries are often linked to revelations, or revaluations, of the techniques used in early Vatican paintings and architecture. For example, the two frescoes in the Pauline Chapel were restored in 1934, cleaned in 1953, and the plaster was subsequently repaired. During this process, the minor repaintings were distinguished from the mass of Michelangelo's own painting; Michelangelo's brilliance of colouring was renewed, and the simplicity of his palette for *buon fresco* observed in his use of natural earth colours including Siena yellow, red, green, jet and lapis lazuli.

The public crowds into the Vatican Museums and can penetrate as far as the 'monuments', which house the marvellous frescoes of Raphael and Michelangelo (but not into the Pauline Chapel), from the entrance in the Viale Vaticano. In recent times, their number has been climbing towards two million a year.

The monuments include, as well as the frescoed chapels and rooms, the Gallery of Maps and the Hall of the Immaculate Conception. The former is a long gallery along the west wing of the Belvedere corridor, where light pours from a score of windows onto the blue and grey marbled floor, and the gilded stuccoes and Mannerist paintings on its barrel-vault. It is famous for the thirty-two sixteenth-century maps of the Tyrrhenian and Adriatic regions of Italy, which are beautiful, intriguing and accurate. The Hall of the Immaculate Conception was constructed in the nineteenth century by demolishing an existing floor between two storeys of the Borgia Tower. It contains paintings celebrating the declaration of the Dogma of the Immaculate Conception by Pope Pius IX in 1854, and the large wooden model made for the dome of St Peter's by Michelangelo, who hoped to prevent its design being changed after his death.

The museums include the Vatican Picture Gallery, the *Pinacoteca* built by Luca Beltrami and opened in 1932 to house the Pope's previously rather mobile collection. The collection ranges from the eleventh to the nineteenth century: from the Italian 'Primitives' before Giotto, and the Byzantine artists, to nineteenth-century portrait painters such as the Englishman Thomas Lawrence, whose portrait of George IV was given to the Pope as an ally in the defeat of Napoleon, and for whom Pope Pius VII sat on several occasions. There are a succession of compelling paintings by Giovanni Bellini, Titian, Veronese,

Pinturicchio, Caravaggio, Van Dyck, and one of Leonardo da Vinci's rare paintings, a monochrome of St Jerome. This unfinished picture was lost and then discovered by a cardinal in two pieces – one, the torso, serving as a lid for a chest in a Roman antique shop, the other serving as a stool-top in a shoemaker's. But for me the high point is the *Transfiguration*, one of three large altarpieces in the gallery which represent virtually all Raphael's artistic development. He painted the *Coronation of the Virgin* when he was twenty and the *Madonna of Foligno* when he was nearing thirty; and the *Transfiguration* was finished after his death at thirty-seven. It was commissioned by Cardinal Giulio de Medici in 1517, and restored under the direction of F. Mancinelli and Redig de Campos in 1972.

The collection does not altogether match up to the grandeur of the Vatican's wealth of fresco paintings, but it is more accessible and offers some marvellous examples of the Papacy's historical dialogue with art. The most tell-tale pictures are in Room XV, where several of the Popes are painted to the life. Clement IX (1667–9), playwright as well as Pope, is lean and bearded and looks as conscientious and kind as he was reputed to be. Clement XIII (1758–69), sits sensuous, fat, and even complacent, for all his worries over the Jesuits. Sixtus V (1585–90), stern reformer and administrator, appears very worn and a little foxy. The future Benedict XIV (1740–58), a great letter-writer, looks sensitive and very plump, doubtless from the good eating of his youth in Bologna.

Near the picture gallery, between the very formal Square Garden of the Vatican and the Cortile della Zitelle, are two terraces one above the other where you can overlook part of the Vatican Gardens, stare along one of the walls of the Belvedere, and see St Peter's ahead of you. The spot leaves a jumble of lasting impressions: of Vatican gardeners lazily pruning trees, of lines of green and blue tiles, masses of yellow brickwork, and the great cupola of St Peter's from yet another angle.

The interplay between the personalities of the Pontiffs and the Vatican's artistic and historical treasures is also evident in the Historical Museum, which was constructed on the wishes of Pope Paul VI in a space of nearly 1500 square metres under the garden near the *Pinacoteca*. The first section presents between massive steel columns an array of carriages that were owned by Popes and cardinals. Among them are three black landaus employed mostly for outings in the Vatican Gardens till the 1920s, two longer-distance travelling carriages, and the lumbering ceremonial coach built for Leo XII and used by several of his successors. There are two sedan chairs, belonging to Leo XIII and Pius IX respectively. In a nearby room there are cars used by Pius XI and Pius XII: a Citroën, a Graham Paige and a Mercedes-Benz.

The second section continues in pomp and circumstance with reminders of the Papacy's state sovereignty and military pretensions. In glass showcases are uniforms of the old Noble Guard, the Gendarmes, the Guard of Honour, the Papal Zouaves and Papal Artillery. There are battle mementoes, from Castelfidardo, Mentana and Porta Pia, where papal troops last prepared to fight. And there is an arsenal of weapons of all sorts, from Venetian sabres and Renaissance canons to fine 78 Remington muskets. The old Regiment of Pontifical Dragoons and Regiment of Pontifical Artillery are recalled by their standards and decorations. The Papal Navy is commemorated by flags and a model of the corvette *Immaculate Conception*.

The other museums of the Vatican cover all periods from the beginning of the history of man. Dr Redig de Campos sees them in triple perspective: as uniquely comprehensive collections of significant art; as symbols of the Vatican's perennial spirit of Christian humanism; and as exemplars of the development of 'aesthetic thought and museum science' beginning with the garden collection of Pope Julius II in the Cortile delle Statue, now the Cortile Ottagono.

As if it were in itself one great work of art or one great idea, the complex of the Vatican Museums invites different levels of approach and interpretation. It provides, for example, an almost unique series of illustrations of the development of the art and science of the museum during the course of four centuries. At the beginning, the criteria for acquiring and exhibiting a work of art were chiefly aesthetic; increasingly, they took account of the artistic and critical importance of the setting in which it was to be placed. It is too idealistic, however, to expect the Vatican displays to demonstrate simply a steady improvement in the way works of art are put on show; they bring out the differing values of different times, as well as increasing sophistication. And all the time, from the Medicis to Montini, there was the collector's urge as well.

The Pio-Clementine to the north of the Vatican is a finely planned eighteenth-century complex, in which classical antiques or copies – statues, mosaics, sarcophagi, reliefs and busts – are displayed to striking visual effect against earnestly contrived neo-classical backgrounds. The shapes or contents of the buildings are indicated by their evocative names: the Room of the Masks, the Cabinet of the Hermes, the Square Vestibule, and so on. A sarcophagus relief in the Hall of the Greek Cross shows cupids picking grapes from a vine. The Circular Hall is paved with Greek mosaics showing battle scenes between men and centaurs. The nine Roman statues that give its name to the octagonally vaulted Hall of the Muses (and inspired a poem by Thomas Hardy) share the space with a statue of Apollo and the busts of famous Greeks, including Pericles, Homer, Socrates and Plato. Three great statues from the collection of Julius II still stand in the Octagonal Courtyard of the Belvedere: the Laocoon, the shapely Apollo Belvedere and the Venus Felix. The victorious young athlete in the Cabinet of the Apoxyomenos – a Roman copy of a Greek bronze by Lysippus – scrapes the oil from his arm in a state of sheer exhaustion.

The Chiaramonti Museum, planned by the Venetian sculptor Antonio Canova in the corridor built by Bramante, commemorates the patronage of Pope Pius VII. It continues into the Lapidary Gallery, reserved for scholars to study Christian and pagan inscriptions, facing each other on opposite walls and at right angles into the austere, uncluttered New Wing with its alternating statues and busts. In the first long section of the Chiaramonti, along walls divided into fifty-nine arched compartments is a daunting assemblage of busts, fragments and figures – Ganymede and the eagle, Penelope seated – inviting study but all too close to each other for comfort. In the New Wing, Julius Caesar is isolated in the centre, between two bronze peacocks from Hadrian's mausoleum; Augustus addresses his soldiers; a reclining statue stands for the heavy Nile.

Greek and Roman antiques and copies fill the Room of the Greek Originals, the Hall of the Chariot (named after the two-horse chariot which was once a papal throne) and the Gallery of Candelabri. Many show the frozen scenes of ancient lusts and violence.

Then centuries and culture shift to still more remote worlds, in the Gregorian Etruscan and the Gregorian Egyptian Museums, spread over various rooms on the north of the Cortile della Pigna. The Etruscan collection was originally formed from finds made during early nineteenth-century excavations in the central Italian area of Lazio (then part of the Papal States). Along with the stone monuments, the ornaments of gold and bronze, the urns, jars and pottery, are some large, striking works of art such as the elegant bronze *Mars of Todi* discovered in 1835 and dated to the late fifth century BC.

The motivations that led to these collections – curiosity, avarice, scholarship, aesthetic instinct – included the belief that they all (even the Egyptian statues) had a part to play in Christian apologetics through the light they cast on the revelations of the Old Testament. Every century and almost every pontificate brings a fresh impulse to the extension and re-ordering of the great Vatican collections. In 1970, the collection of antiquities of the former Lateran Museum was transferred to the new building between the existing museums and the Vatican Gardens. The natural light in the Gregorian Pagan Museum falls on yet another rich collection of classical sculptures, architectural fragments and sarcophagi, populating this corner of the Vatican with familiar classical gods and heroes. Also from the Lateran, galleries of early Christian sculptures and sarcophagi were transferred in 1963 to form the Pian Christian Museum within the city state. The extensive and unique collection is very important to historians of art and religion; and one of the sculptures – the so-called *Good Shepherd*, dating from the first half of the fourth century – has become one of the most famous works of art throughout the world, thanks to postcards and prints, and its uncloying sweetness.

Among the museums recently founded by the Popes was the extraordinary Pontifical Missionary and Ethnological Museum, created by Pius XI at the Lateran in 1926 and later moved by Pope John from a temporary home in the Palazzo San Calisto to two galleries in the new Vatican building. The museum was originally based on 40,000 items from collections and from items shown at a Missionary Exhibition held at the Vatican for

Holy Year 1925. Gifts from various parts of the world continued to arrive abundantly until the beginning of the Second World War, and the practice was resumed with a collection of carpets from Persia, Afghanistan and Bokhara. Today, the museum is divided into sections covering different nations and cultural areas of the world outside Europe, related to their religious or magical beliefs. The whole is an emporium of fantastic variety, impossible to classify, ranging over thousands of items from cooking utensils and clothes to a stone carving of the Mexican god Quetzalcoatl. Here again, informing this gargantuan collecting urge seems to be the instinct to place Christian faith against the background of other religious and materialistic cultures, no matter how outrageous, seeking both significant contrasts and clues to man's common destiny.

Looking after the museums, especially since the incorporation of material from the Lateran, has stretched the Vatican's resources of scholarship and staff to the limit and presents formidable organizational and management problems. Walter Persegati, secretary general of the management board for the Vatican monuments, museums and galleries, works closely with the director general. He became the administrator in 1972, promoted from the Pontifical Commission for Justice and Peace. On the wall by his desk hangs a crude wooden cross from the Philippines, next to a ceremonial mask from New Guinea. There are two small watercolours – of St Peter's and of a family group – as well as the inevitable print of the Pope. Cabinets, steel desk with push-button telephones, on a marble floor, are in the light-grey finish favoured by Vatican decorators.

The vital instrument in Persegati's office is the closed-circuit television set by the window overlooking the slope of the Viale Vaticano. Usually the screen shows the coaches and crowds arriving at the steps leading up the doorway of the museums. The picture can be changed to any corner of the complex of museums and buildings for which Persegati has responsibility in the areas of finance, administration and – most demandingly –security and safety.

Among the Vatican monuments, the Sistine Chapel still functions as a church as well as an art gallery and museum. Sometimes Persegati is informed – at short notice – that the chapel is needed for, say, a special religious service or a private visit by a distinguished foreign ecclesiastic or a head of state. Visitors to the museums, buying one ticket that includes right of admission to the Sistine, have to be diverted for an hour or so. This is a minor problem, but it indicates the flexibility needed in the administration of the museums. The growth of the museum complex over centuries has taken in rooms that were meant for worshipping or dining or even bathing, as well as the functional galleries constructed specifically to display what they contain. And the museum complex, with gardens and loggias and underground apartments, straggles and winds its way over about twenty acres.

A ticket for the Vatican museums cost, in 1981, less than a pound, but the admission fees barely cover salaries and wages. A small income comes from the sale of reproductions, including casts for museums, throughout the world. But the Vatican museums have to be subsidized. The budget of the museums management board is annually approved, and strictly controlled, by the seven cardinals of the Pontifical Commission for the Vatican City State. Once the figures have been approved, they must be 'inserted' into the budgets of all the other state sectors. The Vatican museums do not acquire new works of art other than through gifts or internal transfers. Restoration work, however (carried out in the Laboratory for the Restoration of Works of Art founded by Pope Pius XI), absorbs a big proportion of the budget. So do salaries and wages for the total staff of about 250, and spending on cleaning equipment, uniforms, radio transmitters, alarm systems and safety devices.

Persegati is consulted about personnel, finance and restoration problems by the curators (one Polish, one German and the others Italian) of the main sections of the museums – Classical Art; Medieval; Contemporary Religious Art; Oriental (mostly Egyptian); the Etruscan Museum; the Ethnological and Missionary Museum; the Archives and Research. His responsibility for safety and security extends to all the areas of the museums and galleries, including the Sistine.

'Connected with security,' he says, 'is the difficult problem of how to get people safely through the museums without their being thrown into a panic or suffocated, and with the chance of enjoying themselves. We have an average of 4800 visitors a day. In a year, we will get about 1,500,000 visitors. In Holy Year, 1975, there were over 1,800,000. Sometimes more than 15,000 come on a single day; 10,000 is common. And with all our museums and galleries born at different times, harbouring hundreds of different kinds of art objects, with very few doors, we have a baffling task trying to reconcile safety and security with comfort and the possibility of logical appreciation.

'In ensuring the security of our art treasures, the main problem is certainly not the thief. In a way, the thief is a "clean" problem. Thieves want to preserve the value of what they take, and they don't want to be discovered. Often a good alarm system will be enough to make sure the transgressor is discovered. But, today, we face more of a threat from vandals, from people wanting to demonstrate, or those with disturbed minds. They want to attract attention. Unwittingly, television and the press can become their abettors. Some of them want to destroy. They say they would rather harm works of art than people. All this constitutes a new kind of threat.'

The Vatican authorities deploy a range of weapons against the new vandals. New forms of physical protection have been developed, including bullet-proof glass. But, if too thick, the glass can ruin appreciation of the colours of pictures; if it is processed to give less refraction, it quickly sheds strength. For statues, the apparatus of protection makes the all-round view impossible.

The most notorious example of vandalism at the Vatican in recent years was in May 1972 when Michelangelo's *Pietà* was damaged with hammer blows. The restoration took seven months and gave one or two Vatican civil servants the chance to hold the hand of the Madonna in their own. The statue is now behind thick glass.

Distinctions in the Vatican between the Holy See and the city state, like distinctions between the sacred and the secular, are less simple than the organizational charts show. The cultural activities of the Papacy overlap the divisions between various organizations answerable to different authorities under the Pope. Thus, the governing body of the Vatican Monuments, Museums and Galleries comes under the authority of the Vatican City State, as do the directors of the Pontifical Villas, the Vatican Observatory and Vatican Radio. The observatory, the pontifical villas and most of Vatican Radio are all located outside the Vatican State. Along with the officials responsible for the fabric of St Peter's Basilica and the managers of the Vatican's newspaper publishing house and printing press, the Secret Archives and the Apostolic Library of the Vatican form part of the *Amministrazioni Palatine*. This is the select group of Vatican services organized outside the structure of the Curia and answering directly to the Pope as head of the Holy See.

The Pope is the owner of the secret archives and has absolute authority over their management and use. The admission of students is thus a personal concession of the Pope.

A respected, sharp-minded Italian prelate, with years of curial experience (formerly Prefect of the Sacred Congregation of the Discipline of the Sacraments) has been at the head of the Secret Archives of the Vatican since 1974. Cardinal Antonio Samorè is both cardinal archivist and cardinal librarian. His position is not simply ornamental, since the use of the archives is often still a sensitive matter for the Vatican and may demand decisions at the highest level. However, the day-to-day administration of the archives is carried out by the prefect, Mgr Martino Giusti, who has the services of a vice-prefect and five archivists among his professional staff of nineteen. Giusti is a short, elderly man, who looks as fragile as a leaf but is a bustling functionary. He occupies several other posts including those of President of the Pontifical Commission for the Ecclesiastical Archives of Italy, and he is a consultor to the Sacred Congregation for the Causes of Saints. He lives in a modern book-filled apartment communicating with the area where the secret archives are stored. He is proud of being in charge of 'the most important archives in the world' but not untroubled by the responsibility. It is like sleeping by a vast graveyard where from time to time the dead rise up to confound the living. Much of the material in the secret archives is unclassified and unsorted. It is all inert till a scholar comes along to study and transcribe.

Then there may be historical revelations of the kind concealed in the Vatican Library under the reference Latin MS. 4030. This is the text of the fourteenth-century Inquisition Register of Jacques Fournier, Bishop of Pamiers in Ariège, which furnished the basic material for Le Roy Ladurie's rich revelation of medieval life, the story of *Montaillou*.

The history of the secret archives justifies its air of mystery and intrigue. They were originally the working documents at the service of the Pope and his court – and they are still presented as such within the Vatican. Primarily, they are intended to contain all the acts and documents relevant to the government of the Roman Catholic Church. The history of the secret archives is almost as old as the history of the Papacy, but the reliable history of Vatican documentation begins only with the fifth century and – strangely and sadly – few documents survive from before the end of the twelfth century and the reign of Pope Innocent III.

Material relevant to the Papacy accumulated in various centres during the Middle Ages and the Renaissance, and responsibility for the documents which survived crises such as the Great Schism and the Sack of Rome remained uncertain and divided. Pope Paul V is credited with founding the true central archives of the Catholic Church. A brief of his dated to 1612 appointed an archivist and mentioned the transfer of documents to three rooms in the Vatican Library, which are still used as the first floor of the archives in Bramante's western corridor, with their original reddish-coloured wooden book-cases intact.

In 1630, the archives were given a governing body distinct from that of the Apostolic Library, and their first sole prefect. They continued to swell through routine deposits and the gathering of material from Avignon and Castel Sant'Angelo. They suffered serious loss and damage when Napoleon carted them off to Paris. They assumed more or less their present shape and importance when Pope Leo XIII made one of his own new cardinals their prefect, gradually lowered the barriers against students, and in 1883 in a famous *Letter to Three Cardinals* resoundingly declared that the Papacy had nothing to fear from history.

Since then, the main limitations on students (who must be qualified in Latin and palaeography) have been the hours of work (8.15 a.m. to 1.30 p.m.); the rather clumsy systems of cataloguing and ordering; and the date set for the 'closure' of the secret archives. The date of closure – 1878 for many years – was changed by Pope John Paul II to 1903, the end of the reign of Leo XIII. This gave the Vatican an ungenerous seventy-five-year rule for public access to diplomatic documents, compared with thirty years in Britain. Important material later than 1903 has, however, been published by the Vatican, notably concerning its controversial role in the Second World War. Headaches among the officials of the secret archives, caused in the past by eruption of scandal over, say, the record of the Galileo trial or the Burchard diary passages on the Borgias, are more likely nowadays to be caused by the Sisyphean task of equipping and extending their building to deal with the never-ceasing inflow of material. Recent voluminous additions have poured in from the files of institutions closed down by the Pope (such as the Noble Guard and the Palatine Guard, the Papal Chancery and the Datary); from papal missions throughout the world and from the various departments of the Curia, including the Secretariat of State, which also still maintains its own jealously guarded records. Today all the rooms occupied by the secret archives are filled to capacity. But the rules of secrecy insist all the archives remain within the Vatican City State. Pastor's 'ocean' (as this historian of the Popes called the secret archives) is flooding the shores, and a vast new reservoir has been built underground to contain it.*

The material at the archives is chiefly useful for its collections, in thousands of volumes, of official papal letters – the authentic copies of bulls (sealed with lead) and briefs (sealed with wax). The oldest among the series is the collection of volumes, numbering over two thousand, known as the Vatican Registers (*Registra Vaticana*) and comprising bulls written on parchment in various papal offices from Pope Innocent III in the twelfth century to Pius V in the sixteenth. Near to these, the Avignon Registers in 349 volumes contain mostly bulls of the Popes and the anti-Popes who lived in Avignon for seventy years during the fourteenth century. The largest series of registers (though half of them were lost when the archives were shipped to Paris) are the Lateran Registers, with nearly 2500 volumes extending from the end of the fourteenth century to the end of the nineteenth century, from Pope Boniface IX to Leo XIII. They deal mostly with the small coin of papal diplomacy: benefices, indulgences, dispensations.

*On 18 October 1980, the Pope inaugurated new premises for the archives in the basement of the Cortile della Pigna, incorporating 50,000 metres of shelves.

The substantial number of bulls is exceeded by the many thousands of copies of briefs and collections of minutes, along with a collection of original briefs and letters to princes. Another extensive series (7365 paper volumes), the Register of Supplications, covers the period from Pope Clement VI in the fourteenth century to Leo XIII. Other substantial collections in the archives include documents of the Apostolic Datary and the Apostolic Camera (dating from the thirteenth century), and from the Sacred College of Cardinals and the Sacred Consistorial Congregation with a series on Conclaves (dating from the fifteenth century). The especially important material from the Secretariat of State covering the Papacy's worldwide concerns is split into two collections: before and after Napoleon. Material from the former age is classified according to the rank of the persons concerned; from after 1814, according to subject matter.

All the above material is central to the history of the Popes and the Curia and provides an unparalleled source of information, still largely undigested, for medieval historians in particular. The archives also hold more extraneous collections ranging from documents on critical events in the history of the Catholic Church (classified, for example, as the *Council of Trent*, the *First Vatican Council*, the *Archive of Pius IX*) to the records of Roman patrician families closely linked to the Popes (such as the *Buoncompagni*, the *Borghese*, the *Patrizi-Montoro*). Miscellaneous documents stored in fifteen big cupboards range over a thousand years of history and cover an amazing variety of subjects from oriental religions and witchcraft to the cases of Calvin and Luther. Another collection of miscellaneous registers is still 'open' – the *Instruments Miscellanea* – far from being fully explored, and full of fascinating historical side-notes on, for example, the early Inquisition or the Popes' banking negotiations in the early Renaissance.

The diplomatic archives include about 8500 documents originally lodged in Castel Sant'Angelo. Again they cover a thousand years and contain international treaties, letters from rulers, and many of the most important declarations of the Roman Pontiffs.

Tours are not encouraged, but the best guide to the constantly expanding bookshelves of the Vatican Secret Archives is one of the longest-serving archivists, the Scottish priest Charles Burns. In the words of the historian Professor Denys Hay he is, to many scholars, 'a friend inside the mystery'. Plump, fresh-complexioned and blue-eyed, bubbling with enthusiasm but with a sharp tongue and mind, Mgr Burns, although totally dedicated and exceptionally knowledgeable, seems full of wonderment at where he is and what he is doing there, nearly a quarter of a century since he first set foot in Rome. He came to the Vatican when already a priest to study palaeography and diplomatics at the school attached to the archives. In October 1962 he became a *scrittore* at the secret archives, and in 1968 was promoted to archivist.

The location of the archives as well as their contents is eloquent of intimate papal history that goes back centuries and is still being made. The courtyard of the Belvedere, Mgr Burns recalls, was asphalted a few years ago to make a car park and then tiled very beautifully on the orders of Pope Paul. During the digging, a sharp lookout was kept for historical remains. The courtyard had been used for jousting in Benvenuto Cellini's day. The famous elephant presented to Pope Leo X was known to have been buried there, but nothing of it was found.

The neighbouring *Torre dei Venti* (Tower of the Winds) was handed over to the secret archives in the nineteenth century. It was first built as an observatory, on the orders of Pope Gregory XIII, to help implement recommendations made at the Council of Trent for a revision of the Julian calendar. From the roof, you can see an astonishing panorama of Rome, looking utterly still and clean-edged with the Tiber hidden, and filled with towers and tiled roofs packed together, dominated by the landmark of the Pantheon and a rarely seen perspective of St Peter's. When I was hurried there on a winter's evening, before the light abruptly faded, the sky seemed to run with eddies of black ink formed by the swarming, wheeling and diving of thousands of starlings. To be inside the Vatican at such moments is to be made almost sensually aware of its austere timelessness. Past and present seem one.

Observations in the Meridian Room, at the top of the Tower of the Winds, provided the data for the new Gregorian calendar put into effect throughout the Catholic world in 1582. Colourfully painted on one wall of the empty room is a scene of the storm on the Lake of Galilee. The opening in the mouth of the figure of the triton representing the south wind admits the shaft of sunlight which falls on the black meridian line in the white marble circle on the floor.

Artificial lighting used to be forbidden in the tower, as a safeguard against fire and intruders who, unlike the experienced staff, would need to light their way through its winding passages. It now heightens the dazzling effect of decorations that include frescoes by the famous Bril and the scarcely known Pomarancio.

In the main building of the secret archives, the same wealth of allusive historical material surrounds the seemingly endless stacks and files of mostly loosely bound papers and documents. (The late Eugène Tisserant, Cardinal Librarian, Dean of the Sacred College, once nodded approval of the idea that it should all be bound, and was then told this would take a hundred years.) One room is frescoed riotously with cherubs and heavy-breasted nymphs; when it was prepared for Queen Christina of Sweden – as far away as possible from the Pope's bachelor apartments – a Latin motto saying that all evil came from the north was hurriedly removed. On another floor, which houses the papal bull that divided the known world between Spain and Portugal, a large painting depicts the English Pope Adrian IV in feudal manner grandly handing over Ireland for ever to King Henry II of England. (A reason why, it is said, few Irish Catholics are called Adrian.) Elsewhere, a Pope is shown receiving England as his vassal state. The same Pope refused to accept the validity of Magna Carta, on the grounds that he had not been consulted as feudal overlord.

Among the secret archives themselves, many items are intrinsically precious and aesthetically pleasing, as well as being historically valuable. The archivists and a few privileged visitors can hold in their hands the exquisite richly illuminated fifteenth-century codex of Cardinal Niccolo d'Aragona, *De Sicilie regno*, as well as the momentous papal bull that pronounced the excommunication of Luther, and the one that excommunicated Queen Elizabeth I, letters signed by Michelangelo or Erasmus, or by Lucrezia Borgia writing to her father in a most accomplished hand. In the locked cupboard of a small room are the choicest items ranking both as treasure and as historical evidence: the splendid collection of heavy gold seals, a long letter on parchment from the nephew of

Genghis Khan to the Pope, the letter on silk from the Empress of China, and the red seals of all the Tudor peers of England. Above is deposited the signed testimony of Galileo at his judicial process.

For the intellectually curious, the branches of possible exploration spread out within the secret archives in tempting profusion. In the archives you can research very adequately, say, the evolution of writing materials or brigandage in the old Papal States. (Documents on the latter subject look as if they have not been touched since they were stored. In some areas of the archives there is evidence of an attempt at cataloguing, and then despair. Elsewhere, the progress is respectable.)

The prefect of the archives, Mgr Martino Giusti, who lives in the Vatican, insists that the primary aim of all who work there is the service of the Holy See, and specifically the service of the Pope. But the archives and the library possess considerable cultural and educational value for vast numbers of scholars from all over the world. The series of exhibitions mounted during the past decade or so have been outstanding: they have included the manuscripts of Queen Christina, the designs of Borromini, a Bible exhibition (with UNESCO), the magnificent bindings of the library, and Belgian and Bulgarian manuscripts.

The Vatican Secret Archives and the Apostolic Library were born together and are still linked like Siamese twins, though since the beginning of the seventeenth century they have developed different characters and even a kind of rivalry. Smollett did not distinguish between, nor applaud, them when he dropped sourly into Rome from his convalescence at Genoa in 1765. He wrote to a friend:

> I have nothing to communicate touching the library of the Vatican, which, with respect to the apartments and their ornaments, is undoubtedly magnificent. The number of books it contains does not exceed forty thousand volumes, which are all concealed from the view, and locked up in presses: as for the manuscripts, I saw none but such as are commonly presented to strangers of our nation: some very old copies of Virgil and Terence; two or three Missals, curiously illuminated; the book *De Septem Sacramentis*, written in Latin by Henry VIII against Luther; and some of that prince's love letters to Anne Boleyn.

It is certainly true that a high proportion of the Vatican's portable valuables seem to be stored away. 'You should see what treasures tumble out when you open a cupboard at the back of the Sistine Chapel,' said a monsignore to me, when we were conversing about the discoveries still to be made in the Vatican Archives or among its books and pictures.

The treasures of the Vatican Library – manuscripts, books, coins, medals and works of art – are safeguarded for the Pope by its patron, Cardinal Samorè, who is librarian as well as archivist of the Holy Roman Church. Its prefect is a sprightly, silver-haired Austrian Salesian priest, Don Alfons Stickler, a noted canon lawyer, the first rector of the Pontifical Institute for Latin, and a prolific writer on his own subject. He is a busy administrator, living above the library, where he enjoys one of the best views of Rome. He is assisted by the vice-prefect, Mgr José Ruysschaert, an authority on palaeography, and by a senior staff of thirty-five, of whom five are priests.

The ancient origins of the library can be traced back to the fourth century (or even, it could be said, to the four evangelists.) It had a chequered history of dispersal and migration during the Middle Ages and was founded in its surviving form by three Renaissance Popes. Nicholas V (1447–55), the patron of Fra Angelico, employed agents to search Italy for codices, copyists to transcribe for him, and humanists to annotate and translate. He bequeathed a library of over a thousand Latin and Greek manuscripts. Sixtus IV (1471–84) enlarged the collection to over three thousands and stored it in three beautiful halls on the ground floor of the Palace of Nicholas V, with desks for reading, a special room for the librarian, his assistants and a bookbinder, and a formal lending system. Sixtus V (1585–90) employed his favourite architect Domenico Fontana to design the site and building which, with momentous artistic and practical consequences, divided the Belvedere courtyard from what is now the Cortile della Pigna.

The library is based on the same site today, though greatly enriched and extending in various directions and long distances from its first building. On the upper floor of Fontana's building, the Sistine Hall measures 250 by 50 feet and is 30 feet high. It is divided into two arched aisles. The complex of Sixtus V includes two square rooms, a gallery and a vestibule, luxuriantly decorated, on the vaults, pilasters and walls, with frescoes which illustrate the history of manuscripts and printed books and scenes from the life of Pope Sixtus. Sixtus V also added a private section in the Gallery of Pius IV (the Sistine Rooms) to the parts of the library accessible to outside students.

Since the seventeenth century, glittering satellites have come into being around the Vatican Library proper through the acquisition of collections from noble or princely families. Among these prizes have been the looted Palatine Library of Heidelberg; the manuscripts from the fabulous Library of the Dukes of Urbino; manuscripts collected by Queen Christina of Sweden; large collections of codices from the Capponi and Ottoboni families; the Barberini Library, with furniture as well as manuscripts and printed books.

The progress of the Vatican Library over four centuries seems almost organic in its unceasing growth and adaptation to pressures and crises. These include one tragic accident, when the two central pillars of the Sistine Hall collapsed a few days before Christmas in 1931 and killed a library assistant and four workmen. Earlier, the idea of making the library a museum as well as a collection of books sprang from the decision to embellish a particular gallery (the Clementine) with ancient vases, because there were no frescoes on the walls. This development led to the acquisition of coins and antiques which are now housed in the Numismatic Rooms, the Sacred Museum and the Profane Museum. The relentless extension of the Vatican Library, however, was chiefly a planned response to the need for more book space and more convenient facilities for scholars. The first wave of extensions took the library into the western arm of Bramante's corridor (the Gallery of Pius IV and then the Borgia Apartments) till it acquired a huge T shape.

Pope Leo XIII relaxed the rules for research in the archives and opened the way for a more generous attitude in the 1880s to outside users of the library, traditionally the nicely situated preserve of members of the Curia, some of whom are still often to be seen there, reading quietly of an evening. Pius also created a Leonine Library by adapting the space exactly under the great Sistine Hall for several commodious reference and reading rooms. The Vatican Library's most important collections – the manuscripts – were subsequently transferred from the Sistine Hall to the new Leonine Library, as it in turn began to spread its wings. The Sistine Hall has since been used primarily for display purposes. Pope Pius XI renewed the library's equipment, gave it a new entrance from the Belevedere courtyard, and acquired more whole libraries such as those of the Chigi and Ferraioli families. Pope Pius XII prudently agreed to a continuing process of photographing and microfilming the Vatican manuscripts and rare printed books, for storage in the United States.

Today, the complex of libraries numbers over 700,000 printed volumes, 100,000 maps and engravings, 100,000 autographed items and 65,000 manuscript volumes. The quantities surpass those of many national libraries. By focussing attention chiefly on its great collection of manuscripts, and facilitating reference to them, the Vatican Library provides for scholars from all over the world a unique research institution at university level.

Its most impressive sight is still the majestic Sistine Hall. From the windows on one side, you can see the grandest section of the old Belvedere courtyard, sweeping towards the Vatican Palaces; on the other, the Cortile della Biblioteca (Library Courtyard) and the flank of the New Wing, parallel to the hall. Between the tall recessed windows, the two marbled and frescoed aisles give an impression of luminosity and space. The huge reference room, running under the Sistine Hall, is contrastingly crammed with long desks and chairs; the surfaces of the walls dividing the two aisles, and the lower part of the outer walls, are solid with bookcases. The room glows with light reflected from the furniture, or shed from evening lamps.

Among the most famous and valuable of the books is the Hebrew Bible, which once rested on a brass eagle in the centre of the Hall of the Palace of Urbino. It is beautifully adorned with miniatures and bound in gold and silver brocade. Along with the exquisite Masses of SS. Francis and Anne, it is kept in the so-called Little Gallery of the Library. In the Sistine Hall, the most precious Greek manuscripts include the fourth-century uncial Bible text (Codex Vaticanus B) and a sixth-century St Matthew's Gospel written in gold and silver on purple parchment. In Latin there are several fourth- and fifth-century editions of Virgil – the best known with fifty-nine miniatures – and a fourth-century palimpsest of Cicero's *De*

Republica, the earliest known Latin manuscript. The autographs include those of St Thomas Aquinas, Castiglione, Savonarola, Tasso and Petrarch. Inside an elephant's tooth is a letter to Pope Pius IX from the Emperor of Burma.*

Music has been pressed into the service of the Vatican, principally through choral singing, from the sixth century, when Pope Gregory the Great instituted a *Schola Cantorum* in Rome, a school of singers which developed plain chant, Roman and Gregorian, to a position of foremost importance in Christian Europe. In the Renaissance, the Julian Choir was founded for choral service in St Peter's, the Sistine Choir for the Sistine Chapel. Although he was at one stage made to retire from papal service, on the grounds that he was married and had composed madrigals, Palestrina (*c*.1525–94) was re-employed by the Pope and exerted a decisive influence for restraint and purity, which was sustained even when baroque experiments and extravagances captured the choirs of St Peter's.

After Palestrina and his glorious Mass of Pope Marcellus (who, like John Paul I, reigned for just a few weeks) the Popes patronized a succession of great musicians including Domenico Scarlatti, Marco Marazzoli, Gregorio Allegri (who wrote the plaintively exalted *Miserere*, which the young Mozart copied note by note from memory) and the astonishing soprano, Francesco Grossi. In his *Italian Journey*, Goethe, who went to Italy in 1786, recorded the effect that visiting the Sistine could have on a sensitive ear and heart:

> The music in the Sistine Chapel is unimaginably beautiful, especially the *Miserere* and the so-called *Improperi*, that is, the Crucified's reproaches to His people, which are sung on Good Friday. The moment when the Pope is stripped of his pontifical pomp and steps down from his throne to adore the Cross, while all the others stay where they are in silence, until the choir begins – *Populus meus quid feci tibi?* – is one of the most beautiful of all these remarkable rites. . . .

* Over 200 items from the archives were put on public display at the Vatican during 1981 to mark the centenary of their being opened to outside scholars.

After an extraordinarily turbulent period before and after the Italian seizure of Rome in 1870 (during which another soprano singer, Domenico Mustafa, the last of the *castrati*, was its colourful and aggressive 'Perpetual Director'), the Sistine Choir was reformed by Pope Pius XI and had its management and finances overhauled by Pope John XXIII. Today, it maintains the traditional function of supplying singers for ceremonies over which the Pope himself officiates, and the right to elect its leader from its own ranks. There are fifteen full-time male singers, under the direction of a Florentine priest, the *Maestro Direttore Perpetua*, Domenico Bartolucci. Another priest, Fr. Giovanni Catena OSM, works with him as *Maestro dei 'pueri cantores'* (maestro of the boy singers) and there are two lay assistants: a *segretario cantore* and a *decano cantore*.

The Sistine Choir, the *Cappella Musicale Pontifica*, is grouped with one of the offices of the Roman Curia, falling like the Swiss Guards among the institutions immediately around the person of the Pope. There are three other papal choirs, also associated with the Pope himself. The Julian Choir, under the direction of Armando Renzi, performs at all the important ceremonies in the Basilica of St Peter's. Like the papal choirs of St John Lateran and St Mary Major, both the Sistine and the Julian Choirs have found it increasingly difficult to find boy singers in recent years. In April 1977, women sang in a papal choir for the first time.

The Pontifical Institute of Sacred Music, with offices outside the Vatican in the Piazza S. Agostino, is a modest institution, with a small academic staff that can be counted on one hand, but with the heavyweight, near-octogenarian Cardinal Gabriel-Marie Garrone, Chancellor of the Pontifical Gregorian University, as its titular head. It is listed by the Vatican authorities among the 'Cultural Institutions' which are both Rome-based and international, and which all respond to the initiatives and directives of the Holy See. The Cultural Institutions include the Holy See's five Roman universities and various institutes; forty-seven Catholic universities outside Rome and many faculties for ecclesiastical and religious studies; eight Pontifical Academies; and scores of Roman seminaries and priests' colleges.

The Pontifical Academies are, among other things, a living expression of the powerful synthesizing tendencies of the Holy

See. One of them, the Pontifical Ecclesiastical Academy, is a teaching institution. The others, ranging over theology, art, religious practices and the natural sciences (and not all explicitly called Pontifical) are: the Pontifical Roman Academy of St Thomas Aquinas and of Catholic Doctrine; the Pontifical Roman Theological Academy; the Pontifical Academy of Our Lady Immaculate; the Pontifical International Marian Academy; the Liturgical Academy; the Distinguished Pontifical Academy of Arts of the Pantheon *Virtuosi*; the Pontifical Roman Academy of Archeology; the College of Devotion to the Martyrs; the Pontifical Academy of Sciences.

The first of these, the Academy of the Arts, was founded in 1543, the last, the Marian Academy, in 1946. The Popes who founded them or singled each of them out for pontifical recognition were personally devoted to the academies' intellectual pursuits or theological persuasions; usually they were called into being for specific ideological purposes related to current historical developments. The Academy of Catholic Doctrine, for example, combated the errors of the French Revolution; Pius X founded the Pontifical Institute of Sacred Music to strengthen the revival of plain chant.

The academies are scattered throughout Rome, except for the most famous of them, the Pontifical Academy of Sciences. This academy provides a notable example of the two cultural facets of the Vatican: the material culture, of the Vatican's buildings, monuments, artifacts and so forth; and the spiritual and also social culture that finds expression through them. As mentioned in Chapter 1, the headquarters of the Pontifical Academy for Sciences has since 1922 been in Pirro Ligorio's casina of Pius IV, to which a new wing was added by Pope Pius XI.

The casina, to the north-west of the Vatican Gardens, half-way between St Peter's and the Vatican Picture Gallery, is sheltered by trees on gently rising ground. It is composed of a palace or villa and a loggia, separated by an elliptical courtyard enclosed by a little wall, with a fountain in the middle. The casina seems to be emerging from a classical cocoon into a baroque fantasy. The architectural plan of the two buildings is simple; the façade of the two-storeyed villa is covered with a rich variety of ornamentation. The ceilings of the villa and the loggia were decorated by Federico Zuccari, Federico Barrocci and Pierleone Genga.

Here, the Pontifical Academy holds a plenary session every two years, and a study week, attended by about twenty-five scientists. Their meeting provides an occasion for the Pope to make a scientific address, in the presence of members of the College of Cardinals as well as the academicians, and to announce the winner of the Pius XI medal for a young scientist. It was the kind of occasion which the prolific Pope Pius XII especially enjoyed. In the winter of 1979, Pope John Paul II seized on the occasion of a session of the Pontifical Academy to pay tribute to Galileo as a Christian, a step which pushed home his earlier message that he would dedicate a great deal of his attention to the problems of culture, science and the arts.

The Pontifical Academy of Sciences has a president, at present Carlos Chagas, Professor of Biophysics at the Federal University of Brazil, and a president emeritus, an Australian Jesuit, Fr. Daniel O'Connell, former Director of the Vatican Observatory. The academicians are appointed by the Pope for life, to a total of seventy; at present, as well as two Vatican-nominated supernumeraries, Mgr Giusti from the secret archives and Mgr Stickler from the library, there are sixty-one academicians, mostly professors from European and American universities. They qualify through their original scientific research, and need not be Catholics.

The Papcy's practical attitude towards science and its willingness to be involved in applied science and technology as an aid to religion are exemplified in the Vatican Observatory, the *Specola Vaticana*. The Popes' interest in astronomy was based on the research needed for reform of the calendar, for which Pope Gregory XIII built the Tower of the Winds in 1576. In the nineteenth century, important astronomical work was carried out at the Roman College Observatory, notably by the Jesuit, Pietro Angelo Secchi, who invented the meteorograph. In 1870, the Italian government took the observatory over, and in 1888 Pope Leo XIII re-established the Vatican's own research facilities in the Tower of the Winds.

A Jesuit priest, Fr. J.G. Hagen, was director of the observatory from 1906 to 1930, during which time it was moved to another medieval tower inside the Vatican, and a ten-volume catalogue was prepared, recording the position of half a million stars. Since Fr. Hagen, the directors, indeed all the staff, of the observatory have been recruited from the Society of Jesus.

In 1930, Pius XI had the observatory moved to Castel Gandolfo and equipped it with new telescopes and an astrophysical laboratory. Today the small Jesuit community of six, under Fr. George Coyne as observatory director and Fr. Emiel De Graeve as their father superior, study the motions of the stars in the Vatican zone of the sky and carry out research on interstellar polarization and the classification of stellar spectra.

Like Vatican Radio, the Vatican Observatory is an organization of the Vatican City State, not of the Holy See, but a significant expression of the culture of the institutional Papacy. This culture is astonishingly rich. It carries along with it the relics of the Papacy's virtually imperial past, adapted to a still-powerful position in the present. The fountains in the Vatican City, for example, are splendid to see and listen to, and a reminder that it was the Popes who built all the marvellous fountains of Rome: the Tortoise Fountain, the Three Fountains of the Piazza Navona, the Bee Fountain, and the Fountain of Trevi – to construct the latter Pope Urban VIII increased the tax on wine. Inside the Vatican walls the pride of the Popes is manifest in the *Fontana dell'Aquilone*, the Fountain of the Great Eagle, designed by the Flemish sculptor Giovanni Vasanzio with dragons, tritons and its great bird of prey on top. Another fountain of Vasanzio's – a display of frenzied waters gushing through foliage – is constructed round a huge dragon from the arms of the Borghese family. Carlo Maderno's fountain, near the Belvedere, sports a lead galley whose cannons spout water – the device wanted by Pope Clement IX.

While the fountains play, a few scholars in an office in the Vatican's Via della Tipografia, under their Swiss president, Abbot Carlo Egger, are working to preserve the use of Latin in the Church and translating messages sent by the Pope and the Secretariat of State into that language. They are a dedicated group of seven priests and laymen, with six directors who include Walter Persegati, from the museums, and one of the few women working in the Vatican, Christina Mohrmann. They like to talk Latin among themselves over lunch.

Every year, on the feast of the Apostles SS. Peter and Paul, a huge floral construction in the symbolic form of a fisherman's net is suspended between the two tall columns of the main entrance of St Peter's Basilica. St Peter's itself is the greatest of the Vatican monuments and the best-known example of a culture which centres on the Papacy yet influences millions at many levels of sophistication through its international appeal. The main criticisms of this culture are that it is still too Italian, too European, too clerical and too materialistic to be compatible with the spiritual mission of a universal Church. But, like the Incarnation itself, the fact of the Church being in the world and of the world in actual human history – an aspect of the so-called 'scandal of particularity' – is the essence of historical Christianity.

The scandal is seen again in the tradition of St Peter's burial place.

Between the floor level of the old Constantinian Basilica and the central nave of the present Basilica are the Vatican grottoes which extend to about half the length of the nave. The oldest section dates from the sixth century, when a crypt was built around the apse of the old church to provide access to the tomb of the Apostle. A new crypt with three naves – and a semicircular ambulatory stretching round the old crypt – were built in the sixteenth century. Ten rooms were added in this century, to the north and south of the main crypt. The grottoes contain four chapels cut from the base of the piers supporting the great dome of the Basilica.

The rooms, chapels and passages of the grottoes are a strange, silent storehouse of religious relics and works of art. They house early Christian sarcophagi and architectural remains and monuments from the Constantinian Basilica. There are some delicate frescoes from the early Renaissance, and the mosaic head of an angel attributed to Giotto. There are old mosaics and statues: Arnolfo di Cambio's Boniface VIII and Pollaiuolo's monument to Sixtus IV outstanding among them.

But, above all, there are the tombs. Mostly, these leave one slightly awed but unmoved. Among those of the princes are the tombs of the last Stuarts and of Christina of Sweden; among the tombs of the Popes are those of the first Borgia Pontiff, Calixtus III, and of the only English Pope so far,

Nicholas Breakspear, who became Adrian IV. The sight of them makes one thoughtful; the sight of fresh flowers before the tombs of John XXIII, Paul VI and John Paul I reminds one that when a cardinal is crowned Pope he is very near his burial place.

The scene changes abruptly if you go down from the grottoes to the necropolis, where the air grows colder and you pass from the subdued triumphalism of medieval and modern funereal pomp and marble to ancient burial urns, narrow passages, brown Roman brickwork, uneven floors and plain symbols from the historical edge of Christianity. The Roman necropolis was discovered in 1940 when work was being done on the tomb of Pius XI in the grottoes. Excavations – which had already been ordered by Pius XII in 1939 and continued to 1949 – revealed a large burial ground beneath the Basilica. It contained urns, graves and sarcophagi and showed a change from cremation to inhumation. The necropolis contains two rows of chamber tombs aligned from east to west, built originally across a hillside dropping from north to south. The mausoleums (adorned with mosaics, stuccoes and frescoes) belonged to rich pagan families and some of them were later owned by Christians. Part of the hill had to be levelled and some of the burial ground filled in for the foundation of the Constantinian Basilica.

Here, it is supposed, is the location of the tomb of St Peter. Four of the excavated mausoleums form a quadrangle directly under the main altar of the Basilica. The excavations revealed a red wall (dated to the period 147–161 AD from the maker's stamps on five of the tile bricks) with a niche and marble slab signalling the presence of an important grave. Two collections of bones were unearthed, among them the bones of a big man. When the Emperor Constantine built his Basilica in the fourth century – on a slope, over the burial places – the small monument was carefully protected and left visible in the centre of the presbytery. The recent excavations strongly support the tradition that St Peter's was built on the tomb of the first Pope, but whether the bones are those of St Peter is unverifiable. The imagination stirs when you peer through the opening in the red wall and remember that the road past the Gate of the Bells through which you get to the necropolis passes parallel to the ancient road which skirted the circus of Nero and Caligula.

9

The Balance Sheet of Papal Wealth

When Michelangelo was painting the Sistine Chapel, Pope Julius II wanted him to spread rich colours and gold on the frescoes he was re-touching. 'Holy Father,' he said pointedly, 'in those days men did not bedeck themselves in gold, and those you see painted there were never very rich. They were holy men who despised riches.'

In the days of the early Church, the 'mysteries' of the new religion, in the sense of its sacred words and acts, were kept secret from recent converts as well as from the unbelievers. To modern Catholics, as well as to those outside, the finances of the Vatican have been among the deepest mysteries. Those who have inquired have never been given hard figures, and have had to content themselves with being told, for example, that the income of the Vatican was about the same as that of a large American diocese such as Chicago.

The Pope carries no money, but his head appears on Vatican coins. From time to time, he has to take grave decisions on financial policy. He may even intervene abruptly to order an urgent financial transaction. This very direct involvement of the Pope, and the sense of being in a position of trust felt by those who are in charge of the Vatican's financial affairs, account for the notorious reticence of Vatican officials when the conversation ever turns to money.

Three bishops of the Pope's personal suite (the *Famiglia Pontifica*) accompany him at formal occasions (acting rather like bunches of flowers for the photographs, one of them has said). They are the Prefect of the Papal Household, the Vicar General of Vatican City, and the Almoner of His Holiness, Archbishop Antonio Travia, who is Director of the Holy Father's Welfare

234

Service, *Servizio Assistenziale del Santo Padre*. This is the modern name, imposed by Pope Paul VI, for the old *Elemosineria Apostolica*, which can be traced back as a formal office of the Papacy to the thirteenth century, though well before then officials were entrusted with the Popes' personal acts of charity. Apart from his ceremonial duties, the Pope's almoner supervises several institutes which depend on the Holy See, and runs a small office with a staff of about half a dozen.

Cardinal Egidio Vagnozzi, President of the Prefecture for Economic Affairs until his death in December 1980, was appointed partly because of John XXIII's appreciation of his experiences in the United States and Manila, where he had studied the 'marvellous' success of a local priest in reforming church finances. It was to the Pope, he said, that he presented his department's consolidated budget and balance sheet; just as it was to the Pope that the Vatican 'Bank' – the *Istituto per le Opere di Religione*, most of whose accumulated funds are not those of the Holy See – was answerable. At the *Prefettura*, the cardinal added, 'the president acts as the eyes of the Pope in regard to the material and economic activities of the Holy See. . . .'

The present form of the Prefecture for the Economic Affairs of the Holy See dates from 1967, when Pope Paul VI re-organized the departments of the Curia. It is the nearest organization in the Holy See to the US or British Treasury, and the president is the Pope's treasurer. 'It is not easy to make a comparison between the Holy See and a secular state,' Cardinal Vagnozzi told me, 'but under various aspects the Prefecture has something in common with a ministry of the budget, an exchequer and audit department, a treasury.'

Before the reform of the Curia, the various administrative departments of the Vatican prepared their own annual financial statements and balance sheets, each according to its own different method. Muddle was rife, though more tolerable before the years of spiralling inflation and mounting expenditure. The Prefecture now imposes common criteria for the annual reports, inspects and advises on them, and consolidates the figures into one balance sheet. In addition, the Prefecture prepares a consolidated budget and detailed budget report covering the whole financial picture, including the shady areas if there are any, since it has the authority to initiate criminal or civil action in financial matters.

The Prefecture is meant to probe, to check, where necessary to refer back, and finally to approve and consolidate, the financial reports of the departments, without, Cardinal Vagnozzi commented 'any prejudice to the autonomous exercise of the institutional functions of each body'. Anyone knowing the strong-mindedness of cardinals, and the bitter battles fought in the secular sphere between treasuries and spending departments, will appreciate the need Cardinal Vagnozzi felt to link the official activity of the Prefecture 'with personal efforts to explain, convince and persuade the heads of the individual administrations at conferences, meetings and so forth . . .'.

Above all, the Prefecture answers to the Pope, whom the president sees when he needs. Its most important responsibility, Cardinal Vagnozzi emphasized, 'is to let the Holy Father know the actual economic situation and the state of the patrimony of the Holy See in total, and to suggest initiatives that could lead to opportune improvements in the structure and organization of the departments, always from the viewpoint of efficiency and productivity'.

The offices of the *Prefettura* are in the Palazzo delle Congregazioni, a fairly modern building opposite one of the arms of the Bernini colonnade, in the Largo del Colonnato. There are usually a few business magazines in the waiting room, such as *Ecos*, the review of the Italian State company ENI. The atmosphere is quiet and unhurried. The cardinal president takes the lift every morning to his pleasant third-floor office from where he can see the Apostolic Palace through his windows.

A commission of three cardinals is responsible for the *Prefettura*: Giuseppe Caprio in succession to the Roman-born Egidio Vagnozzi; Giuseppe Maria Sensi, an Italian curial cardinal with a diplomatic background; and Josef Höffner, Archbishop of Cologne. The secretary is a bishop, Mgr Giovanni Abbo, and there is a further staff of eight, including four laymen and two women.

Vagnozzi was a shrewd representative of the old-school Curia. He was a lean, grey-haired man in his mid seventies, looking rather sombre behind his pale-rimmed spectacles, but willing to talk freely and wittily about his lifetime's experiences and diamond-hard religious opinions. There were bright colours in his office and flashes of gold from the carriage clock ticking on his desk, his pectoral cross and the ring on his right hand. He reminisced about his career as an apostolic delegate, and stabbed himself dramatically in the ribs with his fingers as he recalled that there were always 'two thorns in my sides – the ultra-conservatives and the ultra-progressives . . .'. He said that, in the fifty years of his 'priestly life', the greatest historical event was the Second Vatican Council – 'it was beneficial to the Church and it was necessary'.

On the subject of the Vatican's finances, however, the cardinal proved less forthcoming. The key to his attitude, shared widely in the Curia, is that, even if the Vatican were to publish complete information about its financial affairs, it would still encounter abuse and disbelief. In fact, the cardinal's responses to questioning – not denying this and not confirming that, praising one source and condemning another – led me towards a fairly reliable estimate of the financial position of the Vatican.

From discussions with officials of the *Prefettura*, it is plain that the Vatican today feels poor even if it looks very rich. Cardinal Vagnozzi commented that the Catholic Church had no fixed or fiscal 'contributions' flowing into the centre from affiliated bodies, such as the World Council of Churches enjoys. The Vatican needed a steady income 'for the sake of all the Church'.

Inflation has undermined the Church's financial stability throughout the world, the cardinal reminded me. In the United States, for example, the financial problems of Catholic schools and universities had also been worsened by the dip in 'vocations' and the need to employ more lay people. The Vatican, too, was having to look outside the religious orders and the priesthood for staff as its burden of work grew heavier. Overall, salaries were low. A cardinal earned less than an Italian senator, Cardinal Vagnozzi commented, not without indignation. 'We don't live in palaces nowadays.' In fact, after ten years' service in the Curia, a 'higher prelate of the first class' – such as the Archbishop Vice Secretary of State, the *Sostituto* – earned 650,000 lire (say, £350) a month, with benefits. (This was before the 1980 'review', which gave adjustments of 50 per cent on the basis of 1970).

The Prefecture keeps its eye – the eye of the Pope –

principally on five administrative organizations which are concerned with the property of the Holy See and the Vatican City State. The administration or government of the state (the *Governatorato*), with its eight departments under a commission of cardinals, spends on Vatican Radio and the museums, salaries and the upkeep of buildings, and derives an income from the museum charges, stamp and coin issues, retail sales of one kind and another. The overall result has usually been in the black.

The *Fabbrica* of St Peter's (St Peter's, Michelangelo said once, was a meadow on which many fat oxen had grazed . . .) under its octogenarian president, Cardinal Paolo Marella, committee of administration, and four permanent architects, is in charge of the preservation and maintenance of the Basilica, the archives, the mosaic factory and the excavations of the necropolis. Offerings from visitors and income from sales of tickets for the cupola and the necropolis provide an income which generally balances the expenses.

The Apostolic Chamber meets the cost of offices and staff in the Apostolic Palace servicing its own college of priests and the Cardinal Camerlengo. Its history of financial and judicial responsibility goes back to the eleventh century. Since Pope Paul VI's reform of the Curia, it is meant to administer the property of the Holy See when the papal throne is unoccupied, in a period of *Sede Vacante*.

The Sacred Congregation for the Evangelization of the Peoples (Propaganda Fide) derives most of its substantial income from donations from Catholics throughout the world. It produces its own annual report. Usually, it ends the year with a surplus. Unlike other congregations, it has kept the administration of its assets in its own hands, and enjoys virtual financial autonomy, though its property is the property of the Holy See, and its financial affairs are supervised by the Prefecture.

So, too, are the financial affairs of the second of the Vatican's three main financial bodies, the Administration of the Patrimony of the Holy See (APSA). This also emerged in its present form from Pope Paul's reforms of 1967. Its commission of five cardinals is headed by the Secretary of State, Cardinal Casaroli followed by Cardinal Sebastiano Baggio, Cardinal John Knox, Cardinal Pericle Felici and Cardinal Joseph

Schröfleis: the names of seasoned warriors in the service of orthodoxy and the Pope. They direct a large organization, which is probably the most professional and, over details, among the most secretive in the Vatican, and which employs a staff of about forty lay people (mostly Italians), four priests and two nuns.

Cardinal Caprio held the position of head of the Commission of APSA from 1979, when Pope John Paul II made his first batch of important curial appointments, until 1981. The move caused some surprise, as it moved APSA from the direct control of the Cardinal Secretary of State imposed by Pope Paul VI. 'The intention,' comments Cardinal Caprio, 'was to allow more time to be given to our work.' However, on the death of Cardinal Vagnozzi, Casaroli regained the position that was laid down for him under the 1967 constitution.

Cardinal Caprio discussed the history of the APSA with me from when the Popes were in exile at Avignon and the treasurer worked in a room in the Palace, just below that of the Pope. 'This showed the importance of the charitable work of the Papacy.' Like Cardinal Vagnozzi, he spoke in favour of the veil of secrecy that has covered most of the financial interests and operations of the Holy See. Information would too easily be interpreted out of context. 'And, in any case, do we have the right to reveal not only the details of the income of the Holy See but also of the expenditure – how much, for example, the Holy Father gives to this charity or that? It would stir up all sorts of confusion and controversy.'

Cardinal Caprio, in a beautifully furnished, yellow-carpeted room in the Apostolic Palace, explained for me the main policy decisions taken by APSA. 'The important questions of property or investment land on this desk.' Behind him, he has years of experience as a Vatican diplomat in the Far East, including mainland China, and the knowledge and authority that comes from following Mgr Benelli for two years in the influential position of *Sostituto*. He is a short, round-faced man from the south of Italy with a direct gaze through his half-rimmed glasses, and a gurgling chuckle, whose hands dance as he talks. He confesses he misses the Far East and the world of diplomacy, 'but we cardinals do as we are told . . .'.

Do accusations about the wealth of the Church worry him? 'Not at all. Only the problems worry me. And they are very simple. Fifty years ago the revenues of the Holy See were sufficient for the management of the Curia and the Vatican City. Since then, income has risen about three or four times, whereas salaries have jumped, say, twenty times. Our pressing task is to provide the funds for running the central government of the Church. We have no taxes. Our only source of revenue is from the Catholics of the world. . . .'

This message is also emphasized by APSA's secretary, Archbishop Lorenzo Antonetti, who, when I met him, was still digesting the changes in command that had suddenly taken place, after his two years in the secretarial post. Before that, a long career in the diplomatic service took him to Nicaragua, and for four years to Zaire. For Archbishop Antonetti, pale and affable in his gold-rimmed spectacles, one of the main problems is how to alert Catholics to their responsibilities. The Church belongs to the whole world; the whole Catholic world should give the Church the financial support it needs at the centre: a theme that was to be heard by the cardinals when they were called to the Vatican in the autumn of 1979.

The APSA hands over 1 per cent of its revenue for the running expenses of the Prefecture for Economic Affairs, to which, as we have seen, it submits its own accounts. It is divided into two sections, both of them housed nearby in the Apostolic Palace. The Ordinary Section, under a clerical delegate, Mgr Luigi Sposito, deals with the day-to-day administration of the Curia. It is responsible for the salaries of practically all those working for the Holy See in the Curia, for the running costs and maintenance of the Curia's buildings and offices, and of the Apostolic Palaces, for the day-to-day outlays of the Curia (excepting Propaganda Fide), for the expenses of the College of Cardinals, the Synod of Bishops, and some of the institutions of the diocese of Rome.

The other half of APSA, the Extraordinary Section, is the successor to the financial body created by Pope Pius XI to look after the funds given to the Vatican by the Italian government in 1929 under the settlement terms of the Lateran Treaty. Its delegate is an Italian layman, Benedetto Argentieri, who is directly answerable to the secretary, Archbishop Antonetti and the cardinals mentioned above, but who heads a large staff of laymen. The Extraordinary Section of APSA controls a large proportion of the liquid assets of the Vatican – equity shares, bonds – and some of its real estate, and is responsible for the vital, if controversial, investment policy of the Holy See. Along with the Vatican 'Bank', it draws the hottest fire of the moralist critics of the Vatican's wealth and financial involvements.

Argentieri's own office is two floors up in the Apostolic Palace, and the way there from outside is through the bronze doors to the right of St Peter's, past the Swiss Guards, then the doorkeepers. The delegate's room is like an old-fashioned banker's parlour. It is large and quite dark, full of leather furniture and oil paintings in gilt frames. It overlooks St Peter's Square and had a good, uninterrupted view until ceremonial scaffolding was left in place in front of it, to save expense. Argentieri, a slim, middle-aged, soberly suited family man, talks about his work with a charming attitude of reserve and enthusiasm, directness and discretion. 'We are the direct collaborators of the head of the Church,' he says solemnly, in the English he learned as interpreter with a British infantry regiment.

Responsible to Cardinal Casaroli and under the supervision from the *Prefettura*, Argentieri's financial section maintains its now traditional stance of independence: 'We are a kind of government agency which is independently managed,' he said, though since we last met, the authority of the Secretariat of State has been reaffirmed. His most influential predecessor, head of the Special Administration set up by Pius XI, was also a layman, Bernardino Nogara, an engineer and vice-chairman of the Banca Commerciale Italiana. Nogara was a long-sighted financier. He invested intelligently and made careful provisions regarding Vatican property, including the transfer of funds to the United States in good time before the Second World War.

In the 1960s, Pope Paul became increasingly sensitive to the idea that the Church should be seen as a financial entrepreneur, and the department began to shed Vatican investments in Italian companies. 'That was before my time,' Argentieri goes on, 'before I came here after fifteen years' experience abroad. It was providential. Look what happened to the market. . . .' This comment sounds incongruous, uttered a few yards from the Pope's own apartments, but Argentieri reminds you that 'we have to provide the resources for the life of the Holy See'. And this, logically, dictates a prudent but opportunistic investment policy. 'We have a highly diversified portfolio. All the time, subject to the ban on investing in certain kinds of industry, we are looking for a good return. We review our portfolio formally at periodical intervals. I and my collaborators here have some discretion on selling on a day-to-day basis.'

On rare occasions, a move to raise liquid funds through selling is initiated directly by the Pope himself, as when Pope Paul sought money for relief help to Colombia. Normally, Argentieri's section, with its double signing for transactions other than the cardinal president's, its daily *Financial Times* and *Wall Street Journal*, its own computer and worldwide banking links, pursues a conscientious free-wheeling course, under the authority of Cardinal Casaroli and Archbishop Antonetti.

The APSA is treated as a central bank by the World Bank, the International Monetary Fund and the Bank for International Settlements. For running the business of the Vatican, it more or less, in Argentieri's words, 'declares a dividend every year'.

The offices of what is popularly called the Vatican Bank are on the ground floor beneath the Pope's apartments. Its customers come to the Tower of Nicholas V, a few hundred yards from St Anne's Gate. Its proper title is the Institute for Religious Works, *Istituto per le Opere di Religione (IOR)*. It is an office which was founded by Pope Leo XIII about ninety years ago for the express purpose of gathering and administering funds for religious purposes of the Church. It provides clearing-bank services, chiefly for those who live or work in the Vatican, for diplomats, for heads of religious orders, and for some Italians with Vatican connections of one sort or another. It also acts as a merchant bank, forging international connections and advising on investments.

The Holy See receives the profits the bank makes on its transactions as a business, though a large proportion of its investments and their yield belong to the religious orders. Pope Pius XII modified its status in the 1940s to make it responsible for 'the custody and administration of monies (in bonds and in cash) and properties transferred or entrusted to the institute itself by fiscal or legal persons for the purposes of religious works and works of Christian piety'.

The bank's supervisory commission of five cardinals includes the Cardinal Secretary of State. A staff, mostly laymen, run the offices and the bank counter, which – for all its marble floors, patient queues, papal bust and crucifix – is not so different in atmosphere from a branch office of Barclays or Chase Manhattan. I have had my cheques cashed there by courteous favour. There are three priests on the staff, but their main work is not financial. At the top, the president of the department is the American bishop, Paul C. Marcinkus, the best-known of all Vatican figures in world banking and financial circles. The delegate on the administration – Sig. Luigi Mennini – is a close collaborator of Bishop Marcinkus and also serves on the boards of many Italian companies in a personal capacity. One is warned not to conclude that the Vatican Bank therefore has a shareholding in those companies.* Bishop Marcinkus enjoys considerable freedom of action, escaping the direct supervision of the Prefecture for Economic Affairs but responsible to the government of the state, and reporting either directly to the Pope or through the Cardinal Secretary of State.

Bishop Marcinkus, who is of Lithuanian extraction, was born and brought up in Cicero near Chicago, Illinois – as his accent betrays. He is a fast thinker and good talker, in fair command of several languages. He is a genial extrovert, who is at home on the golf course. A heavy man, with grey, thinning hair, over six feet tall, he still shows the physical toughness that won him the job of bodyguard and organizer for Pope Paul VI on the Pope's foreign expeditions. He is said to have saved Pope Paul's life during the assassination attempt in the Philippines. He was appointed by Pope Paul first as secretary, then in 1968 as president, of the bank. Under Pope John Paul II, he has continued to be concerned with the Pontiff's personal safety, to accompany him on journeys, and to check arrangements beforehand.

When he is not travelling with the Pope or busy at the Villa Stritch (the Roman residence for American priests on Via della Nocetta), Bishop Marcinkus can be seen most weekdays crossing the floor of the Vatican Bank to his own office, where he plays a key role in policy-making. He has been a controversial and reticent figure over the past decade, a

---

*Charges of alleged fraud were brought against Sig. Mennini in connection with Banca Privata Italiana in 1981.

victim of the repercussions of financial dealings between the Vatican and the Sicilian financier, Michele Sindona, for which he accepts no responsibility.

These dealings are worth summarizing. The Sindona affair has exasperated those who are critical of any Vatican involvement in international finance, and embarrassed those who accept the need for it to possess capital and income but wish it to be seen to be whiter than white in its dealings. The importance of the Sindona affair is that, fairly or not, it has sharpened scepticism about the competence and even the integrity of the Vatican in financial matters and fuelled the demand for more disclosure.

The background story is that, in the mid 1960s, on the insistence of Pope Paul VI, the main financial institutions of the Vatican, particularly APSA, further diversified their already widespread interests and shed their majority share-holdings in companies. The motives were mixed: investment ought to be more international; the Vatican should not be able to dominate any single large company. Moreover, in 1968, the Italian authorities finally made the Vatican's investments in Italy subject to dividend tax.

Michele Sindona (well known in Milan as a good Catholic entrepreneur) seemed to offer an attractive solution in regard to one Vatican investment in particular: the holding of a one-third controlling interest in the Italian property and develop-ment conglomerate, Società Generale Immobiliare.

The discussions are said to have taken place initially, in 1969, between Sindona and Mgr Sergio Guerri, then secretary of APSA, who was the consultor to the Vatican Bank before Pope Paul made him a cardinal in 1969.

The Società Generale Immobiliare, whose president had been Governor of the Vatican City State, owned a wide spread of property which included the Rome Hilton and the Watergate building in Washington. Sindona was to handle the sale of the Vatican's shares in the company as agent through his own international banking interests and connections, and retain some of the stock himself. Sindona transferred Vatican shares in Immobiliare to an amount then worth about £16 millions to a Luxembourg tax-haven subsidiary, Parisbas Transcontinental. The stock eventually ended up in the hands of Charles Bludhorn, the president of an American conglomerate company. The Vatican sold and re-invested its financial interest in other Italian companies.

In the late 1960s and early 1970s, Sindona bought shares in two financial institutions which the Vatican Bank had helped to set up: Banca Unione and Finabank. Through his own financial instrument, Banca Privata Finanziaria, he acquired majority control equity in the two banks, leaving the Vatican Bank as minority shareholders. The Vatican Bank set out to divest itself of its holdings and did shed most of them before the crash of Sindona.

Cracks in the Sindona edifice appeared, after he failed – against Bank of Italy opposition – in an expensive takeover bid for the Bastogi group, Italy's largest holding company.

In 1972, Sindona switched operations to New York, starting with the bid to buy a controlling interest in the ailing Franklin National Bank. In 1974, the bank was forced to close; an investigation revealed losses on foreign exchange dealings of £20 millions, and the Securities and Exchange Commission started fraud proceedings against Sindona and several officials of the Franklin. (The SEC had brushed against the Vatican Bank itself in 1973, over the bank's inadequately documented acquisition of a share in the American Vetco Industries through an intermediary. The misunderstanding was resolved amicably and with no financial damage.)

Sindona had created a jungle of nominee shareholdings, multiple directorships and 'front' operations. In the summer of 1974, his enterprise began to crumble. Partly because of the Franklin failure, he had to ask support for his newly merged Banca Privata Italiana in Rome, from the Bank of Italy. His own Bankhaus Wolff in Hamburg failed shortly after. After taking his 38 per cent shareholding in Immobiliare as collateral for its loans, and seizing and closing down the Banca Privata Italiana, the Bank of Italy uncovered a huge deficit in the bank's operations. In the autumn of 1974 a warrant was issued by Milan magistrates for Sindona's arrest on charges of falsifying the accounts of the Banca Unione in 1970. In January 1975, Sindona's Finabank was closed by the Swiss government, with reported losses of at least £25 millions.

In June 1976, Sindona was tried in Italy *in absentia* on separate charges of violating the bank laws, and he was sentenced to three and a half years' imprisonment. He had begun his protracted exile in an apartment in Manhattan, protesting his innocence, resisting an extradition order issued by the Italians, and facing an indictment for fraud (on ninety-nine counts concerning the Franklin National Bank) from the Americans. He disappeared, and was reported to have been kidnapped, in New York in 1979, and at last came to trial and was sentenced in 1980.

Before the collapse of the Sindona empire, Cardinal Guerri, in his capacity as pro-president of the government of the state, was reported to have withdrawn Vatican money from the Sindona affiliate property company, SGI. Paper losses were made as the Vatican sold a large portion of its shares in Sindona-controlled enterprises during the weeks and months leading up to the débâcle, but it is said that the total holdings fetched, at the end of the day, $28 millions more than had been paid for them.

Vatican officials are loath to comment on the Sindona affair. In the view of Cardinal Vagnozzi, most of what had been written about it was 'hearsay' and did not correspond to reality. Bishop Marcinkus himself, writing to me after his visit to Turkey in the autumn of 1979, said that he could not speak about the relations Sindona might have had with the Vatican; though, as far as he knew, the only business venture involved the sale to Sindona of a number of stocks which the Administration of the Patrimony of the Holy See had in its possession – Immobiliare and two or three minor ones. Pope Paul VI never met Sindona, except perhaps at a general audience, and any references to Sindona as a 'papal financier and consultant' were without foundation. In regard to his own personal relations with Sindona, Bishop Marcinkus commented that he met him on several occasions at very social functions and found him pleasant company, 'but I never had any business dealings with him and never used him as an adviser or consultant'.

The dealings between Sindona and the *Istituto per le Opere di Religione* concerning Banca Privata Finanziaria led to the latter's suffering only a paper loss 'since we had more than recouped our investment and, in fact, made a substantial gain'.

Bishop Marcinkus informed me that he had never participated in any of Sindona's financial operations, even though 'certain opportunities' had on occasion been presented by Sindona, whose talent he respected. His policy was and always had been, to avoid operations with too commercial a character. 'I maintain that the monies which the Church has at its disposal are a means to achieve the goal, our religious goal, and that if we become too involved in commercial matters we would lose our identity as an institute for religious works.'

But the organization of the Vatican necessitates involvement in commericial matters. The marvellous buildings of the city state and all their contents, despite their tremendous value, incur costs rather than generate income. The running of the city state and the world mission of the Holy See demands more and more cash income, either from gifts or investment, or both.

The treasures of the Vatican include the priceless contents of the Basilica of St Peter's, the Vatican galleries and museums, the treasure of St Peter's, the Vatican grottoes and necropolis, and all the accumulation of furniture, furnishings and ornamentation with which the buildings and courtyards of the Vatican City are embellished and enriched. 'Priceless' is a word used advisedly, since the sale of these treasures – Michelangelo's glistening white *Pietà*, let us say, or the Apollo Belvedere – other than in token fashion, is unthinkable. The best indication of the financial worth of all this may come from remembering that the sum that Michelangelo's single marble *tondo* of the Madonna, owned by the Royal Academy in London, was estimated in 1979 as likely to fetch, if sold, was £20 millions sterling.

'Token' sales have been made and will probably continue to be made of items that the Pope can consider personally his own. But the Vatican treasures as such are held by the Pope on trust, as covered by the Lateran Treaty, which stipulated that students and visitors must be able to inspect them, as the patrimony of all mankind. The Pope does not think of himself as the personal owner of the property belonging to the Holy See. Yet the law of the Church, which lays down strict rules for the administration of property by ecclesiastical authorities throughout the world, leaves the Pope free to dispose as he wishes of all or some of the property that belongs to the Papacy. The practical rule is that a Pope can give away anything

247

which he or his predecessor has received. Anything received by an earlier Pope than his predecessor (presumably one would omit John Paul I) becomes, so to speak, part of the entailed patrimony of the Holy See, and is not given away. Thus, when Pope Paul gave away the papal tiara for the benefit of the poor, he gave away the tiara which he himself had been given on his election by the people of Milan, not the tiaras his predecessors had used.

However, the sight of the Vatican's wealth of gold and silver, marble and mosaic, precious stones and vestments, statuary and painting, and fine books and manuscripts, all the relics and all the riches of modern art, seems to shock as many people as it delights.

The golden, or perhaps purple, thread to understanding the Vatican's wealth today begins with the Lateran Treaty of 1929. Under the agreement, the Italian government handed over to the Holy See, partly in compensation for humiliating losses of territory, the sum of 750 million lire in cash and one billion lire (face value) in consolidated 5 per cent bonds, actually worth 800 million lire. The fund was entrusted by Pope Pius XI to the newly established Special Administration of the Holy See (the predecessor of the Extraordinary Section of APSA) which in the 1930s also administered the funds flowing in from Peter's Pence. A proportion was devoted to ecclesiastical building in the south of Italy, to constructing the Palace of S. Calisto in Rome, and to reorganizing the Vatican Library and Art Gallery. APSA's present-day property holdings are estimated at about $300 million. After decades of careful investment, the fund forms what the Vatican describes as the 'productive capital of the Holy See' in deposits or investments within Italy and abroad. It excludes the Vatican's deposits with its own 'in-house' bank, the *Istituto*, and is generally taken to mean its dividend-paying share portfolio.

Among the Curia cardinals concerned with finance, as so many are, the need to increase the income of the Holy See has become a pressing anxiety. Projected budget deficits for the early 1980s have been forecast as at least $20 millions a year. These possible deficits apply strictly to the annual financial budgets of the Roman Curia, whose administrative costs are constantly rising and whose income, in the late Cardinal Vagnozzi's words, is 'extremely limited and totally insufficient'.

Cardinal Vagnozzi said he had never indicated any 'precise amount' concerning the worth of the Holy See's productive capital. If he were to say that the amount invested were 70 or 75 billion lire, people would ask whether it was really needed. In fact, the amount the cardinal suggested – in terms of order of magnitude – is far less than the estimates usually given, at $60 millions in 1978. 'Different publications have disseminated items on the finances of the Holy See which are extremely far from the truth,' Cardinal Vagnozzi said, rather bitterly. Whatever the capital, it yields a contribution towards the running of the Curia which is increasingly inadequate.

The Cardinal-President's 'consolidated budget' at the Prefecture for Economic Affairs, which showed a mounting deficit during the 1970s, covers the administration of the Vatican City State; the department administering the two sections of the Patrimony of the Holy See; the Sacred Congregation for the Evangelization of Peoples (Propaganda Fide); and the Administration of the Basilica of St Peter's. It does not include the finances of the Vatican Bank, the Institute for Religious Works, whose operations contribute substantially to the income of the Holy See. Unofficial estimates of the value of the bank's total deposits range from £1000 millions to £2000 millions. Of the assets of the Vatican Bank, its deposits and investments in Italy and throughout the world, the Vatican share (including Propaganda Fide but excluding the religious orders and other institutions) is reckoned to be well over 50 per cent.

There also exists a sterile but appreciating capital reserve of gold lodged in the vaults of Fort Knox. I have been told that the sometimes quoted figure of $5 billion as the total for this would be absurd – 'even $20 millions would be too much'.

The income contributed to the Vatican by APSA and the Vatican Bank derives from a broad spread of interests ranging from straightforward bank charges to real estate, earnings on deposits, government bonds and portfolio investments in quoted and non-quoted companies. APSA's Special Section seeks advice on its buying and selling operations from such associates as Rothschilds and Hambros in London; Morgan Guaranty, Chase Manhattan and First National City Bank in New York; Crédit Suisse in Zurich. Its investments have in recent years included shares in blue-chip companies such as

IBM, Shell, Gulf Oil, General Motors, General Electric. 'Since we have to provide the resources for the life of the Holy See,' remarks Benedetto Argentieri, 'we look for a good return.' The rules stipulate that there should be no investments in companies dealing in armaments or making contraceptive pills.

Shrewd and flexible policies by the Vatican's financial experts – who aim for a good spread, a high degree of liquidity, a respectable return – provide the Vatican's basic income. This is supplemented chiefly by Peter's Pence, a fund whose origins can be traced back to King Canute and an annual tax of a penny per household collected in midsummer in medieval England and sent to the Pope. The tax was abolished by the English Reformation Parliament in 1534 and restored, on a global basis, by loyal French and English Catholics in 1860. Today, the collection is taken by local churches once a year. It is paid to the Pope (in Britain through the apostolic delegate) who uses most of it for charitable ends, though it also helps to finance the diplomatic activities of the Papacy and, as we have seen, to help balance the budget for the multifarious activities of the Curia.

The amounts received by way of Peter's Pence in recent years have climbed to an estimated £17 millions, or at least enough to more than cover the £10 million or so deficit of the Holy See. Figures have been kept closely guarded by the Secretariat of State, though revealed to the cardinals at their meeting with the Pope in 1979, some of whom might have blushed if this had been done on a national basis.

From the richer Catholic countries, the Pope's income for charitable purposes is supplemented by special contributions such as the $400,000 a year sent by the bishops of the United States, through their Episcopal Conference, from the overseas relief collection in the churches.

In addition, there is a constant flow of money to and from Rome, supervised within the Vatican but not entering into the complex financial system of the Curia itself. For example, Propaganda Fide, which pays for its administration mostly from its own property investments, controls the work of the Pontifical Mission Aid Societies, whose council in Rome collects and distributes about £50 millions throughout the national Catholic Churches of the world every year.

The Vatican spends money on generous works of charity and aid, on the salaries, wages and pensions of its 3500 employees in Rome and overseas, on the upkeep of its buildings and monuments, on the running costs of the many new departments set up since the Second Vatican Council, including the International Commission for Peace and Justice and the Synod of Bishops, on a growing diplomatic service and an ever more ambitious international presence. Its regular ceremonies are costly, as, in the recent past, have been the funerals, installations and travelling expenses of Popes.

A Domesday Book of the Vatican, or of the still highly centralized Catholic Church throughout the world, might be useful but is clearly an impossible task. How would one assess, for example, the extent to which the assets of national Churches are, in effect, held in trust for the Vatican, and the worth of the assets of national Churches, which are mostly in buildings? In May 1979, for example, Archbishop John Quinn of San Francisco announced that he would sell his episcopal residence – a magnificent, spacious building – to help balance the archdiocesan budget. Maintenance bills would be saved when this was done and the archbishop would move to a vacant convent; income would be generated. Along with other financial economies, the decision would probably cut the budget deficit from about $4 millions to $100,000. In December 1979, Cardinal Hume welcomed a 'remarkable' cut of about £750,000 in the debt of his Westminster diocese, whose expenditure in 1978 was about £1.2 million.

Inside the Vatican, when they are examined informally, many of the mysteries of Vatican finance disappear. Not because the facts and figures are readily available – they have not been so – but because the lack of hard information has been caused as much by the jealousy of officials for the sovereign integrity of the Vatican City State and for the dignity of the Holy See as by past scandal or recent incompetence. The argument that the Catholic Church is being hypocritical in condemning the principles and practices of modern capitalism (in, for example, the encyclical *Populorum Progressio* of Pope Paul VI), while investing in capitalist enterprises including multi-national companies, passes most of these officials by. Nor were they very susceptible, when I met them, to the demand for at least a little more disclosure concerning the sources and extent of the Vatican's wealth, even if the publication of balance sheets was anathema.

In 1980, the quarrels over Vatican finance became more shrill. There was growing criticism from outside over the lack of information, and growing irritation within the Curia over the 'guestimates' published by sometimes very hostile critics. All the events of 1978 (Conclaves, papal funerals, papal elections), the activities of the new Pope, the ravages of inflation, and the generally lackadaisical response of the world's Catholics to the financial needs of the Holy See cried out for an initiative. When it came, it was tied to an appeal to the cardinals of the Church to help the Pope with their advice and their generosity.

The Sacred College of Cardinals, the Pope's Senate, found the economic condition of the Vatican as the third item on their agenda when they met in Rome from 5 to 9 November 1979. After the Pope's address, in which he said that a 'widespread fairy tale about the finances of the Holy See' had done a great deal of harm, the cardinals were 'briefed' by Cardinal Casaroli, Secretary of State, on the subject of curial organization; by Cardinal Garrone, Prefect of the Congregation for Catholic Education, on cultural matters, and by Cardinals Vagnozzi and Caprio on the financial situation. After the last report, Cardinal Casaroli added more financial comment, at the explicit request of the Pope, who sensed, or was told about, the cardinals' thirst for better information.

The final communiqué after the full assembly of cardinals lifted a corner of the veil from the subject of Vatican finances but held out only a faint prospect of more revealing disclosure. It had been made clear, the communiqué stated, that the Holy See's income from property and investments, and its other possible institutional sources of income, were 'absolutely insufficient' to cover the cost of the central government of the Church and the Pope's universal mission.

For 1979, the deficit was forecast at 17,000 million lire, or about $20,240,000, rising in 1980. It had been possible to cover the deficit thanks to voluntary offerings from the Catholic world, and especially Peter's Pence. Within a few years, however, the Holy See would find itself hard-pressed to provide adequately for the central government of the Church and for her mission of evangelization and charity.

There was more heated discussion among the cardinals than this suggests, especially over the challenge of more disclosure. They were asked to send their further views on the meeting to the Vatican during the following three months; and meanwhile it was noted that 'in due course' the proposal to publish information on the subject of Vatican finances might be favourably considered. Thus, when finance was fully debated for the first time among the cardinals of the modern Church, the official emphasis was on fund-raising rather than on revelation and reform. This looks likely to remain the case, whatever progress is made towards releasing certain figures.

The reformers, whose impatience and dismay may increase, should recall the experience of the early Cistercians who fled from the worldliness and complacency of the Benedictine establishment only to find, after settling on the edge of civilized Europe, that they had moved to precisely the place that economic prudence would have dictated for future success.

This story would appeal to Pope John Paul II. He has listened sympathetically to requests for more openness about the management of the Vatican's finances; but he has also responded sympathetically to his advisers in the Curia who tell him that burgeoning activities of the Holy See – vastly increased through his own pontifical zeal – demand larger and more stable sources of finance. The Pope's deep engagement with the world, dramatically manifested through his travels, is costly and yet helps to solve the problem of finance by arousing the loyalty and generosity of faithful Catholics. The labourer is worthy of his hire.

Epilogue

With nearly 600 headquarters of religious orders and a score of universities and institutes of higher education, the city of Rome is a solid link between the Vatican and the Catholic world. But it is also the Pope's own diocese, with about 300 parishes, 1700 religious communities, and nearly 30 groups of enclosed nuns. The Pope's position as a bishop is vital to an understanding of the modern Papacy.

By electing Karol Wojtyla as Bishop of Rome, the cardinals of the Church made him Pope, the successor to St Peter, collaborator with all the bishops of the Church, the successors of the Apostles. The most important document to emerge from the Second Vatican Council in the 1960s was the Constitution on the Church, *Lumen Gentium*, which said that, just as St Peter and the other Apostles constituted one Apostolic College, so the Roman Pontiff and the bishops were joined together.

The theology of 'collegiality' has profound implications for the future organizations and development of the Catholic Church. As we have seen, however, neither the Pope nor the Curia has shown signs of wanting to quicken the process of constitutional reform to give practical effect to the religious theory. This may come gradually, or with a future Pope.

Pope John Paul II's role as bishop is performed practically and dynamically. He delegates the running of his own extensive Curia of the diocese of Rome to his vicar general, Cardinal Ugo Poletti, who is supported by a viceregent and auxiliary bishops. But he throws himself enthusiastically into the activities of the diocese whenever possible, and fosters friendly personal contacts with his clergy.

Practically, too, the Pope's own role as a bishop and his keen sense of ordered structures furnishes him with the apparatus for the most effective communication from the Holy See to the world through his contacts with national episcopacies. These he receives regularly in Rome; to the local bishops he delivers his most important, most confidential, messages when visiting their countries.

For example, to the 300 and more bishops of Brazil (with its immense, mostly Catholic, population of 120 millions) he carefully spelled out his political and social message at Fortaleza during his visit to Latin America in 1980.

In a spontaneous gesture, stirred by the poverty he saw in a Brazilian *favela* the Pope eased off his gold ring and handed it to the parish priest (who said later that it would be kept for remembrance and not sold). With vibrant sincerity – 'a brother among brothers' – he praised and pleaded for unity among the bishops themselves. Their principal task as bishops was evangelization: in the words of Pope Paul VI, 'to testify in a simple and direct way to God revealed by Jesus Christ in the Holy Spirit'. The bishops must proclaim the prophetic message of 'the world beyond'. It was against the background of this pattern of metaphysical thought that the Pope believed the Church could 'contribute to the transformation of society by helping it to become more just,' but without having recourse 'to means that are foreign to her . . .'.

The pattern established in Brazil – a dynamic approach to the problems of social justice combined with the assertion of traditional Catholic teaching – was repeated when John Paul II visited Germany in the autumn of 1980, the first time a Pope had done so for nearly a thousand years. His first speech contained a condemnation of artificial contraception; later, he made a sincere and impassioned plea for Christian unity. On the subjects of religion and politics, Church and State, Communism and Catholicism, papal authority, Christian marriage, the nature of the priesthood, divorce, contraception and abortion – to cite some disparate issues on which the Holy See has pronounced – Pope John Paul II has responded to outside pressure with strong and predictable orthodox responses, ruling the Church almost in the style of the authoritarian paternalism of his austere predecessor, Pope Pius XII.

This is not to beg the question of what is meant by orthodox. Nor to say that the Pope's pastoral approach lacks compassion. Nor to suggest that the insights of the Second Vatican Council have passed him by. Nor that he will not be a reforming Pope. It is to seek an understanding of the modern Vatican through a better grasp of the reason for – almost the necessity of – the *predictability* of the Pope.

Among Roman Catholics, there has been no polarization over the Pope as there might be if his 'conservatism' lacked human warmth or his organizing drive disregarded traditions. By the time of the 1980 Synod of Bishops, 'radical' or 'progressive' Catholics had long since realized that they could not blame what they found distasteful in Roman decisions or pronouncements on a reactionary Curia: they were nearly always the Pope's own voice. Outside the Catholic Church, the novelty of the Pope's ebullient appearance in one country after another throughout the world had worn thin; but not in the spots actually visited. The weighty personal appeal of John Paul II was sustained as he consolidated his unique position as a world leader, demanding as his tribute a self-denying moral and spiritual response. The authority which the Pope asserts (both instinctively and through his intellectual conviction about the nature of his office) seemed, at the beginning of the 1980s, to give millions in the world at least a glimpse of what they were yearning for, in the way of order, certitude and hope.

Does this mean that under Pope John Paul II the Vatican has been unchanging? The wise ruler, Machiavelli said, must so arrange affairs that one change in the state leaves a toothing-stone or projection for the next. Some instinct among the Roman Catholic cardinals and the Curia – perhaps providence – selected after the sensitive, often indecisive, Pope Paul VI a non-Italian Pope determined to stabilize the Church and, with his long, painful experience of aggressive Communism, to strengthen its internal authority and resilience against certain storms. But the changes made and implied by the Second Vatican Council cannot be undone, and they leave their projections for new development in the future.

There are some fresh faces within the Vatican and several new sights to see, since the year of the three Popes. But, inside the walls, you still encounter the old defensiveness of Vatican officialdom and the edgy pride of the Curia, shaken somewhat maybe by the whirlwind of the present Pope's activities. None the less, the Vatican moves – and decisively – in response to developments in the world of which it is so incredibly a part. The changes include the growth of the perception of the international stature of the Holy See; the increase of Catholic populations in Africa and Latin America; the clash of old religions and ideologies on a continental scale; the re-emergence of religious faith in China. In response to all this, the Vatican has to be flexible and positive and therefore to change – just as on a lesser scale in Italy it has had to relax its stiff political posture following the new emphases of the Vatican Council, and the decline of clerical influence on the ground.

Can a judgement be made as to the effectiveness of the Vatican? Its influence in the modern world is often most clearly sighted through the hostility it can provoke, either directly or through local churches and bishops – from many German electors in 1980, for example; from critics nearly everywhere in the West of its official ban on contraception. Many in the Catholic Church would like the Vatican to be assessed in terms of the value of its contribution to human peace and progress – the effectiveness of its struggle against poverty, radicalism, so-called institutional violence and so forth. The balance sheet would be hard to draw up, though I must remark in passing that such a book as this may distort the picture of the Holy See and the Catholic Church by only lightly sketching in their charitable and welfare initiatives throughout the world. However, the contemporary Catholic Church, as far as the Pope and his fellow bishops are concerned, has not for the most part altered the score by which it would want to be judged effective: with evangelization as its purpose and the greater glory of God as its motive. There is no measuring rod for this.

For a comment on the future let me recall a comment from the past. A famous passage on the Papacy in Lord Macaulay's review of Ranke's *History of the Popes* runs:

> There is not, and there never was on this earth, a work on human policy so well deserving of examination as the Roman Catholic Church. The history of that Church joins together the two great ages of human civilisation. . . . And she may still exist

in undiminished vigour when some traveller from New Zealand shall, in the midst of a vast solitude, take his stand on a broken arch of London Bridge to sketch the ruins of St Paul's.

Macaulay's explanation for the longevity of the Papacy was that 'divinity, properly so called, is not a progressive science'. In other words, so he thought, men were as capable of believing an absurd or false religion in modern or future times as they were in ancient times.

The Roman Catholic believes that the Papacy endures because the Pope is the successor of St Peter – that his commission comes from the divine founder of a visible Church which is guaranteed against the triumph of error for all time. This belief allows for a wide range of interpretation.

When Pope Paul VI was still alive, and I was discussing the approach to this book with a Benedictine monk in Rome, he said that I might be carrying out an especially useful exercise, by recording the last days of the old Papacy. What he meant was that the forces of change, more or less as expressed in the Second Vatican Council, were gathering strength, and that the advent of a new Pope was almost certain to see a transformation.

The Curia would be made more international and more responsive to the whole of the Church. The Bishops' Synod would share authority and exercise power more often alongside the Pope himself. The Papacy would shed the more pretentious ceremonies and adopt a less autocratic culture. The centralizing and closed system of the Roman congregations would be made more liberal and open. A more compassionate spirit would inform the internal discipline of the whole Church.

In its organization, the structure of the Church would be adapted to the new, or reformed, ecclesiology, with far greater emphasis in its government on the powers of the bishops and dioceses, on conferences and regional synods of bishops, local and general councils and so forth.

The laity of the Church in turn would come to share in the spirit and implementation of 'collegiality'.

Measured against this prospectus, we still mostly have the old Papacy, but with a Pope who presents it to the world with remarkable appeal, campaigning urgently for human rights as if time were not on his side, with a rosary in his hand. The situation is full of paradox.

Because of John Paul's world vision, the Vatican has grown more aware of the currents of political change running in Latin America, Africa and the East particularly, and is assuming a more international aspect.

The composition of the College of Cardinals and of the Curia is changing, the latter more slowly but no less definitely than the former, towards the same wide internationalization. This will transform the atmosphere of the Vatican during the last part of this century; but the newcomers may well take from the past elements of the old Papacy which seem out of fashion in the West today.

The Roman Curia
and its Chief Officials

SECRETARIAT OF STATE
(Secretaria Status seu Papalis)

Secretary of State: Cardinal Agostino Casaroli
Sostituto (deputy): Archbishop Eduardo Martinez Somalo
Assessor: Mgr Giovanni Battista Re

COUNCIL FOR THE PUBLIC AFFAIRS
OF THE CHURCH
(Consilium pro Publicis Ecclesiae Negotiis)

Prefect: Cardinal Agostino Casaroli
Secretary: Archbishop Achille Silvestrini
Under-Secretary: Mgr Audrys J. Backis

SACRED CONGREGATIONS

Congregation for the Doctrine of the Faith
(Sacra Congregatio pro Doctrina Fidei)
Prefect: Cardinal Franjo Seper
Secretary: Archbishop Jean Jérôme Hamer OP

- International Theological Commission
- Pontifical Biblical Commission

Congregation for the Bishops
(Sacra Congregatio pro Episcopis)
Prefect: Cardinal Sebastiano Baggio
Secretary: Archbishop Lucas Moreira Neves OP

- Pontifical Commission for Latin America
- Pontifical Commission for the Pastoral Care of Migrants and
  Itinerant People

260

Congregation for the Oriental Churches
(Sacra Congregatio pro Ecclesiis Orientalibus)
Prefect: Cardinal Wladyslaw Rubin
Secretary: Archbishop Mario Brini

- Special Commission for the Liturgy
- Pontifical Mission for Palestine

Congregation for the Sacraments and Divine Worship
(Sacra Congregatio pro Sacramentis et Cultu Divino)
Prefect: Cardinal James Robert Knox
Secretary: Archbishop Luigi Dadaglio

- Department for the Sacraments
- Department for Divine Worship
- Special Commissions

Congregation for the Clergy
(Sacra Congregatio pro Clericis)
Prefect: Cardinal Silvio Oddi
Secretary: Archbishop Maximino Romero de Lema

- International Council for Catechetics

Congregation for the Religious and for Secular Institutes
(Sacra Congregatio pro Religiosis et Institutis Saecularibus)
Prefect: Cardinal Eduardo Pironio
Secretary: Archbishop Augustin Mayer OSB

- Department for Religious Institutes
- Department for the Secular Institutes

Congregation for the Evangelization of Peoples or 'De Propaganda Fide'
(Sacra Congregatio pro Gentium Evangelizatione seu de Propaganda Fide)
Prefect: Cardinal Agnelo Rossi
Secretary: Archbishop D. Simon Lourdusamy

- Theological Commission
- Review Commission
- Pastoral Commission
- Catechetical Commission
- Other committees and offices

Congregation for the Causes of Saints
(Sacra Congregatio pro Causis Sanctorum)

Prefect: Cardinal Pietro Palazzini
Secretary: Archbishop Giuseppe Casoria

– Judicial Office
– Office for the General Promotion of the Faith
– Historical-hagiographical Office

Congregation for Catholic Education
(Sacra Congregatio pro Institutione Catholica)

Prefect: Cardinal William Wakefield Baum
Secretary: Archbishop Antonio M. Javierre Ortas SDB

TRIBUNALS

Apostolic Penitentiary
(Sacra Paenitentiaria Apostolica)

Cardinal Penitentiary: Cardinal Giuseppe Paupini
Regent: Mgr Luigi De Magistris

Supreme Tribunal of the Apostolic Signatura
(Supremum Signaturae Apostolicae Tribunal)

Prefect: Cardinal Pericle Felici
Secretary: Archbishop Aurelio Sabattani

Roman Rota
(Sacra Romana Rota)

Dean: Archbishop Heinrich Ewers

SECRETARIATS

Secretariat for Christian Unity
(Secretariatus ad Christianorum Unitatem Fovendam)

President: Cardinal Johannes Willebrands
Vice-President: Bishop Ramon Torrella Cascante
Secretary: Mgr Charles Moeller

– Commission for Religious Relations with Judaism

Secretariat for Non-Christians
(Secretariatus pro Non Christianis)

Pro-President: Archbishop Jean Jadot
Secretary: Mgr Pietro Rossano

– Commission for Religious Relations with Islam

Secretariat for Non-Believers
(Secretariatus pro Non Credentibus)

Pro-President: Archbishop Paul Poupard
Under-Secretary: Mgr Jacqueline Bernard

COUNCILS, COMMISSIONS AND COMMITTEES

Pontifical Commission for the Laity
(Pontificium Consilium pro Laicis)

President: Cardinal Opilio Rossi
Vice-President: Bishop Paul Cordes
Under-Secretary: Mgr Peter Coughlan

Pontifical Council for the Family

Pontifical Commission for Justice and Peace
(Pontificia Commissio a Iustitia et Pace)

President: Cardinal Bernardin Gantin
Secretary: Father Jan Schotte
Under-Secretary: Mgr William F. Murphy

Pontifical Commission for the Revision of the Code of Canon Law
(Pontificia Commissio C.I.C. Recognoscendo)

President: Cardinal Pericle Felici
Secretary: Bishop Rosalio José Lara Castillo SDB

Pontifical Commission for the Revision of the Code of Oriental Canon Law
(Pontificia Commissio C.I.C. Orientalis Recognoscendo)

President: Cardinal Joseph Parecattil
Vice-President: Bishop Miroslav Stefan Marusyn

Pontifical Commission for the Interpretation of the Decrees of the Second Vatican Council
(Pontificia Commissio Decretis Concilii Vaticani II Interpretandis)
President: Cardinal Pericle Felici

Pontifical Commission for Social Communications
(Pontificium Consilium Instrumentis Communicationis Socialis Praepositum)
President: Archbishop Andrzej Maria Deskur
Vice-President: Bishop Agnellus Andrew
Secretary: Rev. Romeo Panciroli

– Press Office of the Holy See
Director: Rev. Romeo Panciroli
– Vatican Film Unit

Pontifical Commission for Latin America
(Pontificia Commissio pro America Latina)
President: Cardinal Sebastiano Baggio

Pontifical Commission for the Pastoral Care of Migrants and Itinerant People
(Pontificia Commissio de Spirituali Migratorum atque Itinerantium Cura)
President: Cardinal Sebastiano Baggio
Pro-President: Archbishop Emanuele Clarizio
Secretary: Rev. Giulivo Tessarolo CS

Pontifical Commision 'Cor Unum'
(Pontificium Consilium 'Cor Unum' de Humana et Christiana Progressione Fovenda)
President: Cardinal Bernardin Gantin
Vice-President: Archbishop Alfredo Bruniera
Councillor: Bishop Ramon Torrella Cascante
Secretary: Rev. Roger Du Noyer MEP

Other committees are:
Committee for the Family
International Theological Commission
Pontifical Biblical Commission
Pontifical Abbacy of St Jerome for the Revision and Emendation of the Vulgate

Pontifical Commission for the Neo-Vulgate
Pontifical Commission of Sacred Archaeology
Pontifical Committee of Historical Sciences
Pontifical Commission for the Ecclesiastical Archives of Italy
Central Pontifical Commission for Sacred Art in Italy
Commission of Cardinals for the Pontifical Sanctuaries of
  Pompei and Loreto

OFFICES

Apostolic Camera
(Camera Apostolica)

Chamberlain of the Holy Roman Church: Cardinal Paolo
  Bertoli
Vice-Chamberlain: Archbishop Ettore Cunial

Prefecture of the Economic Affairs of the Holy See
(Praefecttura Rerum Oeconomicarum S. Sedis)

President: Cardinal Giuseppe Caprio
Secretary: Mgr Giovanni Angelo Abbo

Administration of the Patrimony of the Holy See
(Administratio Patrimonii Sedis Apostolicae)

President: Cardinal Agostino Casaroli
Secretary: Archbishop Lorenzo Antonetti

– Ordinary Section
– Extraordinary Section

Prefecture of the Pontifical Household
(Pontificalis Domus)

Prefect: Bishop Jacques Martin
Regent: Mgr Dino Monduzzi

Pontifical Chapel, comprising:
Members of the Pontifical Ecclesiastical Family
Sacred College of Cardinals
Patriarchs, Archbishops, Bishops and Eparchs Assistants to
the Throne
Vice-Chamberlain of the Holy Roman Church
Superior Prelates to the Sacred Congregations
Secretary of the Supreme Tribunal of the Apostolic Segnatura

Dean of the Sacred Roman Rota
Regent of the Sacred Apostolic Penitentiary
Superior Prelates of the Three Secretariats
President of the Pontifical Commission for Social Communications
Abbot of Monte Cassino and Abbots General of the Regular Canons and of Monastic Orders
The Superior General or in his Absence the Procurator General of each of the Mendicant Orders
Auditors of the Sacred Roman Rota
Voters of the Apostolic Segnatura
Members of the Chapters of the Three Patriarchical Basilicas
Consistorial Lawyers
Parish Priests of Rome
Clergy of the Pontifical Chapel
Members of the Pontifical Council for the Laity and of the Pontifical Commission 'Justice and Peace'
Attendants of the Pope

Pontifical Family, comprising:
Ecclesiastical:
Sostituto of the Secretary of State and Secretary of the Cipher
Secretary of the Council for the Public Affairs of the Church
Almoner of His Holiness
Vicar-General of His Holiness for Vatican City
President of the Pontifical Ecclesiastical Academy
Theologian of the Pontifical Household
College of the Apostolic Protonotaries
Supernumary Apostolic Protonotaries
Prelates of the Antechamber
Pontifical Masters of Ceremonies
Prelates of Honour of His Holiness
Preacher of the Pontifical Household

Lay:
Assistants to the Throne
Special Delegate of the Pontifical Commission for the State of Vatican City
General Councillor of the State of Vatican City
Architect of the Apostolic Palaces
Commander of the Swiss Guard
Consultors of the State of Vatican City

President of the Pontifical Academy of Sciences
Gentlemen of His Holiness
Procurators of the Apostolic Palaces
Staff of the Antechamber
Attendants of the Pope

Office for Papal Ceremonies

Pontifical Chapel of Music

Corps of the Swiss Guard

Welfare Service of the Holy Father
(Beneficum Ministerium Summi Pontificis)

Archives of the Second Vatican Council
(Tabularium Concilii Vaticani II)

Office for the Personnel Relations of the Holy See
(Officium Rationibus Habendis cum Administris Sanctae Sedis Praepositum)

Central Office of Statistics of the Church
(Generale Ecclesiae Rationarium)

The Palatine Administrations

Reverend Fabric of St Peter's
– Committee of Administration
– Supervisory Architects
– Administrative Office
– Technical Office
– Legal Department
– Mosaic Studio

Apostolic Vatican Library
– School of Librarianship

Secret Vatican Archives
– Vatican School of Diplomatic and Archival Paleography

Vatican Polyglot Press

Vatican Publishing House

L'Osservatore Romano

The Vatican City State

VICARIATE OF THE VATICAN CITY

Vicar General: Bishop Petrus Canisius Jean van Lierde

PONTIFICAL COMMISSION FOR THE STATE OF VATICAN CITY

President: Cardinal Agostino Casaroli
Pro-President: Cardinal Sergio Guerri
Special Delegate: Marchese Don Giulio Sacchetti

Council of State

President: Marchese Don Giulio Sacchetti
Secretary: Auv. Vittorio Trocchi

ADMINISTRATION
(GOVERNATORATO)

General Secretariat:

Legal Office
Personnel Office
Office of Central Accounts
Philatelic and Numismatic Offices
Office of Posts and Telegraphs
Goods Office
Central Security Office
Pilgrim and Tourist Information Office

General Management of the Pontifical Monuments, Museums and Galleries

Technical Services

Vatican Radio

Vatican Observatory

Archaeological Studies and Research

Pontifical Villas

Tribunals of the Vatican City State

Health and Welfare Fund

Permanent Commission for the Protection of the Historical and Artistic Monuments of the Holy See

Book List

The following are among the reference works and books that I have found helpful, and sometimes quoted from, in writing *Inside the Vatican.*

Annuario Pontificio, Libreria Editrice Vaticana. (Successive editions.)
L'Attività della Santa Sede, Tipografia Pompei SpA. (Successive editions.)
Catholic Almanac, Our Sunday Visitor Inc., Indiana (Annual.)
New Catholic Encyclopedia, 15 vols., McGraw-Hill, New York, 1967.
Statistical Yearbook of the Church, Tipografia Poliglotta Vaticana.
The Vatican and Christian Rome, Libreria Editrice Vaticana, 1975.

Walter Abbott, SJ, (ed.), *The Documents of Vatican II,* London, 1966.
Giulio Andreotti, *A Ogni Morte di Papa,* Milan, 1980.
Baedeker's Central Italy, Leipzig, 1909.
George Blazynski, *John Paul II: A Man from Krakow*, London, 1979.
George Bull, *Vatican Politics at the Second Vatican Council*, Oxford, 1966.
Christopher Butler, *The Theology of Vatican II*, London, 1967.
Dom Cuthbert Butler, *The Vatican Council, 1869–1870*, London, 1930.
Deoclecio Redig de Campos, *Wanderings Among Vatican Paintings,* Milan.
Rock Caporale, SJ, *Vatican II: Last of the Councils*, Baltimore, USA, 1964.

H.E. Cardinale, *The Holy See and the International Order*, Gerrards Cross, 1976.

Eleanor Clark, *Rome and a Villa*, London, 1953.

Mary Craig, *Man from a Far Country*, London, 1979.

M. Creighton, *History of the Papacy during the Reformation*, 4 vols, London, 1887.

Carlo Falconi, *The Popes in the Twentieth Century*, London, 1967.

Michael P. Fogarty, *Christian Democracy in Western Europe 1820–1953*, London, 1957.

Hartwell de la Garde Grissell, *Sede Vacante: A Diary written during the Conclave of 1903*, London, 1903.

Andrew M. Greeley, *The Making of the Popes*, London, 1979.

Margherita Guarducci, *The Tomb of St Peter*, London, 1960.

Augustus Hare, *Walks in Rome*, 2 vols., London, 1876.

Peter Hebblethwaite, *The Christian–Marxist Dialogue and Beyond*, London, 1977.

Peter Hebblethwaite, *The Year of the Three Popes*, London, 1978.

Philip Hughes, *The Church in Crisis: the Twenty Great Councils*, London, 1960.

R.E.M. Irving, *The Christian Democratic Parties of Western Europe*, London, 1979.

Christopher Kininmouth, *Rome Alive*, London, 1951.

Paul Letaronilly, *The Basilica of St Peter*, London, 1882. Reprinted with a preface by Sir Albert Richardson, London, 1953.

Paul Letarouilly, *The Basilica of St Peter*, London, 1882. Reprinted with a preface by Sir Albert Richardson, London, 1953.

Paul Letarouilly, *The Vatican Buildings*, London, 1882. Reprinted with a preface by Sir Albert Richardson, London, 1963.

Georgina Masson, *The Companion Guide to Rome*, London, 1965.

(Photographed by) Fred Mayer, *The Vatican: Portrait of a State and Community*, Dublin, 1980.

David Mitchell, *The Jesuits: A History,* London, 1980.

Peter Nichols, *The Politics of the Vatican*, New York, 1968.

Peter Nichols, *The Pope's Divisions*, London, 1981.

Gerard Noel, *Anatomy of the Catholic Church*, London, 1980.

Mario Olivieri, *Natura e Funzioni dei Legati Pontifici nella Storia e nel Contesto Ecclesiologico del Vaticano II*, Turin, 1979.

Mario Olivieri, *Le Rappresentanze Pontificie*, Rome, 1975.

(Published in English as *The Representatives*, Van Duren, 1980.)

Corrado Pallenberg, *The Vatican Finances*, London, 1971.

Corrado Pallenberg, *The Vatican from Within*, London, 1961.

Peter Partner, *Renaissance Rome 1500–1559*, California, 1976.

Mgr Paul Poupard, *Connaissance du Vatican*, Paris, 1974.

W.A. Purdy, *The Church on the Move*, London, 1966.

Sir Alec Randall, *Vatican Assignment*, Catholic Book Club, 1957.

Leopold von Ranke, *History of the Popes*, 3 vols., New York, 1966.

Anthony Rhodes, *The Vatican in the Age of the Dictators*, London, 1973.

Xavier Rynne, *Letters from Vatican City*; *The Second Session*; *The Third Session; The Fourth Session*, 4 vols., London, 1963–66.

Michael Serafian, *The Pilgrim: Pope Paul VI, the Council, and the Church in a Time of Decision*, London, 1964.

George Seldes, *The Vatican Yesterday, Today, Tomorrow*, London, 1934.

James van der Veldt, *The Ecclesiastical Orders of Knighthood*, Catholic University of America Press, 1956.

Bernard Wall, *Report on the Vatican*, London, 1956.

Richard Webster, *Christian Democracy in Italy 1860–1960*, London, 1961.

Pope John XXIII, *Il Giornale dell'Anima*, Rome, 1964. (*Journey of a Soul*, London, 1965.)

Pope John Paul I (Albino Luciani), *Illustrissimi*, London, 1978.

Pope John Paul II (Karol Wojtyla), *Easter Vigil and Other Poems*, London, 1979.

Pope John Paul II (Karol Wojtyla), *Sign of Contradicion*, London, 1979.

Testamento di Paolo VI, Rome, 1978.

Index